SOCIAL CLASS AND EDUCATION

Social Class and Education: Global Perspectives is the first empirically grounded volume to explore the intersections of class, social structure, opportunity, and education on a truly global scale. Eleven essays from contributors representing the United States, Europe, China, Latin America, and other regions offer an unparalleled examination of how social class differences are made and experienced through schooling. By underscoring the consequences of our new global reality, this volume takes seriously the transnational migration of commerce, capital, and peoples and the ramifications of such for education and social structure. Moving beyond national confines, internationally recognized scholars Lois Weis and Nadine Dolby offer a set of emblematic essays that break new theoretical and empirical ground on the ways class is produced and maintained through education around the world.

Lois Weis is State University of New York Distinguished Professor of Sociology of Education at the University at Buffalo, State University of New York.

Nadine Dolby is Associate Professor of Curriculum Studies at Purdue University.

EDUCATION IN GLOBAL CONTEXT

Series editor: Lois Weis

Education in Global Context takes seriously the transnational migration of commerce, capital and peoples, and the implications of such for education and social structure in global context. Globalization—in the world economy, in patterns of migration, and increasingly in education—affects all of us. The increasingly globalized and knowledge-based economy renders the linkages between education and social and economic outcomes and arrangements empirically "up for grabs" in a wide variety of nations while simultaneously more important than ever. This series underscores the consequences of the global both internationally and here at home while simultaneously stressing the importance of a paradigmatic shift in our understanding of schooling and social/economic arrangements.

Social Class and Education: Global Perspectives

Edited by Lois Weis and Nadine Dolby

SOCIAL CLASS AND EDUCATION

Global Perspectives

Edited by Lois Weis and Nadine Dolby

Routledge
Taylor & Francis Group

NEW YORK AND LONDON

First published 2012
by Routledge
711 Third Avenue, New York, NY 10017

Simultaneously published in the UK
by Routledge
2 Park Square, Milton Park, Abingdon, Oxon OX14 4RN

Routledge is an imprint of the Taylor & Francis Group, an informa business

Library of Congress Cataloging in Publication Data
Social class and education : global perspectives / edited by Lois Weis and Nadine Dolby.
    p. cm.
    Includes bibliographical references and index.
    1. Educational sociology—Cross-cultural studies. 2. Social classes—Cross-cultural studies. 3. Education and globalization—Cross-cultural studies. 4. Comparative education—Cross-cultural studies. 5. Educational equalization—Cross-cultural studies 6. Students with social disabilities–Education—Cross-cultural studies. I. Weis, Lois. II. Dolby, Nadine.
    LC189.S667 2012
    306.43–dc23
    2011037871

ISBN: 978-0-415-88695-6 (hbk)
ISBN: 978-0-415-88696-3 (pbk)
ISBN: 978-0-203-82920-2 (ebk)

Typeset in Bembo and Stone Sans
by EvS Communication Networx, Inc.

Printed and bound in the United States of America on sustainably sourced paper by IBT Global.

CONTENTS

LIST OF FIGURES

LIST OF TABLES

ACKNOWLEDGMENTS

Numerous individuals contributed to this volume and we thank them for their efforts. Catherine Bernard of Routledge encouraged us to produce the volume and has been an integral part of both its conception and execution. We are most appreciative of her efforts on behalf of this book, and the field more generally. It is our privilege to continue to work with Catherine and we are honored by her ongoing support. Authors worked tirelessly to produce outstanding chapters and we are grateful for their intellectual efforts. A group of dedicated PhD students at the University at Buffalo read widely in the area, helping to map the intellectual terrain and provided suggestions with regard to what should be included in the volume. They did so on a volunteer basis and we appreciate their assistance. They include: Amy Stich, Heather Jenkins, Nancy Campos, Kristin Cipollone, Vikas John, Chien-Chen Kung , Miao Li, Yuri Nakajima, and Carolyn Stirling. As Lois's postdoctoral associate, Amy Stich also provided broad-based intellectual and editorial assistance, and Nancy Campos and Qiongqiong Chen were in constant contact with the authors over the course of the project. We are especially grateful to the efforts of Qiongqiong Chen, who joined our team only this summer, tirelessly wrapping up all loose ends and readying the manuscript for final submission to the press. Thanks to all the above individuals. We could not have done this without you.

Lois Weis and Nadine Dolby
August 2011

INTRODUCTION

Social Class and Education in Globalizing Context

Lois Weis and Nadine Dolby

Within the past decade, increasing attention has been paid to issues of social class, reinvigorating a conversation that had waned by the close of the 20th century (Brantlinger, 2003; Burawoy, Chang, & Fei-yu Hsieh, 2010; Lareau, 2003; Massey & Denton, 1993; Patillo-McCoy, 2000; Reay, Crozier, & James, 2011; Torres, 2009; Walkerdine, Lucey, & Melody, 2001; Weis, 2004, 2008). Class has reemerged in two ways. First, there is greater recognition of class as a key signifier of positionality (Lareau, 2003; Reay et al., 2011; Vincent & Ball, 2006; Walkerdine et al., 2001; Weis, 2004, 2008) and second, there is deepening scholarly focus on entrenched and growing social and economic inequalities (Aron-Dine & Shapiro, 2006; Chauvel, 2010; Gilbert, 2003; Piketty & Saez, 2003, 2006; Sherman & Aron-Dine, 2007).

Social class, while perhaps a "phantasmatic" category, organizes the social, cultural, and material world in exceptionally powerful ways (Weis, 2004, 2008). While class is clearly connected to income and occupation, and there is ample evidence that income inequalities are widening both within and between nations across the globe (Chauvel, 2010; Gilbert, 2003; Piketty & Saez, 2003, 2006; Sherman & Aron-Dine, 2007), class must additionally be understood as practices of living—"the social and psychic practices through which ordinary people live, survive and cope" (Walkerdine et al., 2001, p. 27). The books we read (or if we read at all); our travel destinations (if we have them and what they look like); the clothes we wear; the foods we eat; where and if our children go to school, how far and with what degree of success, with whom, and under what staff expectations and treatment; where and with whom we feel most comfortable; where we live and the nature of our housing; where and if we attend and complete postsecondary education, and under what expectations for success and imagined or taken for granted financing (parents, public/state/

national/federal money, on or off campus job) are all *profoundly* classed experiences, rooted not only in material realities but also in shared culturally based expectations and understandings, whether recognized or not .

Families and schools, among other externally relevant institutions, are important mediators of class. Such recognition of both the structuring effects of class and the ways in which class is lived out (Bourdieu, 1979; Bourdieu & Passeron, 1970) has never been more pressing given key shifts in the global economy accompanied by deepening social inequalities both within and between nations. A number of volumes call for intensifying research efforts into how educational institutions, structures, and systems play into the production of class and social structure more generally. However, there is relatively little serious scholarly attention devoted to the relationship between education and social class in a global context. *Social Class and Education: Global Perspectives* takes this goal as its starting point, with specific focus on the ways in which education is still a critically important space where class is struggled over, engaged, produced, and lived out, as we simultaneously resituate the analysis in its global reality.

In this regard, "globalizing the research imagination" (Kenway & Fahey, 2008) has two meanings. On the one hand, it means that we must situate our analyses of education and social structure within a broadened range of countries, including industrialized nations like the United States, Britain, and Germany, among others, as well as new players in the global arena such as Singapore, China, Brazil, South Africa, Mexico, and India. Second, we must take into account how what goes on within one nation is both similar to and simultaneously has increased links to what goes on in the rest of the world. This volume takes both meanings seriously through a clear focus on education and class construction in varying national contexts, while simultaneously acknowledging that transnational and global lenses are now necessary components of all class analysis. In so doing, we invoke a defiant, rather than "compliant territorial imagination," seeking to pry open questions related to education and social class in a global context in new ways.

The increasingly globalized and knowledge-based economy creates a reality in which movement affects the fundamental structures of our lives, whether we ourselves are mobile. Since the 1970s, we have witnessed a massive realignment of the global economy. In the first wave of this realignment, working-class jobs—primarily in manufacturing—were increasingly exported from highly industrialized countries such as the United States, United Kingdom, and Japan to poor countries, where the truly desperate take jobs that pay starvation wages and offer no job protection or benefits. In the current second wave, middle-class jobs are also exported, as members of a new middle class in countries such as India and China are increasingly educated as architects, accountants, medical technicians, and doctors, and are willing to work for American, British, Canadian, and Australian companies (among others) at a fraction of the salary they would be paid for the same work at corporate headquarters. Such movement has implications for the production of social structure and associated class processes in a wide variety of nations.[1]

For example, as Brown, Lauder, and Ashton (2011) argue, the American middle class is being ripped apart by global forces of knowledge capitalism. With the rise of all-consuming processes of globalization, the competition for jobs no longer sits within national boundaries. Rather, the job market increasingly constitutes a "global auction" wherein bidders work across national contexts to obtain the highest quality work at the lowest cost. Although not new in the sense that capital historically sought to minimize costs of labor (and labor, of course, fought back to gain a "living wage"), companies now have myriad options as they increasingly prowl the new global marketplace to lower the cost of doing business. The nation-state, then, no longer constrains the "bidding wars" or the construction of job sites in the way that it once did, setting in motion entirely different processes of class construction and the relationship between education and social structure in any given nation (Reich, 2001, 2007). Brown et al. (2011) note that "college educated Americans were only sheltered from price competition as long as educated talent was in limited supply at home and only found in equally expensive countries like Japan, Germany, or Britain" (Brown et al., 2011, p. 6). As nations such as China and India put massive amounts of resources into building their educational infrastructure, including an increasingly impressive postsecondary infrastructure, the bidding war intensifies, with highly educated individuals in the United States and other first wave industrialized nations now being increasingly disadvantaged in the new globalized context. Although Americans live this loss on a day-to-day basis, most do not comprehend the broad social and economic processes that produce current options, and tend to blame specific policies and practices wholly on elected officials.

Of course, the situation is not markedly better for members of emergent middle classes in societies such as India and China: while they may be able to afford a higher standard of living than most, they still are paid a fraction of what their labor is worth in an industrialized nation. Thus, the globalization of the economy creates markedly altered economic opportunities for people worldwide, as companies seek the cheapest locale in which to situate manufacturing plants, call centers, and so forth, with little regard for the individual and nationally-based economic, social, and human costs of their decisions. Corporations move jobs from the United States to India, and then a year later abandon their Indian call centers for an even less expensive workforce in Mexico, and then, the following year, relocate to China.

Finally, the volume calls attention to how the shifting macrostructure of the global economy interacts with the movement of people. Intensifying transnational migration patterns have implications for education and social structural formation worldwide, as social class formations in a wide range of countries are now being produced and realigned in relation to large numbers of recent immigrants/migrants in nations that are differentially positioned in relation to globalizing capital and culture. This includes those who possess "flexible citizenship", by virtue of possession of high status knowledge—those who can transcend nation-state boundaries with their inherited or earned cultural and intellectual capital (for example, high powered intellectuals, engineers, and medical professionals who are seduced to work in economically powerful nations; Ong, 1999), and those who enter both economically powerful as well as poor nations as immigrants or refugees with little more than the clothes on their back. In point of fact, a relatively high proportion of the latter group of migrants/immigrants do relatively well in school in first wave industrialized nations such as the United States and Canada, in contrast to their predicted educational achievement and attainment based on current class position in their adopted land (Li, 2005, 2008; Rumbaut & Portes, 2001).

Social Class and Education: Global Perspectives underscores the specific consequences of this new global reality in multiple nations, including the United States, Germany, China, India, Spain, Taiwan, and South Africa among others, while stressing the importance of a paradigmatic shift in our understanding of schooling and social-economic arrangements. A primary goal of the volume is to acknowledge, while simultaneously moving beyond, the relatively bounded and taken for granted national context embodied in previous and otherwise important work on social class and education (e.g., Kinchloe & Steinberg, 2007; Van Galen & Noblit, 2007; Vincent & Ball, 2006; Weis, 2008). Building on previous research, then, this volume intentionally pries open questions related to social class and education in the changing global scope and context while at the same time encouraging scholars to move beyond the confines of the nation when studying questions of class and education.

The volume also draws upon previous important and largely theoretical work on globalization, while empirically concretizing aspects of this literature with specific focus on education and social class. Although important theoretical literature on globalization abounds (Apple, 2010; Kenway & Fahey, 2008; Popkewitz & Rizvi, 2009; Torres, 2009, among others), and there are certainly studies in education that take the globalizing economy or the transnational migration of people as its starting point (Apple, 2010; Dolby, 2001; Dolby & Rizvi, 2008; Lee, 2006; Li, 2005, 2007), *Social Class and Education: Global Perspectives* highlights new work related to our increasingly interconnected world and the implications of such for social class formation: what it is; how we study it; what education has to do with it; and how class arrangements, sensibilities, and productions shift inside a changing world context.

Obviously no one volume can address these issues in their entirety. Our intent here is to open up new intellectual territory while analytically drawing together important empirical research conducted in nations differentially positioned in relation to globalizing culture and capital. Through a set of emblematic essays situated in specifically located and varying nations, we offer a template for *ways* of studying education and social class inside the shifting global arena. While we cannot, of course, take into account all geographic areas or the array of specific issues related to education and social class production in any given nation-state, our goal is to showcase important research produced by a diverse group of authors whose empirical work is situated in diverse national conditions. We intentionally highlight a range of perspectives, research methods, and associated designs through which such work can be accomplished. Although much has been made, for example, of the qualitative/quantitative distinction in social research, it is important that we move beyond such staunchly defended methodological distinctions and borders so as to answer critical research questions. This is not a call for a "mixed methods" approach in any simplistic sense (Weis, Jenkins, & Stich, 2008). Rather, it is a stark statement that we need sophisticated quantitative *and* qualitative studies that address education and class in a global context in order to unearth the extent to which and mechanisms through which class and social structure are produced and realigned all over the world. No one method can answer all relevant questions, and we intentionally spotlight research that employs, across chapters in the volume, varied research methods in varying national contexts.

This similarly applies to *narrowly* conceived perspectives, as we can respectfully *disagree* as to the definition of class as well as the drivers of class production, and at the same time use our collective energies to amass research on the production of social and economic inequalities as related to education. It is, in fact, only by understanding the extent of such inequalities and the mechanisms through which inequalities are now produced in a global context that we can engage meaningful ameliorative actions. No single orthodoxy will suffice here. We need broad-based collective engagement and respect across both method and perspective if we are to make meaningful headway in this globally fueled research arena.

The Essays

The essays in this volume are divided into three sections. In section I, "Postsecondary Access, Equity, and Educational Opportunity in the Global Economy," authors Richard Arum, Adam Gamoran, and Yossi Shavit; Yan Zhao Ciupak and Amy E. Stich; and Josipa Roksa focus attention on one of the most central issues in a world driven by technology and information: the role and function of postsecondary education. Once the province of elites, the expansion of postsecondary education is a fundamental site for the examination of how social class positioning is both transformed and reinscribed in a global world. The essays in section II, "Cultural Politics, Transnational Movement, and the Role of Class," by authors Shumin Lin, Daniel Faas, Catalina Crespo-Sancho, and Caroline Foubister and Azeem Badroodien, look specifically at how national dynamics of class are altered by transnational movement, focusing on the everyday lives of women, families, and youth. The closing section of the volume, "Class and the Changing Global Educational Context," includes essays by Jane Kenway and Anna Hickey-Moody; Antonio Olmedo and Luis Eduardo Santa Cruz; Yun-Kyung Cha and Seung-Hwan Ham; and Ruchira Ganguly-Scrase and Timothy Scrase. In this section authors look at, as Ganguly-Scrase and Scrase suggest in the volume's closing essay, the "paradoxes" of globalization, and how inequalities can simultaneously diminish and flourish within this new context.

Section I: Postsecondary Access, Equity, and Educational Opportunity in the Global Economy

In the first section, authors analyze the complicated issue of access to postsecondary education within the larger framework of a rapidly globalizing economy. While it is true that in many nations around the world access to postsecondary education is increasing, this does not necessarily always ensure greater equity of educational opportunity. Other factors, including differentiation and stratification of postsecondary educational institutions, the cultural and social capital possessed by students and their families, and the specific life circumstances and challenges of entering adulthood create a complex web of realities at both macro- and micro-levels. Postsecondary education is a crucial site for engaging with issues of access, equity, and opportunity in the global context. On a structural level, it is the engine that drives national economies; for individuals, postsecondary education provides the key to a middle-class life, and global possibilities.

The volume opens with Richard Arum, Adam Gamoran, and Yossi Shavit's chapter, "Expanded Opportunities for All in Global Higher Education Systems." Based on a comparative study of 15 nations, the authors examine the relationship between changes in the structure of higher education and access within those national contexts. The chapter is particularly concerned with examining three factors related to access: higher education expansion, differentiation between institutions, and market structures. While their findings are nuanced and varied across the 15 nations study, Arum, Gamoran, and Shavit conclude that, overall, expansion of higher education does lead to increased inclusiveness of opportunity, arguing that the importance of extending a valued good (a higher education credential) to a greater proportion of the population outweighs the reality that it is often elites that still possess a relative advantage within a national context.

The second chapter in this section, Yan Zhao Ciupak and Amy E. Stich's "The Changing Educational Opportunity Structure in China: Positioning for Access to Higher Education," explores the consequences of the expansion of educational access in China, a key global economic nation, and one that was not included in Arum, Gamaron, and Shavit's study. While Arum et al. examine questions of access and opportunity from a macropolicy perspective,

Ciupak and Stich are concerned with the personal stories and experiences of Chinese students within a higher education system that is highly differentiated and stratified. Based primarily on interviews with 75 students in both developed and less developed regions of China, the authors focus on how urban and rural students make sense of three specific and key aspects of decision making in relationship to higher education: pathways to college, the choice of institution and major, and the ways in which college serves as a form of accumulated capital as students plan their lives after graduation. Ciupak and Stich conclude that urban students have greater agency in relationship to higher education than rural students do: for rural students, the choice to go to college still involves considerable risk, and unlike urban students, rural students do not see themselves as full participants in global processes.

Josipa Roksa, in the final chapter in this section, "Race, Class, and Bachelor's Degree Completion in American Higher Education: Examining the Role of Life Course Transitions," explores related questions about the complicated nature of access, this time in the context of the United States. While many previous studies have focused on what happens *before* college entrance as a means of understanding comparatively low rates of college completion among minority students, Roksa turns her attention to the "life course transitions" that occur *during* the college years. Using data from the National Longitudinal Survey of Youth of 1997 (NLSY97), a nationally representative sample of individuals born between 1980 and 1984 (ages 12–16 years as of December 31, 1996), Roksa concludes that while academic preparation is a relatively more important factor than life course transitions for understanding racial/ethnic gaps in degree completion, both sets of factors contribute to this phenomenon. Roksa further suggests that future research in this area needs to examine the relationship between particular institutions, students, and their completion rates, because there is some evidence to indicate that minority students continue to be "under matched"; that is, they are enrolled at less selective institutions than their academic abilities and achievement would suggest (Bowen, Chingos, & McPherson, 2010), and that higher degree completion rates are found at more selective institutions.

Taken as a whole, the three essays in this section underscore that access, while important in and of itself, is little guarantee of equity or equality of opportunity. Instead, the essays point to the necessity of continued research on the interplay between institutional and social structures, and how the larger global context is a constant factor in unraveling these dynamics.

Section II: Cultural Politics, Transnational Movement, and the Role of Class

Authors in the first section analyze the macrodynamics of education within national boundaries. In the second section, authors turn their attention to how transnational movement is shifting dynamics within national spaces, in ways that are sometimes small, but still have significant effects on the intersection of education and social class.

In the opening chapter, "Class Wreckage and Class Repositioning: Narratives of Japanese-Educated Taiwanese," Shumin Lin unravels the story of elderly Taiwanese women who were educated under Japanese colonial rule of Taiwan. With the rise of the Chinese nationalist government in 1945, these women lost both their national and social class status, and speaking Japanese was banned in public spaces. Based on 21 months of ethnographic fieldwork, Lin argues that both class struggle and the politics of language are significant factors in the colonial nostalgia these women demonstrate, and that the new dynamics of democratization and globalization within Taiwan now allow these women to reclaim the identities that had been suppressed for decades.

Daniel Faas's chapter, "Producing Class and Ethnic Identities among German and Turkish Youth in Working- and Middle-Class Schools in Germany," focuses attention on one of the most significant social and cultural contexts of contemporary times, the changing racial and ethnic composition of Europe. Faas's work helps to illuminate how race and ethnic identities intersect with class identities in Germany. Though legally still considered "guest workers," the Turkish students who participated in Faas's 2004 study were, in most cases, second generation Germans. Based on interviews and fieldwork, Faas argues that ethnic identities—or links to a common ancestry, language, and tradition—are stronger in working-class schools. In contrast, in middle-class schools, youth had stronger political identities, which in many cases transcended ethnic (e.g., Turkish), or national (German) identification. Instead, middle-class students identified as Europeans. Faas's analysis reminds us that ethnic, racial, and national identities are always inflected and shaped by class positioning, and that access to the "global" (in material goods, or in imagination), is uneven.

In the third essay in this section, Catalina Crespo-Sancho examines another instance of transnational movement, in this case in the United States. In "Transnational Latin American Families in the United States: Parenting and Schooling in the 'Neither Here Nor There'," Crespo-Sancho discusses how one middle-class Latino family uses the social and cultural capital from their home country (Peru) and culture in order to secure educational advantage for their children in their host country (the United States), through strategic decision making regarding neighborhood and school choice. Similar to the other authors in this section, Crespo-Sancho demonstrates that social class must always be a component of social analysis, and that transnational movement has complicated dynamics both within and between national spaces.

In the final essay in this section, "African Migrant Youth, Schooling, and Social Class in Cape Town" Caroline Foubister and Azeem Badroodien explore themes that echo Crespo-Sancho, this time in the context of a rapidly changing South Africa. Though unable to legally work or live in South Africa, in the past decades millions of Africans fleeing chaos, genocide, war, and famine have settled in South Africa's major cities, and have become a significant part of the school population. Based on a study of 20 African migrant students at a school in Cape Town, Foubister and Badroodien discuss how these youth access their social and cultural capital in three areas of their lives (family, friendships, and religion) to survive and often thrive in a desperate and sometimes hopeless situation.

Moving through four continents, the essays in this section underscore that social class is an ever-present and critical context for understanding changing social, cultural, and political dynamics throughout the world. Furthermore, as the authors demonstrate, class can no longer only be understood within a national framework: the transnational context is increasingly crucial for comprehending local realities.

Section III: Class and the Changing Global Educational Context

In this final section of the book, the chapters look at how class intersects with both informal and formal educational spaces within a global context. All of the authors in this section concentrate their analyses on the (sometimes unintended, sometimes deliberate) consequences of globalization in relationship to class: how, despite the veneer of increased opportunity and possibility, in many cases, social inequalities are actually exacerbated. In the first essay, "Global Scapes of Abjection: The Contemporary Dynamics of Some Intersecting Injustices," authors Jane Kenway and Anna Hickey-Moody examine how images of poor and marginalized people throughout the world—but particularly within Australia—circulate and are reinscribed through global processes. In their analysis, the mere existence of global contexts does not create opportunity, but instead can have the opposite effect of producing more informal educational spaces (e.g., media, tourist guidebooks) that marginalize and stereotype people who are already struggling with poverty.

The second chapter, Antonio Olmedo and Luis Eduardo Santa Cruz's "Being Middle Class Is Not Enough: Social Class, Education and School Choice in Spain," expands the discussion of access and opportunity from section I, but in this instance focuses on schools. As Olmedo and Santa Cruz explain, state policies in Spain over the past decades have gradually shifted educational decision making to parents, following global patterns predicated by the dominance of neoliberal policies that favor "freedom" and "choice." Echoing Kenway and Hickey-Moody, Olmedo and Santa Cruz demonstrate that globally inflected and determined policies may not always produce enhanced opportunities. In this case, they analyze how Spanish, middle-class families with varying degrees of economic and cultural capital feel that they must continually strategize how to provide the best possible futures for their children. As the title reveals, these parents understand that simply being middle-class is no longer enough to guarantee future economic security.

In "Educating Supranational Citizens: The Incorporation of English Language Education into Curriculum Policies," Yun-Kyung Cha and Seung-Hwan Ham examine how English has become part of the regular school curriculum in nations around the world. Their analysis is both historical and global, spanning the world and five historical periods from 1900 to 2005. Cha and Ham argue that the rise of English in contemporary school curricula reflects an expansive concept of "supranational citizenship" that grounds decision making and agency in the individual. As they highlight, the constant global rhetoric that positions English language education as a key to global success also has the potential to lead to new forms of social inequity.

The volume closes with Ruchira Ganguly-Scrase and Timothy Scrase's chapter, "Cultural Politics in the New India: Social Class, Neoliberal Globalization, and the Education Paradox." Against the backdrop of neoliberalism, Gaguly-Scrase and Scrase also explore the dynamics of English language education, in this case, in the Indian state of West Bengal. As English language education explodes throughout India, multiple strata of middle-class Indians cling to English as a way to either retain or gain cultural and economic power. Seeing themselves as victims of globalization (despite their relatively privileged position), lower middle-class Indians in Gaguly-Scrase and Scrase's study point to their English language skills as a marker of their modernity, and ability to hold some strategic advantage in their lives.

The essays in this section point to the complex interplay of class and global dynamics. Far from simply opening doors and possibilities, the politics and policies of globalization—tied to neoliberalism—can also create new tensions in cultures and societies, even in contexts which are not as explicitly transnational as those explored in section II.

Note

1 Although not explicitly discussed in this chapter, a form of financialization sits at the center of the increasingly globalized and knowledge-based economy, and this has implications for class processes in nations across the globe. As Kenway and Fahey (2010, pp. 719–720) note:

> Ultimately another manifestation of the capitalist accumulation process emerged in the form of 'financialisation' with the USA at its epicentre, but which swiftly spread around the world. Foster and Magdoff (2009, 45) call this the 'monopoly–finance capital' phase of capitalism. This involved Money to Money (M–M) rather than Money–Commodities–Money (M–C–M) in Marx's terms. The 'new outlets for surplus were in the finance, insurance and real estate (FIRE) sector' mainly, though not exclusively, 'in the form of financial speculation in securites, real estate and commodities markets rather than investment in capital goods' (Foster and Magdoff 2009, 67). Financialisation involves a situation where 'the traditional role of finance as a helpful servant to production has been stood on its head, with finance now dominating over production.' (Foster and Magdoff 2009, 100, as quoted in Kenway and Fahey 2010, p. 719–720)

We aruge in the Introduction that movement affects the fundamental structures of our lives, substantially altering class processes in global context. We agree with Kenway, Fahey and others that such movement is clearly fueled by larger processes of financialization, as outlined above. However, financialization cannot fully account for all forms of movement, as the worldwide movement of peoples is linked to an array of social and political phenomena, not all of which are rooted in the extent to which and the ways in which financialization sits at the epicentre of the increasingly globalized and knowledge-based economy.

References

Apple, M. (2010). *Global crises, social justice, and education.* New York: Routledge.

Aron-Dine, A., & Shapiro, I. (2006). *New data show extraordinary jump in income concentration in 2004.* Washington, DC: Center on Budget and Policy Priorities. Retrieved from chpp. org/7-10-06inc.pdf.

Bourdieu, P. (1979). *La distinction, critique sociale du jugement* [Distinction: A social critique of the judgment of taste]. Paris, France: Editions de Minuit.

Bourdieu, P., & Passeron, J. C. (1970). *La reproduction: Éléments pour une theorie du système d'enseignement* [Reproduction: Elements for a theoretical system of teaching]. Paris, France: Editions de Minuit.

Bowen, W., Chingos, M., & McPherson, M. (2010). *Crossing the finish line: Completing college at America's public universities.* Princeton, NJ: Princeton University Press.

Brantlinger, E. (2003). *Dividing classes: How the middle class negotiates and rationalizes school advantage.* New York: Routledge.

Brown, P., Lauder, H., & Ashton, D. (2011). *The global auction: The broken promises of education, jobs and incomes.* New York: Oxford University Press.

Burawoy, M., Chang, M-K., & Hsieh, M. Fei-yu (Eds.); A. Andrews, E. Fidan Elcioglu, & L. K. Nelson (Assoc. Eds.), (2010). *Facing an unequal world: Challenges for a global sociology (Vol. 3), Conference Proceedings.* Taipei, Taiwan: Institute of Sociology at Academia Sinica; Madrid, Spain: Council of National Associations of the International Sociological Association.

Chauvel, L. (2010). The increasingly dominated fraction of the dominant class: French sociologists facing the challenges of precarity and middle class destabilization. In M. Burawoy, M-K. Chang, & M. Fei-yu Hsieh (Eds.); A. Andrews, E. Fidan Elcioglu, & L. K. Nelson (Assoc. Eds.), *Facing an unequal world: Challenges for a global sociology (Vol. 3),* pp. 87–121, *Conference Proceedings.* Taipei, Taiwan: Institute of Sociology at Academia Sinica; Madrid, Spain: Council of National Associations of the International Sociological Association.

Dolby, N. 2001. *Constructing race: Youth, identity and popular culture in South Africa.* Albany, NY: SUNY Press.

Dolby, N., & Rizvi, F. (Eds.). (2008). *Youth moves: Identities and education in global perspective.* New York: Routledge.

Foster, J. B., & Magdoff, F. (2009). *The great financial crisis: Causes and consequences.* New York: Monthly Review Press.

Gilbert, D. (2003). *The American class structure in an age of growing inequality.* Belmont, CA: Wadsworth.

Kenway, J., & Fahey, J. (2008). *Globalizing the research imagination.* New York: Routledge.

Kenway, J., & Fahey, J. (2010). Is greed still good: Was it ever?: Exploring the emoscapes of the global financial crises. *Journal of Education Policy, 25*(6), 717–727,

Kinchloe, J., & Steinberg, S. (Eds.). (2007). *Cutting class: Socioeconomic status and education.* Lanham, MD: Rowman & Littlefield.

Lareau, A. (2003). *Unequal childhoods: Class, race and family life.* Berkeley: University of California Press.

Lee, S. (2005).*Up against whiteness: Race, school and immigrant youth.* New York: Teachers College Press.

Li, G. (2005). *Culturally contested pedagogy: Battles of literacy and schooling between mainstream teachers and Asian immigrant parents.* Albany, NY: SUNY Press.

Li, G. (2007). *Culturally contested literacies: America's "rainbow underclass" and urban schools.* New York: Routledge.

Massey, D., & Denton, N. (1993). *American apartheid: Segregation and the making of the underclass.* Cambridge, MA: Harvard University Press.

Ong, A. (1999). *Flexible citizenship: The cultural logics of transnationality.* London: Duke University Press.

Patillo-McCoy, M. (2000). *Black picket fences: Privilege and peril among the black middle class.* Chicago, IL: University of Chicago Press.

Piketty, T., & Saez, E. (2003). Income inequality in the United States, 1913–98. *Quarterly Journal of Economics, 118*(1), 1–39.

Piketty, T., & Saez, E. (2006). *Income inequality in the United States, 1913–2002.* New York: Oxford University Press.

Popkewitz, T., & Rizvi, F. (2009). *Globalization and the study of education.* Oxford, England: Blackwell.

Reay, D., Crozier, G., & James, D. (2011). *White middle class identities and urban schooling.* New York: Palgrave Macmillan.

Reich, R. (2001). *The future of success.* New York: Knopf.

Reich, R. (2007). *Supercapitalism: The transformation of business, democracy, and everyday life.* New York: Knopf.

Rumbaut, R., & Portes, A. (2001). *Immigrant America: A portrait* (3rd ed.). Berkeley: University of California Press

Sherman, Q., & Aron-Dine, Q. (2007). *New CBO data show income inequality continues to widen after tax for top 1 percent rose by $146,000 in 2004.* Washington, DC: Center on Budget and Policy Priorities.

Torres, C. (2009). *Globalization and education: Collected essays on class, race, gender, and the state.* New York: Teachers College Press.

Van Galen, J., & Noblit, G. (Eds.). (2007*). Late to class: Social class and schooling in the new economy.* Albany, NY: SUNY Press.

Vincent, C., & Ball, S. (2006). *Childcare, choice and class practices: Middle class parents and their children.* London. Routledge.

Walkerdine, V., Lucey, H., & Melody, J (2001). *Growing up girl: Psychosocial explorations of gender and class.* New York: New York University Press.

Weis, L. (2004). *Class reunion: The remaking the American white working class.* New York: Routledge.

Weis, L. (Ed.). (2008). *The way class works: Readings on school, family and the economy.* New York: Routledge.

Weis, L., Jenkins, H., & Stich, A. (2008). Diminishing the divisions among us: Reading and writing across difference in theory and method in the sociology of education. *Review of Educational Research, 79*(2), 912–945.

SECTION I

Postsecondary Access, Equity, and Educational Opportunity in the Global Economy

1

EXPANDED OPPORTUNITIES FOR ALL IN GLOBAL HIGHER EDUCATION SYSTEMS[1]

Richard Arum, Adam Gamoran, and Yossi Shavit

Introduction

Recent decades have witnessed dramatic changes in higher education systems worldwide. Many systems have experienced rapid expansion and increased diversification. In addition, given public resource constraints, many have increasingly turned to private sources of funding to support student enrollments. How have these profound changes affected inequalities in access? While inequalities could be structured with respect to a multiple broad set of factors (e.g., race, ethnicity, gender, region, etc.), we are focused in this chapter on social class background. We explore the extent to which variation in system-level characteristics of education systems is associated with differences in the likelihood that individuals from disadvantaged backgrounds will be eligible and attend higher education. We examine these relationships over time and across countries to take advantage of the variation produced by shifting world-wide changes in educational systems.

Expansion and Stratification

While educational expansion is associated with many advantages, including enhancement of peoples' general well-being and of societies' macroeconomic development, scholars have observed that, in and of itself, expansion does not reduce class inequalities in education. Raftery and Hout (1993) have argued that inequality between any two social strata in the odds of attaining a given level of education persists until the advantaged class reaches the point of saturation. Saturation is defined as the point at which nearly all sons and daughters of relatively advantaged origins attain the educational level under consideration.

Until that point, the advantaged group is typically better equipped to take advantage of any new and attractive educational opportunities, and class inequalities will persist or even increase as opportunities are expanded. Only when the privileged class reaches saturation at a given level of education, would further expansion of that level contribute to the reduction of inequality in the odds of its attendance because the privileged cannot increase their attendance rates past the 100% mark.

This hypothesis, maximally maintained inequality (MMI), is consistent with results reported by Shavit and Blossfeld (1993) who found that in most countries educational expansion did not reduce educational inequality. More recent studies (e.g., Jonsson, Mills, & Müller, 1996; Shavit & Westerbeek, 1998) found that as primary and secondary education expanded, class inequalities in their attainment declined. This result is consistent with Raftery and Hout's argument because the middle classes have reached saturation with respect to attainment of lower educational levels. In a recent paper, Hout (2007) analyzed data for 25 nations and found that among market economies, socioeconomic inequality in overall educational attainment is inversely related to the prevalence of higher education. This is also consistent with MMI because in societies with market economies, lower levels of education tend to be saturated in the privileged strata.

Although there are also empirical exceptions to MMI (e.g., in some former state socialist societies, inequality is not related to the degree of saturation (Hout, 2006)), it is consistent with most cases and is considered a useful working hypothesis for studies of educational expansion and stratification (Hout & DiPrete, 2006).

Institutional Differentiation and Stratification

Several scholars have argued that concurrent with expansion, qualitative differentiation replaces inequalities in the quantity of education attained (e.g., Gamoran & Mare, 1989; Shavit, 1984). A well-known tenet of organization theory is that organizational growth tends to be accompanied by differentiation (Blau, 1970). Differentiation is viewed as a means to operate more efficiently by dividing "raw materials" or "clients" into more homogeneous units. Educational expansion often follows this pattern, with systems becoming more complex as greater numbers of students enroll. While differentiation is commonly regarded as a consequence of expansion, it may also *contribute* to expansion, as new places become available in new segments of the education system. Whereas a functionalist view suggests that differentiation allows greater efficiency (Thompson, 1967), social control theorists point out that a differentiated system of higher education preserves the elite status of those born into privilege (Brint & Karabel, 1989; Trow, 1972).

The mode of differentiation in higher education varies between countries. In some countries, tertiary education is offered primarily by a single type of institution—usually, a research university. Meek and his associates refer to this type of system as unified (Goedegebuure, Meek, Kivinen, & Rinne, 1996). Unified systems tend to be quite rigid. They are controlled by professorial elites who are not inclined to encourage expansion, either of their own universities or through the formation of new ones. Very few systems still belong to this type. In our comparative project, only the Italian and Czech higher education systems are strictly unified. Other systems consist of a mix of institutions that are stratified by prestige, resources, and selectivity of both faculty and students. A well-known example is the American system, which consists of prestigious research universities, a second tier of private and public 4-year colleges, as well as many 2-year colleges (Brown, 1995; Grodsky, 2003; Karabel, 1972). Meek and his associates refer to this type as diversified higher education (Goedege-buure et al., 1996).

Often, the second tier of tertiary education takes the form of vocational or semiprofessional training (e.g., the German *Fachhochschulen*). This system is labeled as binary because it consists of two main types of institutions: academic and vocational. Some diversified systems are also binary in the sense that second-tier colleges primarily provide vocational training. In other cases, vocational institutions were upgraded to university status in an attempt to transform the system from a binary to a formally unified one (e.g., Britain and Australia).

The co-occurrence of expansion and differentiation is the basis for claims that higher education expansion is primarily a process of diversion, channeling members of the working class to lower-status postsecondary opportunities in order to reserve higher-status opportunities for the elite (Brint & Karabel, 1989). Swirski and Swirski (1997) argued that as the second-tier system expands, first-tier institutions become more selective and class inequalities in access to first-tier institutions increase. An alternative view, however, is that expansion of lower-tier postsecondary education enhances opportunity by bringing into higher education students who would otherwise not have continued past secondary school (Dougherty, 1994). Furthermore, one could argue that as higher education expands, first-tier institutions must compete for students and may lower admission thresholds. According to this logic, education expansion that leads to higher overall rates of tertiary enrollments is a process of inclusion, even if expansion is accompanied by differentiation.

Tertiary Market Structure and Inequality

Many studies of the relation between educational expansion and educational stratification suffer from an important theoretical inconsistency. On the one hand, they assume that expansion is *exogenous* to the stratification process, and that it affects the educational opportunities available to individuals (e.g., Raftery & Hout, 1993). At the same time, these studies assume that educational expansion reflects rising individual incentives to attend school for longer periods of their life course. Some argue that incentives rise in response to changes in the occupational structure (e.g., Blau & Duncan, 1967; Treiman, 1970). Others believe that incentives rise because groups and individuals compete for access to the best jobs (Collins, 1979) or because parental expectations are such that children's education is likely to equal or exceed that found in the prior generation (Erikson & Jonsson, 1996). Regardless of the specific mechanism, these theoretical orientations share the assumption that expansion is *demand-driven*; namely, that schools expand in response to growing aggregate demand by individuals for education.

Systems of higher education vary greatly in the degree to which they rely on public or private provision to support tertiary education. Furthermore, the responsiveness of education systems to consumer demand changes over time. Since the 1980s, some systems have undergone deregulation and privatization that facilitates rapid expansion in response to growing demand. In some systems private institutions aggressively stimulate and generate demand for their services through the use of promotional and marketing strategies (witness the increase in "nontraditional" students, the spread of the concept of "lifelong learning," or the "College for All" campaigns implemented in the United States).

We anticipate that where higher education is largely funded from private sources, enrollment rates exceed those found in publicly funded systems. Privately funded colleges and universities rely on enrollment for revenue and are thus client-seekers. Furthermore, private institutions may engage in demand-generating activities, such as advertising and the development of specialized programs that cater to well-defined groups of potential clients. Expanded funding from private sources can also potentially increase the overall level of support for higher education by supplementing, as opposed to substituting for, sustained public sector resource commitments (Arum, 1996). At the same time, however, some institutions of higher education are also status-seekers. That is, they engage in various activities intended to enhance their prestige in terms of attracting "high quality" faculty and students relative to competing institutions. Most important in this regard is social exclusion in the process of student selection through the elevation of admissions criteria.

Clearly, the imperatives of client-seeking and status-seeking behaviors conflict with one another. Thus, we expect to find greater enrollment rates and more institutional differentiation in market systems than in state-funded systems.

Class inequalities in the odds of progression to tertiary education may also differ between the two regimes, but we are unable to hypothesize a priori what direction these differences might take. Class inequalities in the odds of educational progression are due primarily to class differences in ability (including cultural capital), financial resources, and motivation. It is likely that in regimes that have expanded tertiary education through reliance on private sector funding there is less stringent educational selection on ability and there could thus be lower class inequalities than in more rigid government funded systems. At the same time, in highly privatized systems class inequalities may be mediated more directly by family differences in the ability to pay tuition fees.

Summary of Propositions

The discussion of educational expansion, differentiation, and market structure suggests six propositions as follows:

Expansion and Educational Stratification

1. Expansion is not associated with inequality at the level where expansion occurs, unless saturation is approached (i.e., inequality is maximally maintained).

Institutional Differentiation and Selection

2. Tertiary expansion and differentiation are related, with causal effects operating in both directions: diversified systems are more likely to have higher overall enrollments rates, and vice versa.
3. The differentiation of higher education (both the diversified and binary modes) diverts students away from first-tier enrollment.

Market Structure, Differentiation, and Access

4. On average, enrollment rates are higher in systems with more funding from private sources.
5. Systems with higher levels of funding from private sources are likely to be more diversified than state-centered systems.
6. The degree of reliance on private funding is associated with inequality in access to higher education, but the direction of the association cannot be determined a priori.

Methodology: A Collaborative Comparative Study

This research project employs a collaborative comparative methodology of the kind previously used by Shavit and Blossfeld (1993), Shavit and Müller (1998), Arum and Müller (2004), and others. Research teams in a sample of countries were asked to conduct similar studies of higher educational attainment using nationally representative data. The country studies each applied a common theoretical and methodological framework that had been agreed upon by the teams and was capable of generating findings comparable across countries.

Once the country studies were completed, as the project coordinators we analyzed the findings comparatively and report the results in this chapter.

Our sample of countries is not a probability sample. Rather, we selected countries that represent variation in the main macrolevel variables of interest (extent of expansion, differentiation, degree of privatization), and where researchers were available who were familiar with our paradigmatic framework and had access to the necessary data. The project includes 15 national teams consisting of 34 researchers and focuses on higher education systems in advanced economies, where expansion of secondary and tertiary education is further along than elsewhere.

Variables and Classifications

Higher Education Eligibility and Attendance

The main objective of this research project is to explore systematic inequalities in access to higher education across social strata. We define higher education as tertiary programs that are either academic or occupationally oriented. We operationalize the former as all programs leading to academic degrees such as a BA or BSc (undergraduate degrees), Laurea, Diplom, MA, or MSc (lower-level graduate degrees), or their equivalents. The second tier includes all 2-year college programs, whether vocational or academic, as well as polytechnics (e.g., in the UK), *Fachhochschulen* (Germany), *Srednee Spetsial'noe Uchebnoe Zavedenie* (SSUZy; Russia), or *instituts universitaires technologiques* (IUT; France). We exclude programs that are typically shorter than 2 years or those attended predominantly by students of upper secondary school ages (e.g., vocational and technical programs in Australia and Israel). Students who attended either academic or second-tier programs are defined as having attended higher education. Those who attended academic programs are defined as having attended first-tier programs, except in the United States and Israel. In the former, the first tier was defined as having attended 4-year programs in selective institutions, while in the latter it was defined as having attended a university rather than a college.

Eligibility for higher education is defined as a certificate, or completed course of study at the secondary level, that formally allows continuation into some form of academic higher education.[2]

Modes of Differentiation

As noted, we capitalize on the existence of marked differences between countries in the organizational form of higher education. However, these differences also thwart a strictly comparable definition of higher education across cases. National postsecondary educational programs vary in eligibility requirements,

TABLE 1.1 Classification of Countries by Mode of Differentiation in Higher Education

Country	Mode of Differentiation
Britain	Binary
France	Binary
Germany	Binary
Netherlands	Binary
Russia	Binary
Switzerland	Binary
Israel	Diversified
Japan	Diversified
Korea	Diversified
Sweden	Diversified
Taiwan	Diversified
United States	Diversified
Australia	Mixed/Other
Czech Republic	Unified
Italy	Unified

content, duration, form of accreditation and certification, and in the settings in which they are offered (university, college, private institute, etc.). While educational systems typically exhibit some mix of organizational forms, we follow Meek, Goedegebuure, Kivinen, and Rinne (1996) who classify them into three ideal typical modes of differentiation. Column 2 in Table 1.1 classifies countries by these organizational categories. The classification pertains to the most recent decades covered by the data in each country and is based on information provided in the respective chapters. Six of the cases are binary, six are diversified, and two are unitary. Australia does not fall comfortably into any of the three categories, but whether we include it as a unified case or exclude it from the analysis does not substantially affect the results we report in findings that pertain to mode of differentiation.

Market Structure

Private–public distinctions in education can be proxied in many ways, such as the degree of state institutional control, student enrollments in the private sector, the number of private institutions, and the private–public mix of funding. We conceptualize the market structure of higher education by focusing on the extent to which the system is driven by a consumer logic; that is, the extent to which colleges and universities are dependent on resources provided by private sources. We operationalize this variable as the percent of national expenditures on higher education that come from private sources as reported by the Organisation for Economic Co-operation and Development (OECD) (OECD 1985–92, table II.1.9, p. 50; OECD 1996, table F1.1c, p. 61). We rely on OECD data here because they report reliable and comparable data on privatization for most countries in our sample. Our focus on examining the implications of private compared to public financial support for higher education systems is consistent with resource dependency theoretical orientations from the literature on the sociology of organizations; this approach suggests that institutional dependence on particular resource flows has consequences for the form, structure, and practices of organizations (Pfeffer & Salancik, 1978).

Measures of Inequality

Logit regressions include measures of father's class and parental education. Father's class was measured on an EGP or a very similar class schema (Erikson & Goldthorpe, 1992), and parental education was measured on the CASMIN educational schemas (Müller, Luttinger, Koenig, & Karle, 1989). Both schemas are shown in Appendix Table 1.A. From each equation we extracted the log-odds of attaining a particular educational outcome contrasting respondents whose fathers were in classes I or II (the so-called service classes that include professionals, managers, and owners of large firms) against those whose fathers were in classes V and VI (the skilled working class). We also extracted the log-odds of achieving an educational outcome contrasting parents with higher education against those with only secondary education. The average of these two log-odds statistics provides a composite summary measure of the relative effects of social background on educational transitions and thus serves as our measure of inequality between social strata, for each educational outcome.

Analysis and Findings

Expansion and Educational Stratification

In Figure 1.1 we describe change across cohorts in the rates of eligibility for and attendance in higher education and of the first tier. The horizontal axis of the figure is labeled by the decade during which the birth cohort would have made the transition from secondary to higher education. We see a marked expansion, across the four decades, in all three educational levels. On average, the eligibility rate for higher education increased from about 35% to about 80%, and attendance in higher education increased from under 20% to over 40% on average. Attendance rates in the first tier also increased about twofold during the four decades.

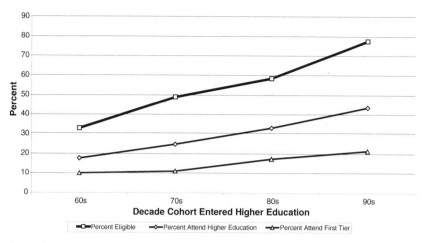

FIGURE 1.1 Average trends in higher education eligibly and attendance in 15 countries.

Following Raftery and Hout's MMI hypothesis, our Proposition 1 suggests that inequality between social strata in the odds of attaining an educational level is stable over time and is unaffected by educational expansion unless the proportion attaining it nears saturation. We begin to assess this hypothesis in Figure 1.2, which depicts the association across countries between eligibility rates and change in inequality of eligibility. The data points in the plot are labeled by the country acronym and the decade during which the youngest cohort attended higher education. We measured change in inequality as the percent difference between the two youngest cohorts in the mean effects of father's class and parental education on the log-odds of eligibility.

Figure 1.2 reveals that inequality in eligibility declined in five countries, was about stable in nine, and increased in one (Italy). The observed pattern is largely consistent with the saturation hypothesis. For this project, we operationalize saturation as educational attainment rates exceeding 80%. In four of the five countries in which inequality declined, eligibility was greater than 80%, and in all but one or two of the countries (Australia is borderline) in which eligibility rates were lower than 80%, inequality was stable or increased over time.

The limitation of Figure 1.2 is that it depicts the relation between changing inequality and saturation, but does not represent expansion. We address this limitation by examining the partial correlations between saturation and expansion on the one hand, and changing inequality on the other hand. We measure expansion as percent *change* between the two youngest cohorts in eligibility rates. The bivariate correlation of expansion with change in inequality of eligibility is weak (0.13). To take account of expansion and saturation simultaneously, we define a dummy variable which is coded 1 for the five cases in which 80% or more of the youngest cohort were eligible for higher

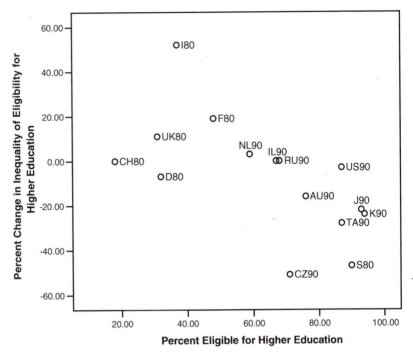

FIGURE 1.2 Associations between percent eligible for higher education and percent change in inequality of eligibility. *Note:* In this and subsequent scatterplots, the countries are labeled by their acronym and the decade during which the last cohort attended higher education. The acronyms are: AU-Australia, CH-Switzerland, CZ-Czech Republic, D-Germany, F-France, I-Italy, IL-Israel, J-Japan, K-Korea, NL-Netherlands, RU-Russia, S-Sweden, TA-Taiwan, UK-Britain, US-United States.

education (i.e., U.S., Japan, Korea, Taiwan, and Sweden) and estimate a linear regression of change in inequality of eligibility on both expansion of eligibility and the saturation dummy ($R^2 = 0.24$). The standardized effect of expansion is virtually null ($r = -0.04$) but the effect of saturation is sizable and negative as expected ($r = -0.50$). This is precisely the pattern of results predicted by MMI and Proposition 1.

Next we repeat the analysis for the transition from eligibility to the actual attendance of higher education. First, we relate change in inequality in the log-odds of making the transition to higher education to the percent of eligibles who attended higher education. We hypothesize that, in the presence of expansion, as the proportion of eligibles who attend higher education exceeds 80%, inequality at that transition point would decline. Figure 1.3 displays the bivariate relation between the percent of eligibles who attended higher education and change in inequality in the transition from secondary to higher education attendance ($r = -0.36$). A detailed inspection of the figure shows that inequality in the transition from eligibility to higher education was relatively stable in 6 of the 13 cases shown (Korea, U.S., France, Britain, Czech Republic, and the Netherlands), increased in three, and declined in four. Of these four cases, the proportion of eligibles who continued to higher education exceeded 80% in two (Israel and Italy). The exceptions are Taiwan and Japan, where inequality declined without saturation. In both cases, after a period of retrenchment and consolidation colleges were allowed to expand rapidly in the 1990s. In both cases, but especially in Taiwan, college enrollments expanded at a much faster pace than the rate of eligibility, and inequality in the transition to higher education declined. Figure 1.3 also reveals one case in which inequality in the parameters examined did not decline despite saturation: in the United Kingdom, rates of higher education enrollment among those eligible were very high, but little expansion occurred over the period covered by the data.

Next, we estimate a regression similar to the one reported earlier, in which we study the combined effects of saturation and expansion on change in inequality of higher education attendance. The dependent variable is inequality in the transition from eligibility to higher education, and the independent variables are two: a dummy variable representing saturation and expansion in the transition rate from eligibility to higher education. The bivariate correlations between expansion and saturation on the one hand, and the dependent

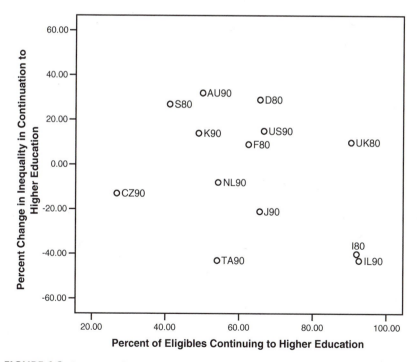

FIGURE 1.3 Assocation between percent of eligibles who continued to higher education, and change in inequality in the log odds of continuation.

variable on the other hand, are -0.36 and -0.45 respectively. However, when both variables are included in the regression equation ($R^2 = 0.21$) their standardized effects are 0.06 and -0.50. Thus, on average, across the 13 countries that are included in this analysis, saturation would seem to reduce inequality while expansion alone does not.

Differentiation and Inclusion

Our next empirical question concerns the extent to which institutional differentiation stratifies opportunities in higher education. Specifically, we address two hypotheses: first, that differentiation and expansion are related (Proposition 2); and second, that the differentiation of higher education diverts students from first-tier education (Proposition 3). To this end, we compare attendance rates in higher and first-tier education in unified, diversified, and binary systems. In addition, we compare inequalities of access to higher and first-tier education between diversified and binary systems.

Table 1.2 examines the relations between expansion, differentiation, and inequality. Although we do not have sufficiently detailed measurement of differentiation nor adequate variation within country over time to model formally the relationship between change in differentiation and change in enrollment, we nevertheless find substantial differences in eligibility rates between diversified systems as well as between binary and unified systems. In the diversified systems eligibility is nearly universal (86%) on average, compared with 42% and 54% in the other two categories. Moreover, diversified systems have the highest tertiary attendance rates. Thus, we find general support for Proposition 2: both eligibility and attendance rates tend to be higher in diversified systems. Table 1.2 does not reveal the mechanisms that link differentiation and higher rates of tertiary enrollments, but the country-specific chapters suggest that more diversified systems tend to have more lenient requirements for eligibility for higher education. In most diversified systems (U.S., Japan, Korea, Taiwan, and Sweden in recent decades) eligibility is conferred upon graduation from secondary school, whereas in most binary systems (Britain, Germany, France, Russia, and Switzerland) students must pass a series of matriculation examinations to be eligible. Matriculation examinations are generally more selective than graduation. Therefore, where matriculation examinations determine eligibility, fewer students are eligible than in systems that require only graduation. In addition, in most binary systems the distinction between vocational and academic education begins at the secondary level, where many students are already diverted from tertiary education (Kerckhoff, 1993).

Proposition 3 suggested that the differentiation of higher education may divert students from first-tier higher education. Column 3 of Table 1.2 contradicts this claim as it pertains to diversified systems: the cohort proportions

TABLE 1.2 Means and Standard Deviations (in Parentheses) of Eligibility, Attendance, and Inequality by Mode of Differentiation

Mode of Differentiation	n	(1) Percent Eligible for Higher Education	(2) Percent Attend Higher Education	(3) Percent Attend First Tier Higher Education	(4) Inequality in Eligibility	(5) Inequality in Higher Education	(6) Inequality in First Tier Higher Education
Binary	6	42.3	30.7	12.2	1.0	0.99	1.6
		(18.2)	(7.6)	(5.0)	(.49)	(.30)	(1.21)
Diversified	6	86.3	51.8	24.2	.77	.80	1.3
		(9.9)	(10.0)	(2.2)	(.29)	(.26)	(.99)
Unified	2	54.0	26.5	26.5	.92	.85	.85
		(24.0)	(10.6)	(10.6)	(.71)	(.33)	(.33)
Total	14	62.8	39.1	19.0	.90	.88	1.4
		(26.0)	(14.2)	(8.1)	(.43)	(.28)	(1.01)

Note: Australia is excluded (see footnote 4). The figures in columns 4-6 are average logit coefficients of fathers' class effects (the effect of the service class versus the skilled manual working class) and parental education (higher versus secondary education).

attending the first tier in diversified and unified systems are similar. By contrast, in binary systems first-tier attendance rates are very low.

Whereas columns 1 to 3 of Table 1.2 respond to questions about differentiation and overall rates of eligibility and higher education attendance, columns 4 to 6 address questions about inequality, as represented by average logit coefficients for effects of parents' educational and occupational backgrounds on eligibility for, and attendance in higher education and its first tier. In column 4 we compare the three modes of differentiation with respect to inequality of eligibility. We find that inequality of eligibility is similar in unified and binary systems (0.92 and 1.0) and is somewhat lower in diversified ones (0.77), consistent with our interpretation that diversified systems have more lenient eligibility requirements. Thus, we conclude that diversified systems are more inclusive than both binary and unified systems: a larger proportion of the population is eligible for and attends higher education, and inequality occurs at a lower rate. The contrast between diversified and binary systems is particularly compelling, favoring diversified systems which exhibit both more expansion and less inequality.

The greater inclusiveness of diversified systems could be illusory, if students from disadvantaged backgrounds lacked access to first-tier higher education. Column 6 suggests this is not the case. Inequality of access to the first tier appears slightly lower in diversified than in binary systems (1.3 versus 1.6 in the logit metric). This contrast is robust to controls for expansion: in a regression on first-tier inequality controlling for percent of first-tier enrollment, diversified systems exhibited lower inequality by the same margin as reflected in column 6.

In both diversified and binary systems, inequality is greater for first-tier enrollment than for enrollment in higher education overall (compare columns 5 and 6). Unified systems have only one tier, so that comparison is not relevant, but it is noteworthy that while diversified systems exhibit lower inequality in higher education enrollment than unified systems, the latter exhibits lower rates of first-tier enrollment inequality. Thus, the differentiation of higher education may come at some cost to inequality of first-tier enrollment, although this conclusion is necessarily tentative since it is based on only two unified cases. The more robust conclusion is that diversified systems exhibit both greater enrollment levels and less inequality than binary systems at all levels of higher education. Thus, we find strong support for Proposition 2 (differentiation and expansion are related), but Proposition 3 (differentiation leads to diversion) is largely refuted. Diversified systems exhibit more first-tier enrollment at lower rates of inequality than binary systems. The relative class-based odds of first-tier enrollment still appear lowest in the unified systems (which have only one tier), but diversified systems offer more access to higher education overall at little cost to enrollment in the first tier.

Market Structure, Differentiation, and Access

Finally our analysis turns to a set of questions that focus on the role of market structure on higher education differentiation, expansion, and inequality (Propositions 4–6). As noted above, we operationalize market structure as the percent of higher education funding that is provided through private sector sources. As was the case in our analysis of differentiation, data limitations prevent formal modeling of changes in funding from private sources within country over time. Nevertheless, we are able to explore the extent to which private sector involvement is related to the scale, scope, and allocation of higher education (i.e., the extent to which it is associated with expansion, differentiation, and inequality).

Figure 1.4 displays the relation between market structure and the size of the higher education sector. There is a strong positive association between these variables ($R^2 = 0.44$), consistent with Proposition 4. However, in supplementary analysis (results not shown), we found no significant relation between private funding and attendance in higher education when the latter was considered only for the subset of the cohort that was eligible. This finding suggests that where higher education is largely funded by private sources, it expands through the adoption of lenient eligibility criteria. Similar results were found when we examined attendance rates solely for first-tier higher education.

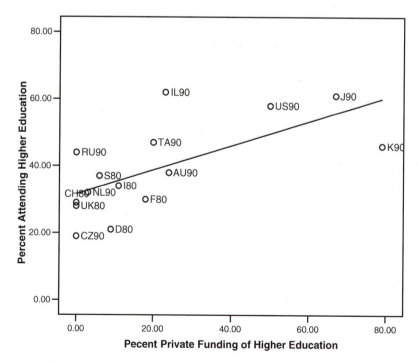

FIGURE 1.4 Association between percent private funding and percent attending higher education.

TABLE 1.3 Private Sector Funding and Mode of Differentiation in Higher Education

Mode of Differentiation	Tertiary Education Reliance on Private Sector Funding		
	Low	Moderate	High
Unified	Italy Czech Republic		
Binary	Germany Russia Switzerland Britain Netherlands	France	
Diversified	Sweden	Israel Taiwan	Japan Korea United States

Table 1.3 examines the relation between private funding and mode of institutional differentiation (classified as unified, binary, or diversified)

Both unified systems exist in settings where tertiary education is funded primarily through public sources. When variation and delineation in organizational type occur in systems with low levels of private funding, it is usually binary rather than the less structured and weakly demarcated diversified form (Sweden is the one exception). Diversified higher education systems appear primarily in countries where higher education relies on private funds to a larger degree. Thus, we find support for Proposition 5: reliance on private sources of funding is conducive to greater differentiation. More important, however, in systems with a high degree of private funding, the mode of differentiation is more likely to be diversified than binary.

Given that greater reliance of higher education on private funding is associated with institutional differentiation, one would also expect increased rates of tertiary attendance in these settings. We find this indeed to be the case. The partial correlation coefficient between private funding and higher education expansion (i.e., change over time), net of the overall original size of the higher education system, is 0.29. Countries with lower rates of expansion tend to have lower rates of private funding and to have either unified or binary institutional forms. This pattern is also consistent with Proposition 5.

Finally, we address Proposition 6 by exploring the relation between the degree of reliance on private funding and inequality in attendance at higher education. When exploring zero-order correlations between our measures of inequality in higher education attendance and the extent to which the system was supported by private sector funding, we found no evidence of any significant association (correlation coefficient = 0.03). We found similar patterns when we examined the association of private funding with change over time in social background effects and when considering attendance solely in first-tier institutions. However, the absence of a direct correlation between private

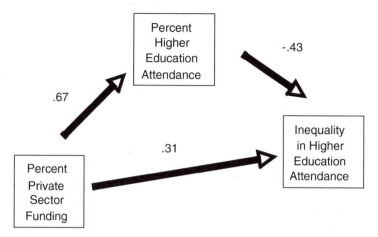

FIGURE 1.5 Path diagram of assocations between private sector funding, higher education attendance, and inequality in higher education.

sector funding and inequality in higher education masks the presence of two contradictory patterns of association underlying this phenomenon of null overall (or "total") effects.

In Figure 1.5, we present a path diagram that captures the extent to which private sector funding is associated with variation in both higher education attendance and higher education inequality. Specifically, private sector funding exhibits a positive direct association with inequality in higher education, as identified by the partial correlation coefficient of 0.31 in the diagram. However, the extent to which private sector funding contributes to increased inequality is mitigated by the indirect link between private sector funding and inequality via higher overall rates of tertiary enrollments. In path diagrams, such an indirect effect can be calculated as the multiplicative product of the two partial correlation coefficients (0.67 × -0.43 = -0.29).

These results indicate that the beneficial effect of private funding is due to its positive effect on increased levels of educational attendance, which in turn reduces inequality of access. Net of this indirect connection, increased reliance on private sources of funding tends to magnify inequality. We suspect that in highly privatized systems, class inequalities may reflect family differences in the ability to pay tuition fees.

Discussion and Conclusions

Our synthesis of country-specific findings indicated that expansion is pervasive, and that under certain conditions, it may lead to declining inequality. In particular, expansion to the point of saturation was associated with declining inequality in eligibility for higher education in four countries (Japan, Korea, Taiwan, and Sweden), and with a decline in inequality in the transition from secondary to tertiary education in two countries (Italy and Israel). With a few exceptions, inequality rates were stable or increased in other cases. These findings supported Proposition 1, that inequality is maximally maintained. Among the exceptions, we took particular note of declining inequality in the transition to higher education in two other countries that underwent sharp expansion after a period of consolidation (Japan and Taiwan). These cases suggest that rapid expansion in a diversified and deregulated system of higher education can broaden involvement in higher education across the social strata, apparently without any greater tendency to divert those of disadvantaged origins to lower-tier institutions.

We also found that expansion and institutional differentiation are related; in particular, diversified systems of higher education exhibit higher rates of eligibility and correspondingly higher rates of enrollment than unified and binary systems (consistent with Proposition 2). Moreover, we found that binary systems divert students away from higher education as a whole and from its first tier. In diversified systems, the proportions attending higher education are much larger than in other systems, and contrary to our expectations (see Proposition 3), the proportions attending first-tier institutions are more comparable to those of unified ones.

Finally, we examined the extent to which variation in private support for higher education was associated with institutional expansion and differentiation as well as stratification of educational opportunities. Our synthesis of country-specific findings suggests that systems with more private sector involvement tend to expand more rapidly and are more diversified (consistent with Propositions 4 and 5). In approaching this project, we hypothesized that while privatization is associated with inequality of access to higher education, we could not specify a priori the shape of the association (Proposition 6). On the one hand we assumed that the client-seeking behavior of private institutions would be associated with expansion, a weakening of social selection, and thus greater inclusion of the lower strata. On the other hand we expected that reliance on private funding could potentially lead to higher tuition fees on average and would increase inequality of access. Our analysis suggests that both mechanisms are likely operative and that these countervailing trends in combination largely balance each other out in their effects. Specifically, privatization is associated with expansion of opportunity and a corresponding lessening of social inequality, but privatization net of expansion is associated with increased inequality of access. Thus, whereas privatization through the indirect effect of expansion tends to draw persons into higher education, it also has direct effects that are exclusive; overall, the total effect of privatization on educational stratification is neutral.

How do these findings stand with respect to claims about inclusion and diversion? Overall, we found much stronger evidence of inclusion than of diversion. Whereas privatization was associated with inclusion and diversion in about equal amounts, expansion and diversification tended to be largely inclusive. First, overall expansion was inclusive in the sense that even when social selection is stable, expansion means that more students from all strata, including those from disadvantaged backgrounds, are carried further into the education system, and for the cohort as a whole inequality is reduced. Second, expansion in a context of saturation often results in declining inequality, clearly a case in which expansion stimulates inclusion. We observed this pattern for both eligibility and attendance of higher education. Third, whereas binary systems tended to exhibit both more inequality and lower rates of tertiary enrollment, diversified systems offered much higher rates of enrollment with no greater inequality overall, and just moderately greater inequality of first-tier enrollment compared to our two unified cases. Diversified systems are thus more inclusive overall than either binary or unitary systems.

Our first claim, that expansion is inclusive even without declining inequality, gives a new interpretation to a familiar set of findings. Previous work characterized cases of rising enrollment and stable odds ratios for educational transitions as "persistent inequality" (Shavit & Blossfeld, 1993). In our view, this conclusion misses an important point: When a given level of education expands, we should expect increasing inequality of enrollment at the next level due to the increased heterogeneity of the eligible population. Consequently, when inequality in an expanding system is stable rather than on the rise, the system should be regarded as increasingly inclusive because it allows larger proportions of all social strata to attend. By this notion, not only should most of our cases be regarded as increasingly inclusive, but so should those reported by Shavit and Blossfeld (1993) despite the stability that they find in the parameters of the educational stratification process. Looking within countries over time, our findings generally mirror those in Persistent Inequality: stable odds ratios, conditional on eligibility (Figure 1.3). Only post-Soviet Russia exhibited increasing inequality. Of the four cases of downward changes in odds ratios, two may be explained by saturation (Israel and Italy) and two by rapid expansion following consolidation (Japan and Taiwan).

Our findings and conclusions have policy implications. *Persistent Inequality* emphasized that expansion enables the privileged classes to retain their relative edge in the process of educational stratification. Our interpretation is different. Of course, we recognize that class inequalities in the *relative* shares of education persist over time and are difficult to change. Much research has shown that in most instances the privileged classes manage to maintain their advantages over time. Given the stability of *relative* inequalities, the most that policy can achieve under ordinary (i.e., nonrevolutionary) political circumstances is change in the absolute size of the educational pie (i.e., expansion). Yet we reach a slightly more optimistic conclusion here: namely that the expanding pie is increasingly inclusive even when relative advantages are preserved, because it extends a valued good to a broader spectrum of the population. Moreover, we found that diversified systems tend to be more inclusive than binary systems—without diverting students from the first tier—and we noted four cases of expansion in which relative inequalities actually diminished somewhat. Our findings thus imply that educational expansion is an equalizing force and that diversification is not inconsistent with inclusion.

In terms of overall lessons to be drawn for sociological understanding the consequences to individuals from disadvantaged backgrounds of shifting world-wide educational configurations, we would emphasize that differences in institutional characteristics are often related to system-level educational expansion. While one might oppose institutional differentiation and privatization for ideological or personal reasons, pragmatically one must recognize that these changes are typically accompanied by overall increased access to higher education. In general, we find that the educational expansion that we observed did not affect the relative odds of different social strata being eligible or attending college. Rather, the expansion was associated with enhanced opportunities for all.

Such changes would be predicted to lead to higher levels of subsequent attainment of college credentials for future cohorts. If students also enhanced their productivity while attending college, the society as a whole would raise its stock of human capital amongst its citizenry opening up the possibility that the economy as a whole potentially might be more competitive and productive. Alternatively, if educational expansion were associated simply with greater distribution of tertiary credentials and only minimal increases in human capital associated with these attainments, a greater level of degree attainment might have effects primarily through affecting the relative position of college graduates in the labor market. In the context of shifting worldwide higher education institutional arrangements, the ultimate consequences for subsequent outcomes of various social strata have yet to be determined.

Notes

1   Adapted from *Stratification in Higher Education: A Comparative Study*, edited by Yossi Shavit, Richard Arum, and Adam Gamoran. Copyright © 2007 by the Board of Trustees of the Leland Stanford Jr. University. All rights reserved. Used with the permission of Stanford University Press, www.sup.org.

2   Higher education systems differ in their eligibility requirements. In some cases (France, Germany, Israel, Italy, Russia, and Switzerland) admission into higher education requires a secondary school matriculation certificate. In the Czech Republic, Japan, Korea, Taiwan, and the United States, completion of secondary education is required. In Australia, it entails completion of Year 12—the preparatory year for university study. In Britain, eligibility for upper tertiary education requires two or more A-level examinations (i.e., advanced secondary qualification examinations). In the Netherlands, there are multiple routes into higher education, but the most common are via the completion of academic 5-year secondary education (VWO) or via 4-year vocational postsecondary education (HBO). In Sweden, the eligibility rules have changed several times during the period of observation. Until the mid-1960s, eligibility for university studies was defined as having passed the examination at the upper secondary level (studentexamen). Since then, it was defined as having completed a 3- or 4-year program of study at the upper secondary level. In all countries, there are both main and alternative routes into higher education. The operationalization of eligibility in this chapter

APPENDIX TABLE 1.A Social Class Origin and Parents' Highest Level of Education

Abbreviation	Description
Class origin	
I	Upper service class; senior civil servants, higher managerial, higher-grade professionals (also self-employed).
II	Lower service class; middle-level administrators and officials, lower managerial, lower-grade professionals.
III	Routine non-manual employees, clerks.
IVab	Self-employed and employers in non-agricultural businesses.
IVcd	Farmers and smallholders, including self-employed fishermen.
VI	Skilled manual workers.
VII	Semi- and unskilled manual workers including unqualified sales personnel.
Parents' education	
1ab	Compulsory schooling
1c	Lower vocational
2ab	Lower secondary/middle level
2c	Upper secondary
3ab	Tertiary

proxies the main routes into higher education in the various countries and tends to ignore the secondary ones. A related limitation is that in some countries different tiers of higher education have different eligibility requirements. For the comparative analysis presented here a uniform definition was required. These compromises are necessary, since modeling such a large number of alternative routes into higher education would not be empirically feasible.

References

Abbott, A. (1992).What do cases do? Some notes on activity in sociological analysis. In C. C. Ragin & H. S. Becke (Eds.), *What is a case?* (pp. 53–82). New York: Cambridge University Press.

Arum, R. (1996). Do private schools force public schools to compete? *American Sociological Review, 61*, 29–46.

Arum, R., & Muller, W. (2004). *The resurgence of self-employment: A comparative study of self-employment dynamics and social inequality.* Princeton, NJ: Princeton University Press.

Blau, P. (1970). A formal theory of differentiation in organizations. *American Sociological Review, 35*, 201–218.

Blau, P., & Duncan, O. D. (1967). *The American occupational structure.* New York: Wiley.

Brint, S. G., & Karabel, J. (1989). *The diverted dream: Community colleges and the promise of educational opportunity in America, 1900–1985.* Oxford, England: Oxford University Press.

Brown, D. K. (1995). *Degrees of control: A sociology of educational expansion and occupational credentialism.* New York: Teachers College Press.

Buchmann, C., & Hannum, E. (2001). Education and stratification in developing countries. *Annual Review of Sociology, 27*, 77–102.

Collins, R. (1979). *The credential society: An historical sociology of education and stratification.* New York: Academic Press.

Dougherty, K. (1994). *The contradictory college: The conflicting origins, impacts, and futures of the community college*. Albany, NY: SUNY Press.

Erikson, R., & Goldthorpe, J. H. (1992). *The constant flux: A study of class mobility in industrial societies*. Oxford, England: Clarendon Press.

Erikson, R., & Jonsson, J. O. (1996). *Can education be equalized? The Swedish case in comparative perspective*. Boulder, CO: Westview Press.

Gamoran, A., & Mare, R. D. (1989). Secondary-school racking and educational-inequality—Compensation, reinforcement, or neutrality. *American Journal of Sociology, 94*, 1146–1183.

Goedegebuure, L., Meek, V. L., Kivinen, O., & Rinne, R. (1996). On diversity, differentiation and convergence. In V. L. Meek, L. Goedegebuure, O. Kivinen, & R. Rinne (Eds.), *The mockers and the mocked: Comparative perspectives on differentiation, convergence and diversity in higher education* (pp. 2–13). New York: IAU Press/Pergamon.

Grodsky, E. S. (2003). *Constrained opportunity and student choice in American higher education* (Unpublished doctoral dissertation). University of Wisconsin, Madison.

Hout, M. (2007). Maximally maintained inequality revisited: Irish educational mobility in comparative perspective. In E. Hilliard & M. Nic Ghiolla Phádraig (Eds.), *Changing Ireland in international comparison* (pp. 23–39). Dublin, Ireland: Liffey Press.

Hout, M. (2006). Maximally maintained inequality and essentially maintained inequality: Cross-national comparisons. *Riron to Hoho* (Sociological Theory and Methods), *21*(2), 237–252.

Hout, M., & Diprete, T. A. (2006). What we have learned: RC28's contributions to knowledge about social stratification. *Research in Social Stratification and Mobility, 24*(1), 1–20.

Jonsson, J. O., Mills, C., & Muller, W. (1996). A half century of increasing educational openness? Social class, gender and educational attainment in Sweden, Germany, and Britain. In R. Erikson & J. O. Jonsson (Eds.), *Can education be equalized? The Swedish case in comparative perspective* (pp. 183–206). Boulder, CO: Westview Press.

Karabel, J. (1972). Community colleges and social stratification. *Harvard Educational Review, 42*, 521–562.

Kerckhoff, A. C. (1993). *Diverging pathways: Social structure and career deflections*. New York: Cambridge University Press.

Meek, L. V., Goedegebuure, L., Kivinen, O., & Rinne, R. (Eds.). (1996). *The mockers and the mocked: Comparative perspectives on differentiation, convergence, and diversity in higher education*. New York: Pergamon/IAU Press.

Muller, W., Luttinger, P., Koenig, W., & Karle, W. (1989). Class and education in industrial nations. *International Journal of Sociology, 19*, 3–39.

Pfeffer, J., & Salancik, G. (1978). *The external control of organizations*. New York: Harper & Row.

OECD. (1996). *Education at a glance*, Paris: OECD.

Raftery, A. E., & Hout, M. (1993). Maximally maintained inequality–Expansion, reform, and opportunity in Irish education, 1921–75. *Sociology of Education, 66*, 41–62.

Shavit, Y. (1984). Tracking and ethnicity in Israeli secondary education. *American Sociological Review, 49*, 210–220.

Shavit, Y., & Blossfeld, P. (Eds.). (1993). *Persistent inequality: Changing educational attainment in thirteen countries*. Boulder, CO: Westview Press.

Shavit, Y., & Müller, W. (Eds.). (1998). *From school to work: A comparative study of educational qualifications and occupational destinations*. Oxford, UK: Clarendon Press.

Shavit, Y., & Müller, W. (2000). Vocational secondary education: Where diversion and where safety net? *European Societies, 2*, 29–50.

Shavit, Y., & Westerbeek, K. (1998). Educational stratification in Italy—Reforms, expansion, and equality of opportunity. *European Sociological Review, 14*, 33–47.

Swirski, S., & Swirski, B. (1997). *Higher education in Israel* (Adva Center Series on Equality, no. 8). Tel Aviv, Israel: Adva Center.

Thompson, J. D. (1967). *Organizations in action*. New York: McGraw-Hill.

Treiman, D. J. (1970). Industrialization and social stratification. *Sociological Inquiry, 40*, 207–234.

Trow, M. (1972). The expansion and transformation of higher education. *International Review of Education, 18*, 61–84.

2

THE CHANGING EDUCATIONAL OPPORTUNITY STRUCTURE IN CHINA

Positioning for Access to Higher Education

Yan Zhao Ciupak and Amy E. Stich

Within only three decades, China has emerged as a major force in the world economy. Numerous social reforms and subsequent large-scale, ongoing foundational transformations have encouraged and simultaneously required China to increase its international competitiveness and build human capital for further economic development. In an effort to reposition itself in these ways, China continues to expand upon its system of higher education while also attempting to bolster the quality of its most established postsecondary institutions. Indeed, "education, broadly defined, is essential to the utilization of human potential for social and economic progress" (Rong & Shi, 2001, p. 108). However, despite the continued expansion and development of China's system of higher education, it is arguably the case that increased educational opportunities have further widened existing inequality of opportunity, particularly between those living within rural and urban contexts (Ciupak, 2008; Rong & Shi, 2001; Yang, 2006). For example, when considering the degree of institutional differentiation within China's system of higher education, students from peasant families represent 56.2% of the enrollment in 2- to 3-year programs and vocational institutes in comparison to less than 18% in prestigious universities, such as Beijing University and Tsinghua University (Yang, 2006). Based upon these statistical findings, researchers conclude that the majority of rural students who gain access to higher education during the expansion enrollment period are concentrated in lower-tier, local institutions wherein they receive neither equivalent resources, opportunities, nor outcomes (Yang, 2006).

Nevertheless, scholars have paid little attention to the personal stories behind the statistics and how these stories are shaped by, and also help to shape, the larger social and economic structure. As a result, we know little about how social and economic changes happening on both local and global scales affect key actors' perceptions, behaviors, and experiences in these newly industrializing economies. In other words, within such a radically shifting, multidimensional context, how are individual and collective identities challenged, negotiated, and reconstructed? What role does education play in these processes of negotiation and reconstruction? Since little research has probed these important changes and their influences on social status attainment and schooling (Weis, 2008), we hope to initiate a larger dialogue through the following empirical response to these timely questions.

More specifically, this chapter qualitatively explores how youth in China are positioned and are also positioning themselves through higher education in China's new social-economic context. We suggest that our understanding of social positioning is achieved through a thorough analysis of the decision-making process at each of three critical moments in Chinese college students' lives: pathways to higher education; choice of postsecondary institution and major; and postgraduation plans. Arguably, the decision-making process at each of these crucial moments relative to higher education effectively reflects the ways social structures and human strategies interact under the new context of local and global economic restructuring.

The Unequal Structure of Higher Education in Contemporary China[1]

Regional disparity in higher education admissions is widely considered by the public as the primary source of inequality affecting education in China, evidenced by differing minimum enrollment scores for different regions. In other words, for the same scores and same universities, the application results differ greatly depending on the applicant's urban or rural residency. Such regional discrimination is exemplified in educational policies that are markedly favorable to the municipalities directly under the Central Government: Beijing, Tianjin, Shanghai, and other key cities. Residents of these cities enjoy higher enrollment quotas and lower minimum enrollment scores. The regional disparity in higher education admissions is directly caused by China's polarized policy of development and the sociostructural characteristics of the socialist state. To be more specific, the uneven distribution of educational resources and the residence registration system *hukou*[2] directly causes unequal access to opportunities in higher education. The socialist registration–residence system, *hukou,* serves as a major political-social mechanism in contemporary China, restricting and directing internal migration, and maintaining local social stratification. The *hukou* system, which in practice protects urban privilege, especially in major cities, is arguably the most prevalent exclusionary practice affecting China's social structure.[3] The conversion of rural to urban status is central to social mobility in contemporary China (Wu & Treiman, 2004). Some researchers call an urban *hukou* the "Chinese dream" for Chinese peasants (Li, 2005). Unskilled migrant workers are still denied a *hukou* in urban areas, so there are few channels available to assist rural peasants to achieve such a conversion. Formal higher education thus becomes an instrumental tool for the children of rural peasants who seek to obtain urban status, despite the rather dim employment situation for college graduates and the increasing number of unskilled employment opportunities in the shifting market economy.

The Study

Data for this research were collected through policy analysis and in-depth interviews with 75 students enrolled in 21 institutions in developed and less developed regions in China. In addition, six administrators and faculty members from various tiers of institutions were interviewed to supplement information. Specific research procedures, sampling techniques, and coding strategies benefited greatly from a grounded theory approach (Glaser & Strauss, 1967; Strauss & Corbin, 1998). In addition, "compositional studies," an approach developed by Weis and Fine (2004), provided important conceptual tools for research design and data analysis. A combination of the two proved to be a powerful analytical tool for theory development, especially with regard to situating groups, lives, and actions in relation to key social and economic structures.

Based upon both Bourdieu's theories and in-depth interview data collected throughout China, this research develops a framework termed "architecture of capital accumulation and transmission." This framework emphasizes the differentiated ways in which individual agents adopt strategies to mobilize, transmit, and accumulate various forms of capital in response to both socialist state institutions regulating capital and socioeconomic structural change. This framework depicts how various forms (species) of capital are highly interconnected, converted, reproduced, and transmitted to enable or constrain educational and social mobility patterns. Thus, this framework contributes to the endeavor of using capital resources or assets as the basis of social stratification analysis. Herein, the authors apply this framework in an effort to explain how the education-related choices and experiences of college students in China connect to local and global changes relative to students' family and institutional habitus, and the availability of various forms of capital. Bourdieu introduced the concept of "habitus" to explain how various species of capital are transmitted through generations (Bourdieu, 1984; Bourdieu & Passeron, 1977). Habitus, loosely defined as the "dialectic of the internalization of externality and externalization of internality" (Bourdieu & Passeron, 1977, p. 72), reflects individuals' internalized sets of dispositions, preferences, perceptions, and expectations through socialization in family or school. In turn, these internalized attitudes create dispositions to act, interpret, and respond to experiences and opportunities, thus constraining or enabling life chances.

We begin with the first of three critical, education-related experiences and opportunities: students' high school pathways to college.

High School Pathways to College

Borrowing terminology from Hossler and Gallagher's higher education choice model (1987), this section focuses on students' choice of college pathway using modified frameworks of "choice" and "biography" during the "predisposition" phase, which is a "developmental phase in which students determine whether or not they would like to continue their education beyond high school" (Hossler & Gallagher, 1987, p. 209). Research employing the choice model argues that higher education choice is a complex decision-making process constructed within the interplay of social and biographical factors through constant negotiation between agency and structure. In addition, Du Bois-Reymond's (1998) distinction of "normal biography" and "choice biography" provides a useful framework to present the data. Du Bois-Reymond characterizes "normal biographies" as linear, anticipated, and predetermined stages of development into adulthood, which are often gender and class specific and rooted in well-established social structures. In "choice biographies," youth "reflect on the available options and justify their decisions … it is the tension between option/ freedom and legitimating/coercion which marks choice biographies" (p. 65). Interview data reveal these biographical distinctions through their responses to the question "why college?"

Students from urban middle-class families often responded to the question with surprise, a chuckle, or silence, which suggests that the decision to attend college was never in question. These kinds of responses fit closely with Du Bois-Reymond's notion of "normal biography." For example, Jian grew up on a college campus where his father works as a chemistry professor and his mother works in administration. To him, going to college is something "everyone" does. When asked why he chose to attend college, Jian states: "Everyone goes to college, so did I. Studying is for final exams; high school is for college. That is the way." Another student, Hasa similarly states: "I never thought of jobs or other things. Maybe because my older brother and sister are all college students, it's something I should do. I didn't think anything more. I didn't know anything else besides the fact that I should go to college." Students from urban middle-class families unanimously talk about going to university as something that is "assumed" and "natural." To these students, higher education is a predetermined path and is something "everyone does."

These short narrations and surprised reactions of urban students are in contrast to the often lengthy, deliberate rationalization recounted by many rural and working-class students. Rural and working-class students, in contrast to those who live in urban areas, are living out a "choice biography." To these students, going to college is a "risk-taking" process infused with anxiety, contradiction, and constant vacillation. Xiang-nan is from rural Northeast China. When asked about her decision to go to college, she thought back to when she was graduating from junior high school. Choosing whether to attend a 2-year vocational school or senior high school was a difficult decision for her. Attending a vocational school meant that she could begin helping with her parents' financial situation in just 2 years. She reflects:

> That traces back to junior high. At that time, I could get into a 2-year vocational nursing school, and then I would be able to begin to earn money. It was a tough decision. I was not sure I could get into a senior high or do well. But I liked English a lot and my English was very good at that time. If I went to a vocational school, I would have wasted my English. Going to a vocational school would be better for the family, since it meant less financial burden, and I could even help out. But going to high school means you are going to try your best to go to a college. You need to wait for 7 years to begin earning money, and a job is not guaranteed. That is, granted that I was able to get into a college. All those ideas preoccupied my mind day and night. My mom felt that was a life decision, but she was clueless, too. She was afraid I'd blame her later if we made a bad decision. So my mom and I went to talk with my English teacher. I asked her whether my English was good enough to survive senior high school and she said so long as I worked hard, I definitely would. Therefore, just relying on those words, I went to senior high school. So, step-by-step, I was pushed to college.

Xiang-nan's elaborate decision-making process contrasts with that of the urban middle-class students who consider higher education as common sense. To poorer rural students like Xiang-nan, the pathway to college is a game involving a great deal of risk at an elevated cost.

These distinctive patterns reflect the subtle, yet simultaneously powerful work of social class in individuals' lived experiences. Through socialization, individuals begin to form practical anticipations, an ability to "sense or intuit what is likely (or unlikely) to befall [them]" (Bourdieu, 1986, p. 466). These practical anticipations, accumulated through daily experiences, help individuals to attempt to "classify themselves and evaluate their positions in relation to others" (Bourdieu, 1986, p.467). Urban middle-class students clearly see attending college as a natural step in their life journey, the fulfillment of an expectation, and the occupancy of a social space that belongs to them. Rural peasant students do not typically associate higher education with "a sense of one's place" (Bourdieu, 1986). Thus, decisions relative to higher education involve a difficult process of "self-classification" and an evaluation of themselves as well as the possible consequences of their actions. The decision-making process relative to attending an institution of higher education offers important insight into how class works through lived (and classed) experiences, and how class is constructed through "choice."

Choice of Institution and Major

Habitus and cultural capital are integral to students' and families' choices (Lareau, 2003; Reay, David, & Ball, 2005); however, in less developed countries such as China, economic constraints play a more significant role in all aspects of social life. In other words, it is less a matter of class-based culture and associated values that decide a child's future. In fact, in many cases, rural families demonstrate urban middle-class dispositions (such as valuing higher education and possessing aspirations toward international culture). It is, however, predictably true that middle-class, educationally oriented parents are more likely to exercise choice within the education market. Less privileged families are less able to formulate and implement the complex strategies that a choice-oriented education market entails. Yet, such a disadvantaged position seems to have a fundamental cause: a lack of resources, such as types of economic and social capital, flexible employment schedules, private transportation, and so forth (Butler & Robson, 2003). Data in the present section suggest that, due to the uneven possession of various forms of capital, both economic and social capital, different social groups are positioned differently to undertake the "work of choice" (Andre-Bechely, 2007).

Choice is a socially embedded and class-differentiated process. Most families utilize their available capital to help position their children, hence the self-maintaining and self-reproduction properties of the social class structure. The fundamental difference, however, lies in the differentiation of the possession and "activation" of various forms of capital, and the power to access, accumulate, and transmit certain forms of capital to their offspring (Lareau & Horvat, 1999). The uncertain global economic shift feeds into the middle-class' "fear of falling" (Ehrenreich, 1989), which further motivates middle-class parents to attempt to transmit and accumulate certain kinds of cultural and social capital for their children. In terms of choosing institution and major, urban middle-class students' university choice involved an elaborate and informed decision, involving a process wherein parents were actively involved, and various forms of capital were strategically mobilized. On the other hand, students from rural peasant families showed a lower degree of control over the institutions or programs in which they enrolled. Their decisions were more random and ill-informed. Quite often, compulsion replaced choice.

Middle-class parents were found to be most actively involved in the choice of universities and major field of study. The ways they were involved and degrees of involvement were based on family habitus, the form and volume of social, cultural, and economic capital, and students' and parents' character. Many children were subject to a process of guiding, channeling, and framing to positively accept the parents' suggested choices that were assumed to be the most beneficial. This finding supports research conducted in industrialized countries on the "family dynamic of choice" among the middle class (Reay & Ball, 1998);

however, we must also note that the acceptance process is not always a "soft landing," but is rather, a complicated process involving contestation as well as the work of habitus.

Bei enrolled in Beijing University of Aeronautics and Astronautics. She comes from a middle-class family in a medium size city in Hunan province, a relatively developed, prosperous province in southern China. The family carefully pointed out a way for Bei to accumulate cultural capital and emerge into the globalizing market economy by obtaining an international trade degree in a city where she would be exposed to a more international culture. Bei and her parents chose to forego her ideal program at a top university because it was not located in a city that is abundant with international culture. When asked about this, Bei replied:

> They expect me to get good social status, get out of our small city, go to a big city, and try to study abroad. My dad thought that only in this way would my life be meaningful. Since junior high, my dad had been suggesting that Beijing is a key city where I could broaden myself and get exposed to some international culture. They wanted me to go to Beijing. But I actually always liked Wuhan University. My interest is actually in engineering, not international trade.

Wuhan University is a higher-ranking institution than her current university and is also located in an economically prosperous region, yet it doesn't meet the family's long-term strategy to position Bei within a globalizing economy. Bei's parents' expectations were similar to many other educated urban middle-class parents—big city, trendy major, and studying abroad. The significance of the international/global dimension in the choices related to education and occupation indicates that the middle class is seeking enrichment in the "language of the global economic subject" (Mitchell, 1997, p. 228). It is not that these families' cultures would necessarily fit into the "school culture" or the global city culture, as Bourdieu's reproduction theory would suggest. Instead, these families are motivated by the desire to accumulate global cultural and social capital, and thus, the desire to be well positioned in an increasingly global society and economy.

The familial experiences of the urban middle-class students resemble what Lareau (2003) describes as "concerted cultivation," an approach to child rearing practiced by middle-class parents in the United States. Through "concerted cultivation" middle-class students establish certain skills (e.g., language, reasoning) and higher educational aspirations that result in early positions of advantage (Lareau, 2003). The present research reaffirms the practice of this approach in that the childrearing practices associated with middle-class culture and habitus equip urban middle-class students with the highly valued cultural capital and global aspirations necessary to better position themselves to grasp new structural opportunities.

Chinese urban middle-class parents do depict a certain degree of anxiety, but it is less a "fear of falling" (Ehrenreich, 1989) as felt by their peers in industrialized countries, as much as it is an "anxiety of competition" in a social class structure in the making. Such anxiety stems from the desire to position their children competitively as local and global change bring about new opportunities. Unlike those who are wealthy and powerful, whose possession of certain types of highly valued capital is such that privilege can be passed down irrespective of external accreditation, members of the middle class largely depend upon the exchange value of credentials in the labor market. The urban middle-class race for more valuable credentials such as prestigious majors and institutions is very similar to what is happening in the United States. However, China and other industrializing Asian countries are unique in that the presumed distinction of credentials occurs with a global dimension. The Chinese middle-class parents are anxious to frame their children's choices around "trendy" majors related to the new global economy and institutions that provide ample amounts of global culture and experience.

Compared to their urban middle-class counterparts, student interviewees from rural peasant families chose institutions and programs on a more individualized, autonomous basis. Data demonstrate that most middle-class parents were actively involved in the decision-making process and many of them attempted to frame and influence their children's choices of universities and majors. Rural peasant students, however, seemed to be free of such channeling and therefore were somewhat autonomous. But, anxiety and uncertainty were pervasive in their accounts due to a shortage of particular types of social and cultural capital needed to help them persist through the complicated college application process. As a result of their uncertainty, their decisions were partially random.

When asked why he chose to attend Beijing University, Jing-nan replied: "Because Beijing University was the only university I had heard of. We lived in a remote area. We got very little information, so I didn't know anything about colleges or majors. I just filled in all these [paperwork for college and majors] blindly." This response is representative of the narrations of rural interviewees about their lack of sufficient knowledge and guidance in terms of their own interests, talents, programs, and institutions. Rural student interviewees in the sample did not possess knowledge of the content or career trajectory of most majors, nor did they have access to college counselors, college students, or graduates. In addition, the kind of negotiation and discussion prevalent in urban middle-class families is absent in these narratives.

At face value, few rural peasant parents were directly involved in the decision-making process or in offering guidance; however, this should not be interpreted as a lack of desire to help their children at such a critical time, rather, these parents lacked the possession of highly valued forms of capital, which ultimately rendered them powerless in the university application and choice process. This shortage of cultural, social, and economic capital also made it impossible for them to enhance their children's applications and chances for admissions, as is often accomplished by privileged parents. Such adult "passivity" is contrasted against the "activity" of middle-class parents, which reflects a differentiated social power and uneven distribution of various forms of capital.

Accumulating Capital: Graduation and Future Aspirations

Chinese urban middle-class students reveal a strong sense of reflexive agency when discussing local and global socioeconomic conditions. Many of them expressively related their graduation plans to the trends in government policies and the global economy. Family and institutional habitus reinforce these plans—the capitals they inherit and accumulate facilitate their implementation. In other words, the ways the actors select, scheme, and implement their actions are deeply rooted in their ongoing and situated structures, reflecting both their past and present habitus and accumulation of certain forms of capital.

Reflexive agency sets the fundamental steps toward meaningful actions. Based on their positioning in China's dual-reward structure, these students are actively accumulating various forms of capital in college. Types of capital are valued differently within different fields, hence the varied actions of capital accumulation. Students planning graduate work in industrialized countries strengthen their cultural capital by improving their English language skills and increasing their involvement in research, and strengthen their social capital by building a larger network of contacts, peer support groups, and often, professional services. Students who plan a government career build up their student leadership profiles and invest in Chinese Communist Party membership as an important component of political–social capital. These two groups of students can be conceptualized as elites in-the-making. They will become the new elites in China's reward system and future social structure, representing the global capital market and socialist redistributive system. The two groups present drastically different characters in terms of working style, commitment, and values, which send intriguing signals about the two competing systems; yet, collectively, the urban middle class reproduces social stratification by securing positions in China's dual-reward structure.

Such a dual-reward system is especially confusing to rural students who lack sufficient amounts of highly valued cultural capital or readily accessible pathways. Their aspirations and perceptions about prospective careers and opportunities are contingent on their inherited and accumulated capitals, their positions in the social and educational stratification, and their perceptions of their opportunities in the various systems. Emirbayer and Mische stress the "projective element" of human agency. They argue that "projectivity encompasses the imaginative generation by actors of possible future trajectories of action, in which received structures of thought and action may be creatively reconfigured in relation to actors' hopes, fears, and desires for the future" (Emirbayer & Mische, 1998, p. 971). The subjective reflection of their own positions and opportunities in China's market and state sectors highly influences the ways in which rural students scheme and implement their plans following graduation. To some degree, their reflexive agency is tempered by their uncertainty as to how they should interpret the new opportunities arising within China's global market economy. Therefore, their reflexive agency fails to result in transformative actions that bring about social change. This point is well demonstrated by the following narration:

> Li-cheng: My starting point is too low. I mean in terms of economic and social status. It is very hard for me to move forward. From my internship experiences, I learned that you need to have *guanxi*[4] even for a secondary school teacher's position in Xinzhou. And I have nothing.... But it's hard to say. Perhaps it's still my own problem. I have some childhood friends in our village who went out to work after junior high and now they already own their own businesses and make a lot of money. So I can't really blame my background too much. It's still my fault that I'm not successful.

The increasing rewards from market activity seem to signal a new route of social mobility for those who are at the bottom of the social or educational hierarchy. The lingering benefits of proximity to the bureaucratic redistribution of power cause resentment among most students, pushing the students to demean the state sector and espouse the market sector. Students who are disadvantaged in social, economic, or geographic capital (proximity to vibrant market economies or political centers) often find themselves caught within a web of confusion and anxiety. Many of them are vocal about the uneven playing field where peers with similar degrees of human capital have different access to opportunities and benefits. Such resentment, however, is tempered by the neoliberal ideology of individualism and meritocracy accompanying the market economy. This sense of uncertainty, unpredictability, and ambiguity was dominant among lower-income students.

Conclusions and Implications

Data in this research reveal certain levels of reflexive agency practiced by both groups of students relative to what is happening in China and the global economy. Improvements in their material lives, changes in their parents' employment, and reforms in educational policies are just part of the lived experiences through which they cope with and reflect upon structural changes. Rapid changes like those occurring in China infuse excitement as well as anxiety. Opportunism and pragmatism prevail in life decisions and choices in hopes of grasping the opportunities arising from structural changes. Indeed, Chinese college students from various socioeconomic backgrounds share many similarities in perspectives and aspirations. More specifically, students in this research show aspirations toward, and admiration for, global culture, urbanity, and modernity. These students also articulate a high level of confidence in China's future; however, the level of confidence in their own future prospects and their corresponding coping strategies vary considerably and are largely based upon the possession and activation of various forms of capital.

As shown, urban middle-class students are not only thinking globally, but they are also acting globally. Urban middle-class parents mobilize highly valued social and cultural capital, as well as economic capital, in an attempt to secure an institution and occupation closely related to the global economy. In this process, the pathway to college is linear and predetermined by the family habitus, although this is dependent upon the activation of class-located forms of capital. Rural peasant students, by contrast, move through a more complicated decision-making process when they decide to pursue higher education. The process is not only complicated by financial constraints, but also by the distraction posed by the demand for waged labor, as well as the "credential race" and college graduate underemployment caused by higher education expansion. Thus, students who do decide to pursue higher education are more aware than their urban middle-class counterparts that this decision bears forgone income and is a form of family investment. Their decision to go to senior high school and pursue higher education is a "risk-taking" process. This mentality and uncertainty in playing others' games, compounded by their lack of proper parental and institutional guidance in the complicated application process, pushes them to take a "risk-averse" attitude and adopt a conservative strategy in choice of major, institution, and occupation. Though the college students from rural peasant backgrounds express admiration for globalization that in a way resembles their urban middle-class counterparts, most of these students are aspiring for globalization and modernity but realistically expect to settle down locally. In other words, they are "dreaming global but planning local."

As local places acquire new meanings through globalization, not only economic meanings, but also cultural meanings, youth construct their biographies partly by imagining and making a place within globally important localities. Gaining education and employment in these localities bears symbolic and material meanings and consequences—they are directly connected to access to, and to the accumulation of, global social, cultural, and economic capitals. Stevenson suggests that the global flow of people, culture, and social movements has connected the local to the global, and that the old slogan, "think globally, act locally", might now be more appropriately framed as "think and act locally and globally" (Stevenson, 2008, p. 354). Other social theorists have also declared a blurring of borders or the "death of geography," arguing that digitalization and globalization have "flattened the world" and empowered the disadvantaged.[5] This work challenges this notion through data collected on urban middle-class students' career aspirations and planning, which provide evidence of "thinking and acting locally and globally." For those students who grew up and attend college in a global city such as Beijing or Shanghai, the distinction between "local" and "global" is arguably becoming blurry. Global is not a dream, but a living condition in which they grow up. Their privilege of mobility is largely based on the various capitals they inherited and accumulated. Rural peasant students, on the other hand, though showing admiration for and aspirations toward globalization and modernity, do not have the luxury of acting globally. The Information Age brings the world closer to these lower-class students, providing them with a telescope through which to look, admire, and imagine, and for some, to plan. Structural barriers limit, if not restrict their mobility in educational systems, social structures, and geographic locations. Their disadvantaged positions within an increasingly stratified higher education system make it hard for many rural peasant students to realize their global dreams. For these students, the boundary between "global" and "local" is still very distinct.

This research demonstrates that Chinese college students possess various degrees of agency as they select, scheme, and implement their future plans in order to position themselves within local and global changes. Yet, all students, irrespective of class or geographic background, yearn for more choices and flexibility within the educational system. Their expressive awareness of structural and societal inequalities highlights the hope for societal changes. On the nexus of local and global, Chinese college students are indeed creatively and strategically positioning themselves in tomorrow's world.

Notes

Data for this chapter were taken from Yan Zhao Ciupak's 2008 unpublished dissertation. Special thanks to the members of Yan's dissertation committe: Lois Weis, Guofang Li, and Robert Stevenson.

1 China's higher education admissions system demonstrates the following characteristics: it is a centrally controlled system, which affords individual institutions little autonomy; it requires students to take an annual standardized test, the National College Entrance Exam (NCEE), which is among a limited set of college admissions selection criteria; and it adheres to a particular quota policy that is based on provinces. The term *province* is used to refer to all first level administrative divisions in China, including provinces and municipalities that are administered by the central government (Beijing, Tianjin, Shanghai, and Chongqing), and autonomous regions. Each year, the Ministry of Education (MOE) creates a human development plan and assigns quotas to these provinces. Quotas are then assigned to individual institutions under the various jurisdictions. Finally, the institutions decide on the enrollment quota for different provinces. In a system such as this, student applicants have very limited control in the application process and outcome.

2 The *Hukou* system was institutionalized in China in the 1950s to provide the state with means and information to secure the socialist political and social order. A Chinese citizen's *hukou* has two components: the place of residence (with the most common classifications being urban and rural), and socioeconomic eligibility (agricultural or nonagricultural). These two related components define one's activities, eligibility for housing, education, healthcare, government welfare, and so forth, within one locality. A rural to urban *hukou* conversion must meet the government's stringent policy and quota. Only a small fraction of those who are rural-born have been able to convert their *hukou* through military mobilization, promotion to senior

administrative positions, employment in the state sector, higher education and subsequent job assignment, and marriage. For government regulations, see Decree of the President of the People's Republic of China, Zhonghua renmin gongheguo hukou dengji tiaoli (Regulations on Household Registration in the People's Republic of China (1984).

3   Urban residents, especially those of the centrally controlled municipalities, enjoy significant state subsidies in housing, healthcare, employment, and especially education. The urban–rural divide and its relationship with the *hukou* system has been substantially discussed in the literature (e.g., Christiansen, 1990), as well as Cheng and Selden (1994) and Mallee (1995).

4   *Guanxi* (pronounced "gwan-shee") refers to social connections or personal network. In contemporary China, *guanxi* often carries the negative connotation of using social ties in exchange for favors. Scholars and researchers have done significant work on the role of *guanxi* in job mobility and other realms in China. Renowned researcher Yanjie Bian suggests that the increased labor market competition and increased institutional uncertainty has caused increased use of *guanxi* in job acquisition in contemporary China (see Bian, 1997). For a collection of recent works on *guanxi* in China, see Gold, Guthrie, and Wank (2002).

5   See Thomas Friedman's best seller *The world is flat: A brief history of the twenty-first* century (2005). Many economic geographers argue against this narrative (e.g., Morgan, 2004).

References

Andre-Bechely, L. (2007). Finding space and managing distance: Public school choice in an urban California district. *Urban Studies, 44*(7), 1355–1376.

Bian, Y. J. (1997). Bringing strong ties back in: Indirect ties, network bridges, and job searches: The rise of Guanxi in Chinese transitional economy. *American Sociological Review, 62*(3), 366–385.

Bourdieu, P. (1984). *Distinction: A social critique of the judgment of taste.* Cambridge, MA: Harvard University Press.

Bourdieu, P. (1986). The forms of capital. In J. G. Richardson (Ed.), *Handbook of theory and research for the sociology of education* (pp. 241–258). New York: Greenwood Press.

Bourdieu, P., & Passeron, J. (1977). *Reproduction in education, society and culture.* London: Sage.

Butler, T., & Robson, G. (2003). *London calling: The middle classes and the remaking of inner London.* Oxford, England: Berg.

Cheng, T., & Selden, M. (1994). The origins and social consequences of China's hukou System. *China Quarterly, 139,* 644–668.

Christiansen, F. (1990). Social division and peasant mobility in mainland China: The implications of hukou system. *Issues and Studies, 26*(4), 78–91.

Ciupak, Y. Z. (2008). *Positioned and positioning in globalizing socialist China: Higher education choices, experiences and career aspirations among Chinese college students* (Unpublished doctoral dissertation). State University of New York at Buffalo, Buffalo, NY.

Decree of the President of the People's Republic of China (1984). Zhonghua renmin gongheguo hukou dengji tiaoli [Regulations on household registration in the People's Republic of China]. January 9, 1958. In Ministry of Public Security (Ed.), *Zhonghua renmin gongheguo gongan fagui huibian 1957–1993* [Compilations of PRC public security regulations (1957–1993)]. Beijing: China People's Public Security University Press.

Du Boi-Reymond, M. (1998). I don't want to commit myself yet: Young people's life concepts. *Journal of Youth Studies, 1*(1), 63–79.

Ehrenreich, B. (1989). *Fear of falling: The inner life of the middle class.* New York: Harper Perennial.

Emirbayer, M., & Mische, A. (1998). What is agency? *The American Journal of Sociology, 103*(4), 962–1023.

Friedman, T. (2005). *The world is flat: A brief history of the twenty-first century.* New York: Farrar, Straus & Giroux.

Glaser, B. G., & Strauss, A. L. (1967). *The discovery of grounded theory.* Chicago, IL: Aldine.

Gold, T., Guthrie, D., & Wank, D. (Eds.). *Social connections in China: Institutions, culture, and the changing nature of guanxi.* Cambridge, England: Cambridge University Press.

Hossler, D., & Gallagher , K. S. (1987). Studying student college choice: A three-phase model and the implications for policymakers. *College and University, 62*(3), 207–221.

Lareau, A. (2003). *Unequal childhoods: Class, race, and family life.* Berkeley: University of California Press.

Lareau, A., & Horvat, E. (1999). Moments of social inclusion: Race, class and cultural capital in family relationships. *Sociology of Education, 71,* 39–56.

Li, Y. (2005). *The structure and evolution of Chinese social stratification.* Lanham, MD: University Press of America.

Mallee, H. (1995). China's household registration system under reform. *Development and Change, 26,* 1–29.

Mitchell, K. (1997). Transnational subjects: Constituting the cultural citizen in the era of Pacific rim capital. In A. Ong & D. Nonini (Eds.), *Ungrounded empires: The cultural politics of modern Chinese transnationalism* (pp. 228–256). New York: Routledge.

Morgan, K. (2004). The exaggerated death of geography: Learning, proximity and territorial innovation systems. *Journal of Economic Geography, 4*(1), 3–21.

Reay, D., & Ball, S. J. (1998). "Making their minds up": Family dynamics of school choice. *British Educational Research Journal, 24*(4), 431–448.

Reay, D., David, M., & Ball, S. J. (2005). *Degrees of choice: Social class, race, and gender in higher education.* Stoke-on-Trent, England: Trentham Books.

Rong, X. L., & Shi, T. (2001). Inequality in Chinese education. *Journal of Contemporary China, 10*(26), 107–124.

Stevenson, R. B. (2008). A critical pedagogy of place and the critical place(s) of pedagogy. *Environmental Education Research, 14*(3), 353–360

Strauss, A. & Corbin, J. (1998). *Basics of qualitative research: Techniques and procedures for developing grounded theory* (2nd ed.). Thousand Oaks, CA: Sage.

Weis, L. (2008). *The way class works: Readings on school, family, and economy.* New York: Routledge.

Weis, L., & Fine, M. (2004). *Working methods: Research and social justice.* New York: Routledge.

Wu, X., & Treiman, D. (2004). The household registration system and social stratification in China, 1955–1996. *Demography, 41,* 363–384.

Yang, D (2006). Gaodneg jiaoyu ruxue jihui: Guoda zhizhong de jieceng chaju. [Access to higher education: Widening social class disparities].*Tsinghua Journal of Education, 27*(1), 19–25.

3

RACE, CLASS, AND BACHELOR'S DEGREE COMPLETION IN AMERICAN HIGHER EDUCATION

Examining the Role of Life Course Transitions

Josipa Roksa

The 20th century was the century of access—the massive expansion of higher education facilitated transition to college for ever growing proportions of high school graduates. Policymakers focused on opening doors to college opportunities while scholars studied enrollment patterns, and in particular, how they varied across students from different sociodemographic groups (see Arum, Shavit, and Gamoran chapter in this volume). In the early 21st century, completion has become a pressing issue. President Obama noted in his first speech to a joint session of Congress in February 2009: "In a global economy where the most valuable skill you can sell is your knowledge, a good education is no longer just a pathway to opportunity—it is a pre-requisite." And he made the commitment that: "We will provide the support necessary for you to complete college and meet a new goal: by 2020, America will once again have the highest proportion of college graduates in the world."

Focus on completion comes amid recent reports suggesting that the United States is losing ground in comparison to other nations. Drawing on Organisation for Economic Co-operation and Development (OECD) data, Goldin and Katz (2008) reported that the United States has the highest share of college graduates among those aged 55 to 64 but trails behind 12 nations on 4-year college graduation rates for young people (those under 25). Similarly, considering educational attainment measured by the mean years of schooling completed for individuals 25 to 34 years old, the United States ranks 11th out of 30 countries for males and 10th for females. Although some observers have questioned these international comparisons (e.g., Adelman, 2009), even looking at the trends at home suggests a slowdown in the supply of college graduates over time (see Goldin & Katz, 2008). Between the high school class of 1972 and 1992, the rate of entry into higher education increased from 48% to 71% while the bachelor's degree completion rate decreased: 51% of the class of 1972 and 46% of the class of 1992 graduated with a bachelor's degree within 8 years (Bound, Lovenheim, & Turner, 2009). Similarly, considering educational attainment of different birth cohorts reveals that over the course of the 20th century the proportion of young adults with some college has increased, but the proportion with bachelor's degrees has at best remained stable (Turner, 2004).

The rates of college completion are not only low and stagnating, they are also highly unequal. While the actual percentages vary depending on the specific samples examined (e.g., high school graduates or college entrants; specific age groups or all first-time college entrants; students who enroll in 2-year vs. 4-year institutions), inequalities by race/ethnicity and social class are clearly evident. Among traditional-age students who enter higher education, approximately half of White students complete bachelor's degrees within approximately 8 years of high school graduation (Table 3.1). At the same time, less than

TABLE 3.1 Percentage of Students Completing Bachelor's Degrees

Dataset Sample	NELS High school sophomores	NELS Postsecondary entrants	BPS First-time postsecondary entrants, 2yr institutions	BPS First-time postsecondary entrants, 4yr institutions
Race/ethnicity				
African American	16.40	30.80	3.20	43.40
Hispanic	11.60	23.10	5.50	44.00
Asian/Pacific Islander	46.10	52.20	7.40	69.10
White	33.30	48.30	11.40	61.90
Parental education				
High school or less			6.00	43.10
No high school	5.90	16.30		
High school	13.30	25.60		
Some postsecondary	25.70	35.80	8.40	50.90
Bachelor's degree	49.40	58.00	16.20	66.30
Advanced degree			25.20	73.90
Master's	65.40	73.30		
Professional/doctorate	73.30	79.80		

Source: Column 1: Digest of Education Statistics, 2009, Table 326; Column 2: Author's calculations based on NELS; Columns 3 and 4: Digest of Education Statistics, 2009, Table 332.

Notes: NELS refers to the National Education Longitudinal Study of 1988, which began with a nationally representative sample of 8th graders in 1988 and followed through 2000.

BPS refers to the Beginning Postsecondary Students Longitudinal Study, which began with a nationally representative sample of first-time postsecondary entrants in 1995-1996 and followed through 2001.

one-third of African American students and less than one-quarter of Hispanic students attain the same level of education. Similarly, while approximately three-quarters of students whose parents hold advanced degrees complete bachelor's degrees, less than a quarter of those whose parents have no college experience complete these credentials.

Scholars have dedicated much more attention to understanding inequalities in access to higher education than in the likelihood of degree completion (Goldrick-Rab & Roksa, 2008). However, as Table 3.1 illustrates, entry into higher education far from guarantees completion, and students from racial/ethnic minority groups and less advantaged family backgrounds are less likely to leave their postsecondary journeys with a degree in hand.[1] Considering these inequalities in degree completion and recent demographic trends, Bowen and his colleagues (Bowen, Chingos, & McPherson, 2009) have argued that increasing the proportion of the U.S. population holding college degrees rests on improving outcomes for students from racial/ethnic minority groups and less advantaged family backgrounds. It is thus crucial to understand what factors contribute to the lower likelihood of degree completion of these disadvantaged groups, even after they pass the hurdle of entry into higher education.

When previous studies have considered inequalities in degree completion, they have often focused on differences with which students enter higher education, particularly academic preparation. Regardless of whether academic preparation is assessed through test scores, high school tracks, or completion of specific courses or curricula, students from disadvantaged family backgrounds and racial/ethnic minority groups fare worse than those from more advantaged groups (Adelman, 1999, 2006; Grodsky, Warren, & Felts, 2008; Kelly, 2007; Lucas, 2001). Academic preparation thus clearly plays an important role in explaining inequalities in degree completion. However, the probability of success is not determined at entry; it is also shaped by what students do after they enroll in postsecondary institutions. In this chapter, I focus on one set of relevant activities that have garnered increasing attention in the higher education discourse: transitions into roles typically associated with adulthood, such as work, marriage, and parenthood. This study addresses two related questions: Do transitions into social roles typically associated with adulthood vary across students from different socioeconomic and racial/ethnic backgrounds? Moreover, do they contribute to the observed racial/ethnic and socioeconomic gaps in degree completion?

Life Course Transitions and Degree Completion

By the time students enter higher education, they enter the phase of the life course when they are increasingly likely to make transitions into roles typically associated with adulthood, such as work, marriage, and parenthood. As individuals stay in school longer and as growing proportions of high school graduates, including those from less advantaged groups, enter higher education, schooling is becoming increasingly intertwined with the traditional markers of adulthood (e.g., see reviews in O'Rand, 2000; Shanahan, 2000). Only approximately one quarter of young adults today follow the traditional sequence of transitions to adulthood, characterized by the completion of schooling, followed by finding full-time work, getting married, and having children (Mouw, 2005). Many others alternate or combine schooling with work, marriage, and parenthood (Pallas, 1993). There is thus no single transition from school to work, nor does postsecondary entry preclude transition into family roles. "Transition" by no means implies a final state: students can transition in and out of different social roles as well as pursue them simultaneously or in different sequences.

While this flexibility in life course transitions may be applauded for signaling an absence of rigid norms and allowing individuals to chart their own trajectories, it appears not to be without consequences. Previous research suggests that employment, particularly at high intensities (such as working full-time), is negatively associated with a range of educational outcomes, including degree completion (for reviews, see Pascarella & Terenzini, 2005; Riggert, Boyle, Petrosko, Ash, & Rude-Parkins, 2006). Similarly, students who transition into family roles, and particularly those who have children, have a lower likelihood of degree completion (Bozick & DeLuca, 2005; Jacobs & King, 2002; Roksa & Velez, 2012; Taniguchi & Kaufman, 2005). And indeed, when students who leave higher education are surveyed about their reasons for departure, 50% indicate that they have left for reasons related to family or work (e.g., need to work, conflicts with job/military, change in family status, or conflicts at home) (National Center for Education Statistics [NCES], 2003).

Given the negative association between life course transitions and degree completion, an important question is whether the likelihood of making these transitions varies across racial/ethnic and socioeconomic groups. Previous research is remarkably silent on this point. While many scholars have considered the overall patterns of life course transitions, they have rarely examined variation across sociodemographic groups. The extensiveness of employment in particular has been well documented, with nearly 80% of traditional-age undergraduates working while enrolled in college, and over a quarter of them working full-time (National Center for Education Statistics [NCES], 2002). A much smaller, but substantial, proportion of traditional-age students also transition into marriage or parenthood before or during the pursuit of higher education (Bozick & DeLuca, 2005; Goldrick-Rab & Han, 2011). Only a few studies have considered whether these patterns of transitions into work, marriage, and parenthood vary across sociodemographic groups after students enter higher education, and they have produced contradictory results. For example, some studies have found a relationship between family background and employment patterns (Cooksey & Rindfuss, 2001; NCES, 2002; Roksa & Velez, 2010) while others have not (Bozick, 2007).

Whether transitions into roles typically associated with adulthood vary across sociodemographic groups and whether they contribute to inequalities in degree completion are important questions to address. Students' commitment to the labor market has been on the rise, both in terms of the percentage of students working and the number of hours spent in the labor market (Scott-Clayton, 2007). Rising tuition, decreasing grant aid, and increasing reliance on loans, have made work an important feature of the higher education landscape. Since students from less advantaged family backgrounds and racial/ethnic minority groups are more reliant on financial aid, employment is likely to play a more prominent role in their journeys through college. Similarly, given the broad patterns of stratification with respect to marriage and parenthood in the society at large, those factors are important to consider when explaining socioeconomic and racial/ethnic gaps in degree completion. Throughout the educational system, students from less advantaged groups follow less favorable pathways, whether researchers examine access to different tracks or institutional types. Does this pattern persist into higher education, leading students from disadvantaged backgrounds to follow less educationally beneficial life course patterns, ones which include transitioning into roles typically associated with adulthood? I address this question and illuminate the contribution of life course transitions to the racial/ethnic and socioeconomic inequalities in degree completion.

Data and Analytic Strategy

To examine whether life course transitions vary across sociodemographic groups and whether they contribute to the lower likelihood of degree completion among students from less advantaged family backgrounds and racial/ethnic minority groups, I use data from the National Longitudinal Survey of Youth of 1997 (NLSY97; U.S. Department of Labor, 2007), a nationally representative sample of individuals born between 1980 and 1984 (ages 12–16 years as of December 31, 1996). The baseline survey was administered in 1997 to 8,984 individuals in 6,819 households, who were selected using a multistage stratified random sampling design. Respondents have been reinterviewed annually, with the latest available follow-up conducted in 2007. This dataset presents a recent sample of young adults and provides detailed information on schooling and transitions into roles typically associated with adulthood (i.e., work, marriage, and parenthood).

I begin by presenting descriptive results for students' transitions into work, marriage, and parenthood. I consider variation in these transitions for students from different family backgrounds and racial/ethnic groups. Family background is captured by two variables: parental education and income. Parental education is coded as the highest level completed by either resident parent, and is divided into four categories: no college (i.e., high school or less), some college, bachelor's degree, and graduate/professional degree. Income reflects the total household income, and due to the highly skewed distribution is divided into four quartiles. Since the two dimensions of family background reveal similar patterns, the descriptive patterns focus on variation by parental education. Race/ethnicity is represented by four categories: White, African American, Hispanic, and other racial/ethnic groups.

I explore variation in racial/ethnic and socioeconomic patterns of transition into three distinct roles typically associated with adulthood: work, marriage/cohabitation, and parenthood. Once an individual becomes a parent, she or he continues to have this role designation, but the other two roles, particularly employment, are reversible. Students can go frequently in and out of the labor market. Consequently, all variables denoting life course transitions are coded as time-varying for every month that the student is in the dataset. Family transition roles—marriage/cohabitation and parenthood—are coded as dummy variables indicating whether respondents are married/cohabitating and whether they have any children. Marriage and cohabitation are combined due to the age of the respondents. Cohabitation has been on the rise over time, with the majority of young women and men today spending some time in cohabitating relationships (Scommegna, 2002). Individuals in their late teens and early 20s, what Arnett (2004) termed "emerging adults," are particularly likely to engage in more transitional forms of behaviors, such as cohabitation. Thus, in the sample examined, cohabitation was more prevalent than marriage. Among students who entered college, 4% were cohabiting and 2% were married in their first month. Both forms of union formation increased over time: approximately 4 years after college entry, 11% of respondents were married and 13% were cohabitating.

Employment is divided into three categories: low intensity (up to 20 hours per week), moderate intensity (21–35 hours per week), and high intensity (over 35 hours per week), with students who are not working serving as a reference. The high intensity employment category captures students who are working full-time, which is one of the markers of transition to adulthood. Since simply contrasting full-time and non-full-time work would not capture the potential differences in gradations of work hours noted in previous studies, I also include dummy variables for moderate and low intensity employment. Most financial aid programs restrict student work to 20 hours per week, making that the logical choice for the boundary of low intensity work. Moreover, working at high intensity in a given month may not be as consequential as working intensely for an extended period of time. Previous studies have shown that specific *patterns* of employment are related to student success (e.g., Mortimer 2003; Staff & Mortimer, 2007). Instead of considering only whether students are working in a particular month, I examine the cumulative number of months students spend in different employment categories.

Following descriptive results, I estimate a series of discrete time event history models (Allison, 1984; Singer & Willett, 2003) to examine the extent to which different factors, including transition into family and employment roles, are related to degree completion and help to account for racial/ethnic and socioeconomic gaps in completion. A discrete time event history model is preferred to a regular logistic regression due to a large number of right censored cases and the importance of including time-varying covariates in estimation. In order to estimate this model, the data file is organized in a person-month format. The person enters the dataset at the point of entry into higher education, and remains "at risk" until they either experience the event (i.e., they complete a bachelor's degree) or exit the sample. The model is thus estimating the risk of bachelor's degree completion in each month, called the hazard, which is the conditional probability that an individual would obtain a bachelor's degree in the time period j, given that she did not do so in an earlier time period. Background variables remain constant through time while variables capturing transitions to adulthood (marriage/cohabitation, children, and work) take on different values in different time periods. The baseline hazard is estimated using a piecewise constant function (Wu, 2003). This specification provides a better fit than either linear or polynomial (square and cubic) specification.

In addition to the key variables of interest, regression models include other demographic controls, including gender and age at entry into higher education, as well as several measures of academic preparation, including test scores (Armed Services Vocational Aptitude Battery; ASVAB), high school grades, and academic track. I also include an indicator of whether students begin postsecondary education in 2-year or 4-year institutions. Although this is not strictly a measure of academic preparation, the two are related, as students who attend 2-year institutions tend to be on average less academically prepared. Moreover, institutional type is related to both social class and life course transitions (Roksa, 2010), which makes it an important factor to consider in presented analyses. Missing data on family background and control variables was dealt with in two steps. First, if the information was missing for a given year, data from the next year was used, not to exceed students' entry into higher education. That step substantially reduced the number of missing cases. The remaining missing data was dealt with using multiple imputation (Allison, 2002). The imputation procedure was based on creating five distinct datasets with imputed values, each of which was analyzed separately and then combined into the reported parameter estimates using SAS PROC MIANALYZE.

Transitions into Work, Marriage/Cohabitation, and Parenthood

Due to the weak link between the educational institutions and the labor market in the United States (Kerckhoff, 2000, 2004), students must construct an "individualized amalgam of school and work" (Mortimer & Kruger, 2000). Students develop complex pathways involving school and work, and those pathways vary

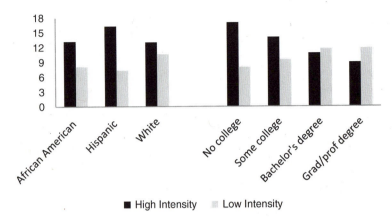

FIGURE 3.1 Number of months college entrants work at high and low intensities, by selected socio-demographic characteristics. *Source:* Author's calculations based on NLSY97. *Note:* Figure represents cumulative number of months worked at high and low intensities during approximately four years since entry into higher education.

across sociodemographic groups. Figure 3.1 reports the proportion of college entrants in selected racial/ethnic and family background groups who are working at high and low intensities. Complete results for all groups, with appropriate statistical tests, are reported in the appendix Table 3.A.

Although African American students were less likely to report working when they first entered higher education, the gap narrowed over time such that 45 months after entry similar proportions of students from different racial/ethnic backgrounds were employed. However, beneath this similarity of participation in the labor market lies substantial variation in the intensity of employment across groups. White students are more likely to be working at low intensity, and over time spend more time in low-intensity employment (working up to 20 hours per week) than either African American or Hispanic students. Hispanic students spend more time in high-intensity employment, and do so increasingly over time. By 45 months after entry into higher education, only 5% of Hispanic students were working at low intensity and almost 50% of them were working at high intensity. As is evident in Figure 3.1, they thus accumulate the most time in high intensity employment over time.

Differences in employment patterns are even more pronounced among students from different family backgrounds. While employment in the medium intensity category is relatively similar across groups, there is a notable trade-off between the low and high intensity employment that distinguishes students from more and less educated family backgrounds. Only 8% of students whose parents hold graduate/professional degrees work at high intensity one month after entry into higher education, while 22% of students from families without college experience do so. All groups increase their participation in the labor market and intensity of employment over time, but students from less educated families continue to work disproportionately at high intensity. The result of this pattern is an increasing gap between students from different family backgrounds over time. As cumulative measures in Figure 3.1 reveal, students with highly educated parents spend proportionally more time in low intensity employment and less time in high employment than their less advantaged counterparts.

The importance of these patterns is illuminated by considering previous research which has shown that high intensity employment has negative consequences for degree attainment, while low intensity employment is positively associated with educational outcomes, including degree completion (Bozick, 2007; National Center for Education Statistics [NCES], 1998; Staff & Mortimer, 2007). Racial/ethnic minority students and especially students from less advantaged family backgrounds thus spend less time in educationally beneficial types of employment and more time in employment categories that have been associated with negative consequences for educational outcomes. Similarly, previous research has suggested that family transitions, particularly having children, has a negative relationship to degree completion, and as Figure 3.2 shows, family transitions also vary across students from different family backgrounds and racial/ethnic groups. The complete results, including relevant statistical tests, are presented in appendix Table 3.A.

There are pronounced gaps in transitions into marriage/cohabitation and particularly parenthood between students from different family backgrounds, both at entry into higher education, and subsequently. Within 45 months after entry into higher education, very few students (5%) whose parents had graduate/professional degrees had children, while 4 times as many (22%) students whose parents had no college experience made this transition to adulthood. Marriage/cohabitation is more prevalent, but still unequally distributed.

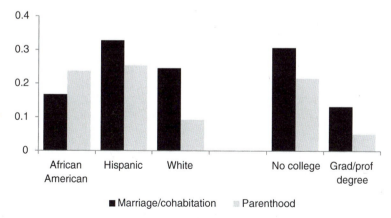

FIGURE 3.2 Proportion of college entrants transitioning into marriage/cohabitation and parenthood, by selected socio-demographic characteristics. *Source:* Author's calculations based on NLSY97. *Note:* Figure represents family transitions approximately four years since entry into higher education.

Approximately 13% of students whose parents completed graduate/professional degrees were married/cohabitating 45 months after entry into higher education. The rate of marriage/cohabitation was twice as high for students whose parents had no college experience, 31% of whom made this transition.

Racial/ethnic differences in family transitions are less pronounced, but still present. Hispanic and especially African American students are more likely to have children at entry into higher education than White students, and although the rate of transition into parenthood becomes more equal over time, the gaps persist. Forty-five months after entry, less than 10% of White students report having children while approximately a quarter of Hispanic and African American students have made the transition into this adult role. Differences in marriage/cohabitation are less pronounced. The same proportion of African American and White students transition into marriage/cohabitation at entry into higher education, but a gap emerges over time, such that a lower proportion of African Americans make this transition. Hispanic students, in contrast, are more likely to make the transition into marriage/cohabitation than White students throughout their educational careers.

Understanding Inequality in Degree Completion

Do these differences in life course transitions contribute to racial/ethnic and socioeconomic gaps in degree completion? To answer this question, I begin by estimating the overall gaps in degree completion between students from different sociodemographic groups. The first set of columns in Table 3.2 represents these baseline differences, based on a model that includes both race/ethnicity and family background (parental education and income). Previous research has shown that students from racial/ethnic minority groups on average come from less advantaged family backgrounds. In a review of the literature Gamoran (2001) concluded that: "the most important reason for educational inequality between blacks and whites is socioeconomic" (p. 137). Indeed, without parental education and income in the model, the gaps in degree completion across racial/ethnic groups are approximately 30% to 40% higher. However, it is notable that even after taking parental education and income into consideration, African American students have 33% lower odds of bachelor's degree completion than White students. The gap is slightly larger for Hispanic students, who have 41% lower odds of attaining this educational credential than their White peers. The gaps in bachelor's degree completion across parental education categories are even more pronounced. Students whose parents had no college experience had 55% lower odds of completing a bachelor's degree than those whose parents held graduate/professional degrees. These findings indicate that even among students who enter higher education there are stark gaps in degree completion among students from different racial/ethnic and family background groups.

TABLE 3.2 Estimated Odds Ratios from Event History Models of Bachelor's Degree Completion [selected results for racial/ethnic groups and parental education]

| | Model 1 | | Model 2 | | Model 3 | | Model 4 | |
| | Baseline | | Life Course | | Academic | | Life Course and Academic | |
	Odds	Difference from reference	Odds	Difference from reference	Odds	Difference from reference	Odds	Difference from reference
Race/Ethnicity [reference: white]								
African American	0.67**	-33%	0.70**	-30%	0.83*	-17%	0.78*	-22%
Hispanic	0.59**	-41%	0.64**	-36%	0.80*	-20%	0.80*	-20%
Other non-white	1.22	22%	0.94	-6%	1.37	37%	1.09	9%
Parental Education [reference: grad/prof degree]								
No college	0.45**	-55%	0.65**	-35%	0.70**	-30%	0.86	-14%
Some college	0.54**	-46%	0.68**	-32%	0.78**	-22%	0.88	-12%
Bachelor's degree	0.85*	-15%	0.91	-9%	1.00	0%	1.00	0%
Controlling for								
Parental income, gender and age at college entry	Yes		Yes		Yes		Yes	
Life course transitions			Yes				Yes	
Academic preparation					Yes		Yes	

*p < 0.05, **p < 0.01

The second model considers the extent to which these differences could be accounted for by differential patterns of life course transitions, including work, marriage, and parenthood. While Table 3.2 presents only selected results, it is important to note that life course transitions are related to the likelihood of degree completion. Getting married/cohabitating, and especially having children, has a negative relationship to the likelihood of degree completion. Moreover, the more months students spend in high intensity employment (working over 35 hours per week), the less likely they are to earn bachelor's degrees. Conversely, the more months students spend in low intensity employment (20 hours or less), the more likely they are to complete their degrees. There is no relationship between moderate intensity employment and degree completion. These results indicate that simply being employed is not necessarily a culprit for low degree attainment. Instead, it is high intensity employment (i.e., transitioning into the adult role of full-time employment), that is negatively associated with degree completion (see also Bozick, 2007; NCES, 1998; Staff & Mortimer, 2007).

Descriptive statistics have revealed some differences in life course transitions across students from different racial/ethnic groups and marked differences across students from different family backgrounds. Given the negative association between life course transitions and degree attainment, it would be expected that these patterns account for some of the inequalities in degree completion. As Model 2 shows, including life course transitions in the model changes gaps across racial/ethnic groups only slightly, but it substantially reduces the gaps across students from different family backgrounds.[2] After adjusting for family and employment transitions, the gaps in degree completion between African American and Hispanic students on the one hand and White students on the other hand remain of similar magnitudes as in the previous model—both racial/ethnic minority groups have approximately one-third lower odds of degree completion than their White peers. The gaps between students from more or less educated families remain pronounced as well, but are of much smaller magnitude than in the previous model. After adjusting for transitions to adulthood, including work, marriage/cohabitation, and parenthood, students whose parents had no college experience had 35% lower odds of degree completion than students whose parents completed professional/graduate degrees—a notable gap, but substantially smaller than in the previous model.

Results suggest that life course transitions play an important role in explaining inequality in degree completion, particularly among students from different family backgrounds. However, they may overestimate the role of life course transitions in explaining inequalities in degree completion because they do not control for other factors that are related to family background as well as the likelihood of degree completion. One factor that is particularly relevant for a discussion of postsecondary educational success is academic preparation. Students from racial/ethnic minority groups and less advantaged family backgrounds score lower on standardized tests (see a review in Grodsky, Warren, & Felts, 2008) and have lower levels of academic preparation measured by other indicators such as coursework completed (Adelman, 1999, 2006), which contribute to their lower likelihood of degree completion. I thus consider the role of academic preparation in Model 3. As would be expected, academic preparation is an important predictor of students' likelihood of degree completion: students who had higher test scores, who were in academic tracks in high school, and who had higher high school GPAs had a substantially higher likelihood of degree completion. At the same time, beginning postsecondary education in 2-year institutions had a negative relationship to bachelor's degree completion.

Do socioeconomic and racial/ethnic gaps persist after controlling for academic preparation? The third model indicates that controlling for academic preparation reduces the racial/ethnic gaps in degree completion by approximately one half in comparison to the baseline model. After controlling for academic preparation, African American students have only 17% lower odds of bachelor's degree completion than their White counterparts. A similar pattern is revealed for Hispanic students. Academic preparation also plays an important role in understanding gaps in degree completion among students from different family backgrounds. After adjusting for academic preparation, students whose parents had no college experience had 30% lower odds of completing bachelor's degrees than those whose parents completed graduate/professional degrees— this is approximately half of the gap that existed in the baseline model.

There are two additional notable findings in Model 3. First, although academic preparation is an important predictor of degree completion, and although there are notable differences in academic preparation across sociodemographic groups, the gaps in degree completion persist. Even after controlling for academic preparation, African American and Hispanic students are less likely to complete bachelor's degrees than White students, and students from less educated families are less likely to attain these educational credentials than students from highly educated families. Another important finding emerges from a comparison of Models 2 and 3. What seems apparent is that academic preparation plays a much more pronounced role in explaining racial/ethnic gaps in degree completion than life course transitions. At the same time, both sets of factors, academic preparation and life course transitions, are consequential for the gaps in degree completion across students from different family backgrounds. Thus, while higher education is stratified by both social class and race/ethnicity, specific factors seem to make unique contributions to the observed inequalities in degree completion.

Since both academic preparation and life course transitions are related to degree completion, and since they both vary across students from different sociodemographic groups, could they jointly explain the gaps in degree completion? This is the question addressed by the final model which includes measures of academic preparation and life course transitions. The first notable finding is that gaps in degree completion across racial/ethnic groups persist. Even after controlling for indicators of academic preparation and life course transitions, African American and Hispanic students have approximately 20% lower odds of degree completion than their White peers. Patterns for parental education are notably different. After controlling for academic preparation and life course transitions, students from different family backgrounds have similar likelihoods of degree completion. Small gaps persist, but those gaps are no longer statistically significant. Neither academic preparation nor life course transitions alone could account for socioeconomic gaps in degree completion; however, considered together, they can help to explain gaps in degree completion between students from more and less educated families.

While this chapter has focused on inequalities in degree completion by race/ethnicity and family background, it is important to mention the issue of gender. Gender has received increasing attention in recent years as women today are more likely than men to complete college (Buchmann & DiPrete, 2006; DiPrete & Buchmann, 2006). Analyses performed for this chapter confirm those patterns, showing that women are substantially more likely than men to complete a bachelor's degree. One relevant question would be whether the relationships between race/ethnicity and socioeconomic status on the one hand, and bachelor's degree completion on the other vary by gender. In the sample examined by Bowen and his colleagues (2009), racial/ethnic minority women had a greater advantage in degree completion than did White women. That, however, does not hold for the sample examined in this chapter. There were no statistically significant interactions between gender and race/ethnicity (or between gender and family background). The issue of gender is thus not explored further in this chapter. However, it is possible that this pattern of a lack of interaction between race/ethnicity and gender is unique to NLSY97 and thus deserves careful attention in future research.

Conclusion

Racial/ethnic and socioeconomic inequalities in American higher education are well documented. While previous research has often focused on studying inequalities in entry into higher education, findings presented here indicate pronounced inequalities in degree completion, even among students who enter postsecondary institutions. These inequalities contribute to the low rates of bachelor's degree completion and require careful consideration if we as a nation are to reach the newly set goals for degree attainment. It is thus crucial to understand what factors contribute to racial/ethnic and socioeconomic gaps in bachelor's degree completion.

When previous studies have considered this question, they have often focused on academic preparation. Since academic preparation is strongly related to degree completion and since students from less advantaged family backgrounds and racial/ethnic minority groups on average tend to have lower levels of academic preparation, academic preparation helps to explain some of the inequalities in degree completion. However, even after controlling for academic preparation, students from racial/ethnic minority groups and less advantaged family backgrounds are less likely to complete bachelor's degrees. What students bring to higher education is important, but it is not sufficient for explaining observed inequalities.

The present study thus focused on what happens after students enter higher education, and in particular, whether they transition into roles typically associated with adulthood, including work, marriage/cohabitation, and parenthood. These analyses illuminate the complexity of higher education trajectories, revealing that young adults today rarely focus exclusively on their studies. Instead, many of them juggle schooling with and against other considerations, including work, marriage/cohabitation, and parenthood. Notably, transitions into adult roles are not randomly distributed: students from racial/ethnic minority groups and especially students from less advantaged family backgrounds are more likely to make these life course transitions. Moreover, transitions into full-time work, marriage/cohabitation, and parenthood are associated with a lower likelihood of degree completion. Additionally, findings reveal that transitions into roles typically associated with adulthood explain a substantial portion of the inequality in degree completion between students from more and less educated families. These transitions play a less prominent direct role in explaining racial/ethnic gaps in degree completion. However, they play an indirect role in the production of racial/ethnic inequality through the association between race/ethnicity and family background. Family background accounts for approximately 30% to 40% of the racial/ethnic gaps in degree completion, meaning that transitions to adulthood are also indirectly relevant for understanding racial/ethnic gaps in completion.

Analyses presented in this chapter illuminate the extent to which different factors, namely academic preparation and life course transitions, contribute to racial/ethnic and socioeconomic gaps in degree completion. Academic preparation is a relatively more important factor than life course transitions for understanding racial/ethnic gaps in degree completion, although both sets of factors contribute to understanding inequalities among students from different family backgrounds. The final set of models present another remarkable set of findings: after controlling for both academic preparation and life course transitions, there are no gaps in the likelihood of bachelor's degree completion among students from different family backgrounds. At the same time, the racial/ethnic gaps, although substantially reduced, continue to persist (see also Lavin & Crook, 1990; Milesi, 2010).[3] These persisting racial/ethnic differences require more attention in future research.

One possible avenue for exploring racial/ethnic gaps in the future is to examine more closely the types of institutions students attend. Several recent studies have highlighted the issue of "undermatching" or students attending less selective institutions than they are academically prepared for. The undermatch seems to be more prevalent among students from less advantaged family backgrounds and racial/ethnic minority groups (Bowen, Chingos, & McPherson, 2009; Roderick, 2008). This can be consequential for racial/ethnic and socioeconomic gaps in degree completion since students who attend more selective institutions have a higher likelihood of degree completion, even net of their own individual characteristics. Moreover, as recent institutional-level studies have shown, colleges and universities vary notably in their racial/ethnic gaps in completion (Carey, 2004). Thus studying the role institutions may play in narrowing the racial/ethnic gaps in degree completion deserves careful attention in future research.

Notes

1   The term *racial/ethnic minority* students used throughout this chapter refers to African American and Hispanic students. Asian/Pacific Islander students have higher degree completion rates than White students and are thus not discussed at length.
2   Although comparing logistic coefficients across models can lead to erroneous conclusions (e.g., Mood, 2010; Winship & Mare, 1984), y-standardized coefficients confirm the reported patterns.
3   Bowen et al. (2009) also show gaps in degree completion net of controls, although that seems to be the case only for men: African American and Hispanic males have lower completion rates than White males, but African American and Hispanic women, along with White women, have slightly higher graduation rates than White men. Also, some studies seem to show no racial/ethnic gaps in degree completion (Adelman, 2006).

References

Adelman, C. (1999). *Answers in the tool box: Academic intensity, attendance patterns, and bachelor's degree attainment.* Washington, DC: U.S. Department of Education.

Adelman, C. (2006). *The toolbox revisited: Paths to degree completion from high school through college.* Washington, DC: U.S. Department of Education.

Adelman, C. (2009). *The spaces between numbers: Getting international data on higher education straight.* Washington, DC: Institutue for Higher Education Policy.

Allison, P. (1984). *Event history analysis: Regression for longitudinal event data.* Thousand Oaks, CA: Sage.

Allison, P. (2002). *Missing data.* Thousand Oaks, CA: Sage.

Arnett, J. J. (2004). *Emerging adulthood: The winding road from the late teens through the twenties.* Oxford, England: Oxford University Press.

Bound, J., Lovenheim, M., & Turner, S. E. (2009). *Why have college completion rates declined? An analysis of changing student preparation and collegiate resources* (NBER Working Paper 15566). Cambridge, MA: National Bureau of Economic Research.

Bowen, W. G., Chingos, M. M., & McPherson, M. S. (2009). *Crossing the finish line: completing college at America's public universities.* Princeton, NJ: Princeton University Press.

Bozick, R. (2007). Making it through the first year of college: The role of students' economic resources, employment, and living arrangements. *Sociology of Education, 80,* 261–285.

Bozick, R., & DeLuca, S. (2005). Better late than never? Delayed enrollment in the high school to college transition. *Social Forces, 84*(1), 531–554.

APPENDIX TABLE 3.A Patterns of Work, Marriage/Cohabitation, and Parenthood of College Entrants, by Family Background and Race/Ethnicity

	PARENTAL EDUCATION				RACE/ETHNICITY		
	No college	Some college	Bachelor's degree	Grad/prof degree	African American	Hispanic	White
Married/cohabitating (%)							
Month 1	0.103	0.076*	0.057**	0.025**	0.055	0.104^	0.067
Month 45	0.307	0.272	0.210**	0.132**	0.167**	0.328**	0.246
Children (%)							
Month 1	0.099	0.063**	0.036**	0.022**	0.157**	0.091**	0.038
Month 45	0.216	0.148**	0.085**	0.051**	0.283**	0.254**	0.093
Employment (%)							
Month 1							
Not employed	0.385	0.395	0.472**	0.580**	0.545**	0.385^	0.427
Low intensity	0.193	0.236*	0.254**	0.204	0.156**	0.191*	0.237
Medium intensity	0.205	0.186	0.142**	0.134**	0.152	0.191	0.177
High intensity	0.217	0.182*	0.133**	0.082**	0.147	0.233**	0.158
Month 45							
Not employed	0.179	0.218*	0.239**	0.271**	0.245	0.211	0.218
Low intensity	0.138	0.163	0.251**	0.239**	0.169**	0.106**	0.203
Medium intensity	0.175	0.205	0.189	0.175	0.158^	0.193	0.188
High intensity	0.507	0.414**	0.320**	0.315**	0.429	0.490**	0.391

(continued)

APPENDIX TABLE 3.A Continued

	PARENTAL EDUCATION				RACE/ETHNICITY		
	No college	Some college	Bachelor's degree	Grad/prof degree	African American	Hispanic	White
Employment (months)							
Cumulative by Month 45							
Low intensity	7.987	9.510**	11.681**	11.820**	8.089**	7.345**	10.588
Medium intensity	8.811	9.004	8.638	7.627**	7.590**	9.179	8.758
High intensity	17.047	14.013**	10.822**	8.942**	13.193	16.291**	13.028

^p<0.10, *p<0.05, **p<0.01 (Reference categories are "No college" for parental education and "White" for race/ethnicity.)
All estimates are weighted and significance tests are adjusted for clustering of individuals within families.

Buchmann, C., & DiPrete, T. A. (2006). The growing female advantage in college completion: The role of family background and academic achievement. *American Sociological Review, 71,* 515–541.

Carey, K. (2004). *A matter of degrees: improving graduation rates in four-year colleges and universities.* Washington, DC: Education Trust.

Cooksey, E. C., & Rindfuss, R. R. (2001). Patterns of work and schooling in young adulthood. *Sociological Forum, 16,* 731–755.

DiPrete, T. A., & Buchmann, C. (2006). Gender-specific trends in the value of education and the emerging gender gap in college completion. *Demography, 43*(1), 1–24.

Gamoran, A. (2001). American schooling and educational inequality: A forecast for the 21st century [Special issue].*Sociology of Education, 75,* 135–153.

Goldin, C., & Katz, L. F. (2008). *The race between education and technology.* Cambridge, MA: Belknap Press of Harvard University Press.

Goldrick-Rab, S., & Han, S. W. (2011). Accounting for socioeconomic differences in delaying the transition to college. *Review of Higher Education, 34,* 423–445.

Goldrick-Rab, S., & Roksa, J. (2008). *A federal agenda for promoting student success and degree completion.* Washington, DC: Center for American Progress.

Grodsky, E., Warren, J. R., & Felts, E. (2008). Testing and social stratification in American education. *Annual Review of Sociology, 34,* 385–404.

Jacobs, J. A., & King, R. B. (2002). Age and college completion: A life-history analysis of women aged 15–44. *Sociology of Education, 75*(3), 211–230.

Kelly, S. (2007). Social class and tracking within schools. In L. Weis (Ed.), *The way class works* (pp. 210–224). New York: Routledge.

Kerckhoff, A. C. (2000). Building conceptual and empirical bridges between studies of educational and labor force careers. In A. C. Kerckhoff (Ed.), *Generating social stratification: Toward a new research agenda* (pp. 37–58). Boulder, CO: Westview Press.

Kerckhoff, A. C. (2004). From student to worker. In J. T. Mortimer & M. J. Shanahan (Eds.), *Handbook of the life course* (pp. 251–268). New York: Springer.

Lavin, D. E., & Crook, D. B. (1990). Open admission and its outcomes: Ethnic differences in long-term educational attainment. *American Journal of Education, 98,* 389–425.

Lucas, S. (2001). Effectively maintained inequality: Education transitions, track mobility, and social background effects. *American Journal of Sociology, 106,* 1642–1690.

Milesi, C. (2010). Do all road lead to Rome? Effect of educational trajecotries on educational transitions. *Research in Social Stratification and Mobility, 28,* 23–44.

Mood, C. (2010). Logistic regression: Why we cannot do what we think we can do, and what we can do about it. *European Sociological Review, 26,* 67–82.

Mortimer, J. T. (2003). *Working and growing up in America.* Cambridge, MA: Harvard University Press.

Mortimer, J. T., & Kruger, H. (2000). Transition from school to work in the United States and Germany: Formal pathways matter. In M. Hallinan (Ed.), *Handbook of the sociology of education* (pp. 475–497). New York: Plenum.

Mouw, T. (2005). Sequences of early adult transition: A look at variability and consequences. In F. F. J. Furstenberg, R. G. Rumbaut, & J. Settersten (Eds.), *On the frontier of adulthood: Theory, research, and public policy* (pp. 256–291). Chicago, IL: University of Chicago Press.

National Center for Education Statistics [NCES]. (1998). *Profile of undergraduates in U.S. postsecondary education institutions: 1995–1996, with an essay on undergraduates who work* (NCES 1998-084). Washington, DC: U.S. Department of Education.

National Center for Education Statistics [NCES]. (2002). *Profile of undergraduates in U.S. postsecondary institutions: 1999-2000* (NCES 2002-268). Washington, DC: U.S. Department of Education.

National Center for Education Statistics [NCES]. (2003). *Short-term enrollment in postsecondary education: Student background and institutional differences in reasons for early departure, 1996–1998* (NCES 2003-153). Washington, DC: U.S. Department of Education.

Obama, B. (2009, Feburary 24). *Remarks prepared for the joint session of Congress.* Washington, DC: White House Press Office.

O'Rand, A. M. (2000). Structuration and individualization: The life course as a continuous, multilevel process. In A. C. Kerckhoff (Ed.), *Generating social stratification: Toward a new research agenda* (pp. 3–16). Boulder, CO: Westview Press.

Pallas, A. M. (1993). Schooling in the course of human lives: The social context of education and the transition to adulthood in industrial society. *Review of Educational Research, 63*(4), 409–447.

Pascarella, E., & Terenzini, P. T. (2005). *How college affects students: A third decade of research.* San Francisco, CA: Jossey-Bass.

Riggert, S. C., Boyle, M., Petrosko, J. M., Ash, D., & Rude-Parkins, C. (2006). Student employment and higher education: Empiricism and contradiction. *Review of Educational Research, 76*, 63–92.

Roderick, M. E. A. (2008). *From high school to the future: Potholes on the road to college.* Chicago, IL: Consortium on Chicago School Research.

Roksa, J. (2010). Differentiation and work: Employment patterns and class inequality at two-year and four-year institutions. *Higher Education, 61*, 293–308.

Roksa, J., & Velez, M. (2010). When studying schooling is not enough: incorporating employment in models of educational transitions. *Research in Social Stratification and Mobility, 28*, 5–21.

Roksa, J., & Velez, M. (2012). A late start: Life course transitions and delayed entry into higher education. *Social Forces, 90*, TBD.

Scommegna, P. (2002). *Increased cohabitation changing children's family settings.* Washington, DC: National Institute of Child Health and Human Development (NICHD), National Institutes of Health.

Scott-Clayton, J. (2007). *What explains rising labor supply among U.S. undergraduates, 1970–2003?* Unpublished manuscript, John F. Kennedy School of Government, Harvard University, Cambridge, MA.

Shanahan, M. J. (2000). Pathways to adulthood in changing societies: Variability and mechanisms in life course perspective. *Annual Review of Sociology, 26*, 667–692.

Singer, J. D., & Willett, J. B. (2003). *Applied longitudinal data analysis: Modeling change and event occurrence.* New York: Oxford University Press.

Staff, J., & Mortimer, J. T. (2007). Education and work strategies from adolescence to early adulthood: Consequences for educational attainment. *Social Forces, 85*, 1169–1194.

Taniguchi, H., & Kaufman, G. (2005). Degree completion among nontraditional college students. *Social Science Quarterly, 86*(4), 912–927.

Turner, S. E. (2004). Going to college and finishing college. In C. Hoxby (Ed.), *College choices: The economics of where to go, when to go, and how to pay for it.* Chicago, IL: University of Chicago Press for NBER.

U.S. Department of Labor. (2007). *NLSY97 user guide.* Columbus, OH: Center for Human Resource Research.

Winship, C., & Mare, R. D. (1984). Regression models with ordinal variables. *American Sociological Review, 49*, 512–525.

Wu, L. L. (2003). Event history models for life course analysis. In J. T. Mortimer & M. J. Shanahan (Eds.), *Handbook of the life course* (pp. 477–502). New York: Springer.

Cultural Politics, Transnational Movement, and the Role of Class

4

CLASS WRECKAGE AND CLASS REPOSITIONING

Narratives of Japanese-Educated Taiwanese

Shumin Lin

In 2006, a Japanese television show featuring Japanese youth traveling around Taiwan aired a segment in which a Taiwanese female elder, Grandma Lee, approached the film crew, greeted them in fluent Japanese, and expressed her strong affinity for Japan. "Hello, my name is Lee, and my Japanese name is Sawajima. I love Japanese people," Grandma Lee told the film crew. She continued, "During the Japanese imperial era, we received much education.... Japanese came to Taiwan and built many things. We are very grateful for this." After the clip was posted on YouTube,[1] it sparked heated debate within Taiwan. The majority accused Grandma Lee of having no national pride and of having no right to speak for all Taiwanese. Others argued for empathy with Taiwanese elders who were educated under Japanese colonial rule (Liu, 2007).

The controversy surrounding Grandma Lee's YouTube video reflects the linguistic dilemma and identity struggle faced by a generation of Japanese-educated Taiwanese whose lives encompassed two distinct eras of modern Taiwanese history: the era of Japanese colonial government (1895–1945), and the years of the Chinese Nationalist *Kuomintang* (KMT) regime (1945–2000). While Japanese-educated Taiwanese were the first educated class in Taiwanese history, their social status changed radically after the KMT came to power in 1945. To establish a national identity tied to China, the KMT imposed a Mandarin-only policy, banning the use of all local languages and Japanese in public.[2] The Japanese language, once a marker of education and modernity, became stigmatized as a signifier of "enslavement" (*nuhua*). After the sweeping arrests and massacres of the February 28 incident of 1947 and the ensuing "white terror" of the 1950s, the Japanese-speaking generation was effectively silenced and rendered invisible or "erased" (Irvine & Gal, 2000) under the Mandarin-only ideology. To the great dismay of local Taiwanese, their brothers from mainland China became another colonial power (Huang, 2010), whose behavior was similar to, and in some ways worse than the Japanese.

Democratization and increased access to global media and air travel since the 1990s have created a new social space for these Taiwanese elders to reclaim their Japanese education, by speaking Japanese, watching Japanese TV, and traveling to Japan. Those who celebrate the era of Japanese colonial government too enthusiastically, however, risk criticism for compromising Taiwanese national pride, particularly from younger Taiwanese who grew up under the KMT regime, and from mainlanders (*Waishengren*) who migrated with KMT forces to the island in 1949.

Since the 1990s, however, the pro-Japanese sentiments of Japanese-educated elders have received increased attention by Taiwanese scholars (e.g., Huang, 2003; Lee, 2004). In general, these scholars argue that contention between native Taiwanese, the KMT regime, and the mainlander group in the immediate postwar period has played a prominent role in structuring these elders' feelings. Little attention has been paid, however, to the issue of class rearrangement in this complex layering of political power and cultural authority. Based on interviews with Japanese-educated elders, this paper argues that class struggle and language politics play a central role in these elders' colonial nostalgia, and that democratization and globalization afford these elders a new space to reclaim their politically erased linguistic and educational identities.

Studies by sociolinguists and linguistic anthropologists have demonstrated that language plays a key role in political processes and in the construction of social inequality (Kroskrity, 2000), and that language is a form of social action—people do things with words (Austin, 1962). In this view, language is not just a set of formal structures, performing a strictly referential function as in the tradition of formal linguistics (Chomsky, 1965). Instead, language is seen as being inextricably linked to networks of sociocultural and political relations. Large-scale historical processes—colonization, state formation, and globalization—create new linguistic markets (Bourdieu, 1991) or linguistic regimes (Kroskrity, 2000) wherein the functional and ideological value of languages get reorganized (Philips, 2004) and individuals' identities and class positions get reconfigured. For example, newly adopted standards in a new regime can become distinct class-stratified varieties and ways of speaking (Gal, 1989).

Multicolonized Taiwan provides a particularly revealing window into the ways in which political changes affect the crucial role of language in class formation and transformation. At the center of this entangled relationship are the Japanese-educated elders, whose class position was erased by virtue of the elision of their educational experiences after 1945. In this chapter I focus on how these elders reconstruct and reclaim their educational identities through the narration of schooling experiences and recurrent use of Japanese in everyday life. These narratives reveal how dialogical and interactional spaces created by democratization and globalization have enabled these elders to reclaim their cultural identities as educated and multilingual Taiwanese. This study thus builds on a growing body of work on language and political economy by showing how social actors are deeply implicated in dynamics of linguistic contact and political struggle in situations where colonial legacies become entangled with nation building and globalization.

Data used in this chapter are drawn from 21 months of ethnographic fieldwork with Taiwanese elders conducted between 2001 and 2006.[3] I focus my analysis on interviews with elderly Japanese-educated women.[4] I analyze their narratives about their Japanese education and their present use of Japanese in everyday life to show how these elders articulate their linguistic and educational identities by positioning themselves in relation to others (their uneducated peers, the younger Mandarin-speaking generations, the researcher, etc.). Observational data is supplemented to complement their narration of their use of the Japanese language.

The structure of this chapter begins with the theoretical framework. Positioning theory offers useful analytical tools to explore how these elders reposition themselves as the educated class through and across the event of narration and the narrated event. In order to make sense of their stories, I then provide a sketch of the history of education in relation to language and class in Taiwan. The centerpiece of this chapter is a detailed discussion of these elders' discursive construction of positive bilingual and educated identities through the narration of their Japanese education and their use of the language.

Narrative Construction of Identity

As many scholars from a variety of fields have pointed out, narrative is a pivotal site for identity construction (De Fina, Schiffrin, & Bamberg, 2006; Goffman, 1979; Koven, 2007; Miller, Fung, & Mintz, 1996; Ochs & Capps, 2001; Wortham, 2001). Narrators manage their roles as narrator, narrated character, and performed character across the event of narration and the narrated event (Koven, 2007; Wortham, 2001). As such, they construct identities through various positionings in and through narrative practices.

Positioning theory offers useful analytical tools to study the processes of identity construction in narrative practices (Davies & Harre, 1990). At the metalevel, "[P]eople construct identities (however multiple and changing) by locating themselves or being located within a repertoire of emplotted stories" (Somers, 1994, p. 614). Within each narrative interaction, there are many levels of positioning relationships: between the narrator and what is being said; between the characters (including the narrator in the story) in the propositional content of the narrative; between speaker and hearer; between the narrator and dominant ideologies, widespread social practices and underlying power structures (De Fina, et al., 2006).[5]

Of particular importance for this analysis is that positioning theory views agency as "bidirectional." On the one hand, historical, sociocultural forces in the form of dominant discourses or linguistic or social policies position speakers in their situated practices and social positions without their agentive involvement. On the other hand, speakers position themselves as active and interactive agents, and choose the linguistic, paralinguistic, and nonverbal resources by which they construct their identities vis-à-vis others as well as vis-à-vis dominant discourses (De Fina et al., 2006). As such, narratives serve as a powerful tool to reveal the agency and voices of historically displaced, linguistically marginalized individuals.

Using positioning theory to frame the analysis, this chapter analyzes Japanese-educated elders' narratives, illustrating how they use multiple linguistic devices to position themselves vis-à-vis others and the master discourses across the narrated event and the event of narration. Through the narration, they construct strong learning and educated identities associated with their Japanese education.

Colonization, Schooling, and Social Class

Before the Japanese colonial government established modern schooling in Taiwan in 1895, traditional education was conducted in *shufang*, usually housed in temples or private houses, where pupils studied classical Chinese.[6] The *shufang* pupils were mainly from wealthy families and were predominantly male.

During the first half of the Japanese colonization period, enrollment in Japanese schools remained low. From the early 1920s on, Taiwanese acceptance of Japanese education was fairly widespread among all classes but particularly among the upper and middle classes (Tsurumi, 1979). Following the outbreak of war in 1937, the Japanese began the *kominka* movement, which aimed to transform the Taiwanese into Japanese imperial subjects. Enrollment increased dramatically during the war years for both genders. Toward the end of the colonization period, 70% of Taiwan's school-aged children were literate in Japanese. Although the majority of Japanese-educated Taiwanese only attended elementary schools,[7] they represent the first educated generation in Taiwan.

Following Japan's 1945 defeat in World War II, Taiwan was handed over to the Chinese Nationalists (KMT) in China. In 1949, after losing a civil war to the Chinese Communists, the KMT and its troops retreated to Taiwan. To establish a national identity tied to China, the KMT imposed a Mandarin-only policy. Mandarin replaced Japanese as the language of instruction at all school levels. All local languages in Taiwan—Hoklo, Hakka, and aboriginal languages—were relegated to the status of *fangyan* "dialects" and banned in public domains, despite the fact that these languages are in fact as different from Mandarin as English is from Spanish. The Japanese language and printing materials were also severely sanctioned, thus turning the Japanese-literate Taiwanese into "illiterates" overnight.

Disillusioned by these and other acts, many Japanese-educated Taiwanese leaders expressed their dissent in the famous uprising of February 28, 1947. The KMT responded by sending troops from mainland China and killing unknown thousands of people (see Kerr, 1965). During the ensuing "white terror" in the 1950s, dissenters were imprisoned, kept quiet, or fled into exile to places such as Japan or the United States (Kerr, 1965). The KMT installed martial law in 1947, which lasted until 1987. Scholars have argued that the KMT's authoritarian rule over Taiwan should be seen as a variation of colonization or an internal colonization (Ching, 2001; Huang, 2010).

Since the mid-1980s, along with the island's democratization and a concurrent localization movement, the newly legalized opposition party, the Democratic Progressive Party, local activists, and social elites have revalorized Hoklo as a symbol of Taiwanese solidarity. This and other positive new re/presentations of Hoklo, however, disguise the enduring legacies of the KMT's Mandarin-only policy, namely linguistic hierarchy and language shift. Hoklo continues to be associated with rurality, backwardness, illiteracy, and low class, while Mandarin retains its status as the language of urbanity, education, literacy, and high class (Su, 2008). There is also a continuing language shift toward Mandarin with each succeeding generation (Huang, 2000; Sandel, 2003). While the postwar generations grew up speaking Mandarin, the prewar generations remained non-Mandarin speaking. According to Huang (1993), an estimated 17.5% of the total population (equal to 3.5 million people) could not understand Mandarin.

In parallel with the revalorization of local languages, the Japanese language began to resurface in public arenas in the late 1980s, especially in the popular culture and youth culture (Lee, 2004). However, this reemergence of the Japanese language does not coincide with a renewed appreciation of the elders' Japanese education and language. They remain invisible in public discourse and in the media. Whenever Taiwanese elders appear on television, they are Hoklo-speaking and uneducated.

Since the mid-1980s, however, globalization, together with local policy changes, have created a new space for Japanese elders to reengage with Japan, albeit in private or with friends and relatives, through, among other things, watching Japanese television, singing karaoke to Japanese songs, or traveling to Japan. Since the Taiwanese government lifted restrictions on international travel in 1979, Japan has increasingly been the major destination for overseas travel, especially among the elders. Japanese television programming became available through unofficial cable network companies in the 1980s, which were legalized in the 1990s. It is precisely in these global flows of media and travel (Appadurai, 1996) that the Japanese-educated elders were able to reconnect with their pasts and reclaim their multilingual educated identities. It is worth noting that while a growing body of literature has begun to examine how globalization affords new spaces for youth to forge "new and unexpected identities" (Dimitriadis,

2008, p. x; e.g., Dolby & Rizvi, 2008), less is known about how the same global forces affect elders' lives and identities. Echoing Dolby and Rizvi's (2008) claim that global mobility is instrumental in producing and reproducing class formations, this chapter is an example of how globalization affords marginalized elders spaces for identity construction and class reconfiguration.

In the following essay, I analyze narratives of Japanese-educated Taiwanese to illustrate how they have used the linguistic and cultural capital acquired through Japanese education to reposition themselves as the educated class. The analysis is divided into two sections: the first is about their narratives of school life and childhood; and the second is devoted to their narratives of using Japanese in their present lives.

Remembering the Past: Japanese Education

Whether elicited or not, accounts of schooling experiences came up repeatedly in my interviews or conversations with these Japanese-educated elders. Their portrayals of school life were unequivocally positive, depicting themselves as smart and studious students and their Japanese teachers as loving and caring. By recounting these stories, these women repositioned themselves as "the educated class," distinct from their uneducated peers. Such representations also serve to counter the dominant master narrative that has stigmatized them or rendered their language and education invisible.

"I loved to Study Most!"

The majority of Japanese-educated elders told stories about their diligence, hard work, and excellent performance at school. One of the topics they frequently related was that they never missed a class. For example, whenever Granny Wang talked about her education, she started with this refrain: "I never missed a class. And I got a prize for that at graduation." The most dramatic and elaborate account of the same topic was from Gao mama. Over the course of my research, she told and retold the following event about how she insisted on going to school even after contracting malaria:

> I loved to study most! When I was a student, I never took a day off! (Um) However sick I was, I still went to school. Once in the Japanese period I contracted malaria. I had fever, and sometimes I was cold and sometimes I felt hot. My grandmother asked me not to go to school. I had my school bag on my back, and half way to the school, the school was very close to our house, half way to the school, I collapsed on the street, and I could not make it back home. The neighbors saw me and they went to get my grandfather to carry me home. I was twelve, and my grandfather had me on his back [laughs]. My legs were long, dangling! And my grandfather took me home!
>
> *(Gao mama, 72 years old, 5 years of education)*

After claiming explicitly that she loved to study most, Gao mama used the example of her insistence on going to school despite being sick to illustrate her point. She mentioned her grandmother, who cared about her health but thought it was all right to skip class, to contrast herself as someone with a strong will to learn. She also depicted a scene in which she collapsed, and her grandfather carried her back home with her two legs dangling. This dramatic and unusual scenario increases the tellability of this event (Ochs & Capps, 2001), as Gao mama repeatedly told the story. Miller and colleagues have called this kind of repeated engagement with certain stories "story attachments," which reveal the narrator's sustained emotional involvement in the narrated events (Alexander, Miller, & Hengst, 2001).

In addition to stories of being studious, accounts of how smart they were as students also dominated the school stories. Gao mama, for example, who was the most eloquent storyteller in the study recounted a fortunate event that contributed to her advancement to the second grade without repeating the first grade, thus enabling her to finish fifth grade instead of fourth grade when colonization ended in 1945. When her grandmother sent her to school at age 7, one year earlier than other students, the idea was for her to study in the first grade twice—so she would be the same age as other students when she advanced to the second grade.

> So I went as a "tagalong" student. Our first semester was taught by a Taiwanese deputy principal surnamed Liao. The second semester we changed to a Japanese lady. Shirasu sensei [in Japanese, Teacher Shirasu]. And Shirasu sensei came to visit. In the past, on April 1, school started after vacation and others graduated. So right before school started again, [she came for] a home visit. Our house was near the school, just a wall and a street away. My teacher said she would visit. And she came and asked me to translate for her. She, a Japanese lady, did not speak Hoklo. She said, "Your granddaughter is smart. She could follow the instruction. Do you want to let her advance to the second grade?" And she asked me to translate. And I translated. And my grandmother replied, "Of course. If she can advance to the second grade, she can study one year less. How can I not let her go up to the second grade? OK. OK." Then I went straight to the second grade. When the war ended, I was already in the fifth grade. Or else, I would have been only in the fourth grade.
>
> *(Gao mama, 72 years old, 5 years of education)*

It turned out that Gao mama was more than a tagalong (*ji-xue*) student in her first year of elementary school. She could learn as well as her classmates who were one year older. With her Japanese teacher's recognition of her talent and active support, Gao mama was able to advance directly to the second grade.

The significance of this event has to be viewed from the context of the unstable situation in Taiwan toward the end of the war, and the capricious nature of education in Gao mama's generation. Air raids by the Allies frequently interrupted school, and after the transition of power, the KMT disrupted the education of many Taiwanese people. As Gao mama recounted, "We didn't study much. Whenever there were air bombings, *kuushuukeiho* (in Japanese), then we did not go to school.... We only studied about half of the time during the last year of the war." Thus, being able to advance to the second grade without repeating the first grade meant that Gao mama was able to attend one more year of school before her education was abruptly discontinued.

It is important to note that Gao mama reconstructs or animates (Goffman, 1979) the dialogue between the Japanese teacher and her grandmother, with her younger self being the third character acting as a translator in the story world. Reported or quoted speech has been discussed as "a pivotal site for seeing how speakers can incarnate potentially multiple, alternative versions of self" (Koven, 2007, p. 100). Through reported speech, narrators can borrow the voices of others to construct their own identity. In the above excerpt, Gao mama used the words of a figure of authority (i.e., her Japanese teacher) to construct her younger self as being smart.

Furthermore, by using the "verb of saying"—"translate"—as a metapragmatic descriptor (see Wortham, 2001, pp. 71–72), Gao mama constructs her younger self as bilingual in Hoklo and Japanese. Examined from the historical context, such bilingual ability is not a given, but a rarity. Only those who were privileged to go to school had the opportunity to learn the Japanese language. Thus, this metapragmatic descriptor is indexical of education. While the propositional content reveals her good fortune in attending an extra year of common school, the examination of these linguistic cues reveals Gao mama's active construction of her linguistic, educated, and smart identities.

"My Teacher Was Very Good!"

In the elders' stories of school experiences, the teachers are always portrayed in a positive light: they were unselfish; they emphasized character education; and they were loving and caring. Several of the elders talked about their teachers offering free classes to prepare them for the middle school entrance exam.[8] Gao mama gave a vivid portrayal of the after-school classes in her teacher's house:

> In the past, 2 years prior to middle school, the teacher picked 10 people to study at her house. After-school learning (*buxi*). Entirely free classes. In the past, the teacher volunteered to do this. And she told us that she was preparing us for middle school. In the past, middle school was 2-year study after common school. The teacher often picked 10 or 12 students to give after-school classes in her house. We all kneeled on the *tatami* [in Japanese, a traditional type of Japanese flooring] and studied. Ah, oh, and her, her mother, our teacher was not married yet. And when she taught, her mother made rice cakes for us to eat. Those were so delicious! It was [the Japanese] New Year and they made rice cakes to treat us. (Oh, So

you went there to have class and you also had delicious food to eat!) Oh, yes, they treated us. So one [Chinese] New Year, my grandmother said, "Your *sensei* often treated you." In the past, we called [teachers] *sensei.* "You take these two big oranges to give to your *sensei.*" [laughs]

(Gao mama, 72 years old, 5 years of education)

In this narrative, Gao mama located herself among those being chosen to receive free classes for entering middle school, which indexes her excellence in academic performance. What's more, the propositional content reveals the close bond between the Japanese teacher and the students: the teacher offered free classes at her home and (the teacher's mother) even provided snacks for the students.[9] Note that she stressed that the classes are free by adding an intensifier "entirely" to emphasize the teacher's unselfish and loving character. Then she provided the historical context "In the past, the teachers volunteered to do this" to contrast the teachers in contemporary Taiwan who offer after-school classes to make money.

In the meantime, by switching to Japanese when she said "teachers" in Japanese, *sensei,* and then providing the translation for me, she performs her identity of a Japanese speaker vis-à-vis a non-Japanese speaker in the storytelling event. Furthermore, by supplying historical contexts ("In the past, middle school was 2-year study after common school."), she gave herself a privileged epistemological position. Although I am familiar with these contexts from reading literature and from my continuing research with Taiwanese elders, I let her inhabit this epistemic stance, which, in a sense, voices the Japanese-educated, whose lived experiences include personal involvement with the Japanese education system.

In addition to portraying the teachers as moral, the elders also told stories of the character education they received from the teachers. Great Aunt Meichi told a story of how her teacher dealt with her transgression in an art and craft class:

Before I was stupid. We needed to make model planes for our art and craft class. We bent bamboos, heated them, and then bent them, and made a model plane.... We went to her one by one with our plane for her to examine and grade. Some students forgot to bring their planes on the grading day. They wanted to borrow mine. I was soft-hearted and agreed. The teacher could tell and challenged the students.... For my mistake, she said, "You can't lend this to others. Too bad you did great work on that. Now I need to deduct your grade." [laughs] The teacher was very good!

Note that she started the story by saying she was "stupid" to commit the transgression of loaning her airplane model to her classmates. And she ended the story with a coda, "The teacher was very good!" This evaluative comment reveals her appreciation of her teacher's moral education.

As is seen in these stories, elders appreciated their Japanese teachers' efforts, and the close relationship they enjoyed with them. This close relationship was also evident in stories about how sad they were when they changed teachers or when the teachers had to leave after the war. Liang mama recounted how nice and unforgettable her Japanese teacher from grades one to three was, and how, when they needed to change to a new teacher at the fourth grade, "the whole class cried!" The 96-year-old Granny Lai told me: "We all cried so hard when we graduated!" This was after she sang the Japanese graduation song and explained the lyrics to me one day in her living room.[10] The departure of the Japanese teachers after the war also drew tears from the students, as Great Aunt Meichi related, "When our teacher needed to return to Japan, we all cried, cried, and cried!"

In summary, through these narratives of the good old school days, members of Taiwan's Japanese-speaking generation evoke a social universe associated with Japanese schooling, filled with characters such as loving teachers and good, studious students. Through the narration, these elders repositioned themselves as the educated class. It is important to note that many of the elders in this study are not unaware of discriminatory policies by the Japanese during the period of colonization.[11] However, they did *not* experience oppression in their lived experience *within* the school. These narratives demonstrate that their interpretive framework for their Japanese education is, in part, derived from interpersonal interactions with the Japanese teachers, not with the colonial government. As commented on by a Taiwanese anthropologist Liu Jih Wann, who was educated during the Japanese period, "Because of colonialism, the government of course was bad, but the Japanese people were very nice" (quoted in 鈴木滿男 [Ling Mu Man Nan], 2002, p. 189).

Using the Past in the Present: Reclaiming the Educated and Linguistic Identity

In addition to the narration of their Japanese education, these Japanese-educated elders also engaged in activities associated with the Japanese language and culture: speaking Japanese (or code-switching a lot between Japanese and Hoklo), eating Japanese food, reading Japanese magazines, watching Japanese television, singing Japanese songs to karaoke, frequently traveling to Japan (as many as one or two times a year for some), visiting their Japanese teachers in Japan, and attending elementary school class reunions. As presented earlier, it is in the context of democratization and globalization that these activities became possible. In addition, advanced age and better financial status allowed time and offered necessary means for these activities. In this section, I focus on their stories of traveling to Japan and watching Japanese television to demonstrate how they reclaimed their linguistic and educated identity through the narration.

"I Love To Visit Japan Most"

All of the Japanese-educated elders in this study had many experiences traveling abroad. Their favorite destination was Japan. According to them, their proficiency in Japanese accounted for this preference. As Chen mama put it, "I love to visit Japan most. There I can read, I understand [what people say], it's more fun."

In addition, when traveling with younger companions, their Japanese language skills advantageously positioned them vis-à-vis younger Mandarin-speaking generations. Great Aunt Meichi talked about "taking my daughter to Japan to study in a language school" and "interpreting for her." Gao mama relished the stories of her many travels to Japan. Most of the trips were funded by her sons, three of whom owned motorcycle shops, or by the sons' main motorcycle companies. In the following excerpt, she proudly recounted how the wives of other motorcycle shop owners in her group depended on her Japanese to shop in Japan.

> I loved to go to Japan most. Because I studied Japanese when I was little, I can more or less communicate. So I love to visit Japan all the more. Some of the bosses' wives, they are young, in their thirties or forties, in that generation. They all loved to be with me.
>
> (I see.) At night when there were no tour schedules, they asked me to shop with them, [laughs], to buy things. (So you can translate for them?) Yes. I said things for them—what they wanted to buy. And then I said to him [the Japanese clerk].

Gao mama thus constructs her Japanese linguistic identity by positioning herself vis-à-vis the Mandarin-speaking younger generation. Her Japanese proficiency functions in a practical sense in helping the young wives to complete transactions.

She then continued with another story in which she helped translate for her neighbor Jinglan on another trip to Japan. Jinglan was a few years younger than her, and never went to school. She was charged fees for watching movies in the hotel, and Gao mama helped translate this situation to the confused Jinglan, who was being asked to pay at the checkout counter. She added an evaluative comment when narrating this incident, "She [Jinglan] did not read Japanese. When she watched, she did not know she would be charged!" [laughs] Taken together, we see Gao mama construct a positive linguistic identity associated with her Japanese education in relation to both the younger Mandarin-speaking generation and her uneducated peer. Through these stories, she enacted a multilingual identity that contrasts starkly with what has been represented in the master narrative, and with official discourse that seeks to erase or stigmatize her education and the Japanese element in her linguistic repertoire.

Great Aunt Meichi had many language-related travel tales as well. After retiring as a post office clerk in 1980, she has made numerous trips abroad. Although Japan remained her favorite destination, she traveled to far more countries than the other elders, including Africa and South America. Several times, she told the following story about how she put her Japanese to good use in South America.

> So that day we went to Peru. We visited Machu Picchu. I was the oldest in that group. I was upset with our own tour guide. A Japanese group was there and they had explanation, but our group did not. They were all there just taking pictures and all that. So I went over to the Japanese group to hear what they were saying and I followed them. And I got lost from my own group! [laughs]

In this narrative, she first identified herself as the oldest in the group. She was in her early 70s then and she joined this group on her own. She then expressed her discontent with the Taiwanese tour guide, who did not provide an explanation of the historical site. While it was likely that other group members were unhappy about the lack of an informative guide, Great Aunt Meichi's Japanese placed her in an advantageous position to "overhear" the explanation in the nearby Japanese group. Furthermore, she presented herself as someone who desired to be informed about the site rather than "just taking pictures," thus implicitly constructing herself as an educated person and a learner who craved knowledge. Such a learning identity was evident in other narratives as well, as when she related how she loved to read Japanese books and magazines loaned from a local bookshop, and how she continued expanding her Japanese vocabulary from watching Japanese television shows.

These travel narratives demonstrate that members of first-generation educated elders deployed the linguistic capital they acquired through a Japanese education to position themselves in relation to both the younger generation and their peer generation who do not speak Japanese, thus implicitly highlighting their educated identity.

In addition to sightseeing, some of the elders' trips to Japan included visiting their former Japanese teachers. Great Aunt Meichi recounted a trip to Japan in the 1980s with 20 classmates from middle school to visit their teacher and concluded: "Our teacher was very happy. She gave each of us some money!" [laughs]

Chen mama told me that on her first trip to Japan with a tour group, she and her elder sister made an effort to visit her teacher:

> We found some free time and took a taxi to visit my Japanese teacher of the fifth and sixth grades. The teacher had visited Taiwan several times and had written to me to tell me that if I visited Japan, I should visit her. When we arrived at the teacher's home, to our distress, we learned that the teacher was heavily ill and was hospitalized. My sister and I cried so

hard there. We gave 8,000 Japanese yen [about $100 US dollars] to the family to express our sympathy. And we promised to come back to see her when she is better.

(Chen mama, 74 years old, 6 years of education)

While Chen mama told me this story, she also showed me pictures of this teacher visiting Taiwan. There were several pictures of her class, all grand-parents by then, and this teacher sitting in a classroom of the local elementary school they had attended decades before. Such mutual visits between Taiwan-ese elders and their Japanese teachers in recent years are not uncommon.[12] In stories like these, the narrated characters are teachers and students who had maintained decades of good relationship. In telling these stories, in which they remained students to their Japanese teachers, they enacted an educated identity. Not only were they educated in their youth, but their social network of class-mates and teachers continued to the present.

"I Love To Watch NHK Most"

Unlike their uneducated peers, who have little choice of television program-ming because they can neither understand the Mandarin-dominant program-ming nor read the subtitles that come with almost every program in Taiwan (Lin, 2009a), these Japanese-educated elders have access to many quality Japa-nese shows. Since the ban on television programming in Hoklo and Japanese was lifted and cable television was approved in the 1990s, Japanese shows have become widely available in Taiwan. During my research, when I saw these elders watch television, most of the time they watched Japanese shows. They stated how much they enjoyed Japanese shows and compared them with poor-quality Hoklo shows. For example, according to Chen mama, "I don't like Taiwanese [Hoklo] serials. It's all fighting and violence. Bad guys bully good guys. I watch Japanese programs."

Great Aunt Meichi watched a lot of Japanese television too, as a result of which she could access world news and other information. Once during my visit, she watched the NHK channel (*Nippon Hōsō Kyōkai*, Japan Broadcast-ing Corporation). She commented with pleasure, "Now it's so good there is NHK!" and went on to report what she just saw on the NHK news, "There was an uprising in Buenos Aires, Argentina. Fortunately I had been there last year." She then went on to tell me what she saw on NHK recently, including one report about "charter schools" in America. She jotted down the term and asked her daughter who had been to America many times what charter schools were. As the NHK channel does not have Chinese subtitles and I had long been aware of the NHK's reputation of producing high-quality programs, I felt envi-ous of Great Aunt Meichi's linguistic advantage that allowed her to understand the NHK shows. Thus I followed up by saying, "It's so good you understand

Japanese!" In this short exchange about television, we coconstructed her Japanese linguistic and educated identity vis-à-vis my non-Japanese speaking identity.

In summary, by narrating their present use of Japanese in their everyday lives in traveling and television viewing, these elders crafted an educated, multilingual identity in contrast to their uneducated peers and the younger Mandarin-speaking generation, including the researcher.

Discussion

I have demonstrated that the Japanese-educated elders used the new space created by more relaxed political and cultural policies in Taiwan and increasing globalization to reconnect with Japan. In narrating their past and present connection with Japan, they interactionally reclaimed their politically erased educated and multilingual identities, effectively recovering their postwar "class wreckage" and staging their own "class reunion" (Weis, 2004) discursively and behaviorally in the new millennium. Similar to Weis's (1990, 2004) longitudinal research on the impact of globalization on the rearticulation of the American White working class, this study demonstrates how globalization, in conjunction with political changes over time, affect the class rearticulation of the Japanese-educated elders.

Positioning theory offers a useful lens through which to see how this class repositioning is achieved via narratives. We see these elders are not only "structured" by the past, but they actively deploy their linguistic and cultural capital to craft and reclaim their educated identity through and across the narrated event and the event of narration. That is, while the content of the stories consists of statements about their past and present connection with Japanese education and language, through the act of telling stories and choosing plots, they reposition themselves as the educated class in relation to the Mandarin-educated and in opposition to the uneducated.

This distinction is of considerable significance given that their class position was erased by virtue of the elision of their educational experiences after 1945. Liu mama's example is particularly illuminating about the Japanese-educated elders' desire and need to distance themselves from their uneducated peers. With 8 years of Japanese education and having retired from a career in nursing, Liu mama once indignantly related an encounter with college students whom she perceived to have conflated her with the uneducated: "Some young college students came to interview me. They asked me, 'Did you have education?' I was very upset. I did not want to answer them. That was rude. How can they ask 'Did you have education?' They should ask 'How many years of education did you have?' I didn't want to talk to them."

This research thus contributes to a growing body of literature on the phenomenon of Japanese-educated elders' colonial nostalgia by revealing the central role that language and class distinction plays in their affinity for Japan. In addition, by examining a unique case of postcolonial language politics and class "erasure" in multicolonized Taiwan, this study builds on a growing body of work on how ideologies of language are linked to social inequality and how both are inflected through the dynamics of linguistic contact and political struggle in situations where colonial legacies become entangled with nation building and globalization.

A particularly intriguing finding in this study pertains to the role of elders. The linguistic dilemma and identity struggle faced by the Japanese-educated elders reveals a seeming paradox: namely, how is it possible that elders are rendered voiceless and invisible in a society that still holds the traditional values of veneration for elders as shown in the cultural concept of filial piety (Ikels, 2004)? Elsewhere I have argued that most Taiwanese elders are faced today with twin dilemmas: their linguistic marginality is unique to their generation as a product of historically layered language and education policies; and traditional practices of filial piety have been transformed in modern society to focus primarily on taking care of the material and physical needs of elders (Lin, 2009a). Thus the belief that filial piety is still being practiced masks the fact that the elders are often linguistically marginalized in daily life, even within the intimate arena of the family (Lin, 2009a). On the other hand, it is also important to keep in mind that the elders' sociolinguistic marginal status did not suddenly appear in their later years. They have lived with erasure and stigmatization for nearly half a century. Their marginalization, therefore, has more to do with generational issues than with the role of elders.

Finally, it is important to note that class repositioning through narratives as demonstrated in this chapter can only be achieved when there is a listener, as any transaction of speaking requires a speaker *and* a listener (Bakhtin, 1981). This paper reveals that these elders were able to complete the speaking transaction within the private space occasioned by the presence of relatives and friends and the interviewer. It remains to be seen whether their stories are "heard" and understood beyond these individual and interactional moments at the societal level. An implication of this study is that the meanings of the subaltern's utterances cannot be understood without locating the speakers in a temporally specific sociohistorical and political trajectory. Notably, beyond the academic circle, in the past few years there is an emerging trend in popular culture (e.g., commercial films and documentaries) that has begun to represent Japanese-speaking elders' lives as situated in the complicated history of Taiwan under the Japanese colonization, the Chinese Nationalist regime's authoritarian rule, and recent globalization.[13] Most of these productions have attracted huge viewership across generations. In so doing, these productions, along with scholarly work such as the present study and others on similar issues, have the potential to educate the general public as to "how we might 'listen' to the voices" of the elders (Fine & Weis, 2005, p. xii).

Notes

1 The clip is available at http://www.youtube.com/watch?v=31alNneqJdU&feature=related
2 The languages previously spoken on the island included aboriginal languages, and two Han languages—Hoklo and Hakka, spoken by settlers who immigrated to Taiwan from China 400 years ago. Since 1945, the ethnic Hoklo comprise 73.3% of the population; Mainlanders (*waishengren*, people who came to the island in 1949 with the KMT), 13%; Hakka, 12%; Aborigines, 1.7%.
3 This study is derived from two related field research projects about the sociolinguistic marginalization of Taiwanese elders. The first is a 6-month study between 2001 and 2002 with my family members, including my Great Aunt Meichi, who received 8 years of Japanese education (Lin, 2009a). Interviews with Great Aunt Meichi form part of the data for this chapter. The other interviews for analysis were based on a second project, which consists of 15 months of fieldwork between 2004 and 2006 in Sunset Mountain (Lin, 2009b). Together, the participants included in this chapter were between 72 and 96 years old and had 5 to 8 years of Japanese education.
4 I only discussed women's interviews because my main field sites of the larger study between 2004 and 2006 are senior education classes, where the overwhelming majority of students are female. Thus I chiefly have access to women's accounts. The issues discussed in this paper apply to males as well.
5 Wortham (2001) suggests five linguistic sources that are windows to how positioning is achieved by the narrator: reference and predication (e.g., that woman); metapragmatic descriptors (...argues/lies/quarrels); quotation; evaluative indexicals ("lexical items, grammatical constructions, accents, or any of a number other linguistic patterns" which get associated with particular groups of people and when used by narrators or characters function as indices of these groups); and epistemic modalizers (expressions that reveal the kinds of access narrators have toward the narrated event and position them in the event in particular ways, as spectator, participant, etc.).
6 The language of instruction was in Hoklo or Hakka.
7 As a discriminative policy against native Taiwanese, the Japanese only allowed a small number of Taiwanese students to receive education beyond the primary grades (Tsurumi, 1979).
8 The middle school exam is based on the materials taught in the elementary schools admitting only Japanese. Taiwanese children needed extra classes to prepare for the examination.
9 In addition to the rice cake during the Japanese New Year, they were offered snacks occasionally.
10 On the 100th anniversary of the elementary school in 2002, some elderly students sang the song in the celebration and gave a copy to Granny Lai.
11 They explicitly named these discriminatory practices in education during the interviews.
12 In a recent documentary, *Taiwanese Life* (Taiwan *Rensheng*), featuring five Japanese-educated elders, one of the elders went to his former teacher's grave in Japan to pay tribute in memory of the teacher's kind encouragement during his school years.
13 For example, the movie Cape No. 7 (Wei, 2008) depicting the connection between a Japanese teacher and a Taiwanese girl and the documentary *Emerald Horizon: Shonenko's Stories* (Kuo, 2006) on Japan's use of child labor during World War II.

References

Alexander, K. J., Miller, P. J., & Hengst, J. A. (2001). Young children's emotional attachments to stories. *Social Development, 10*, 373–397.
Appadurai, A. (1996). *Modernity at large: Cultural dimensions of globalization*. Minneapolis: University of Minnesota Press.
Austin, J. L. (1962). *How to do things with words*. London: Oxford University Press.

Bakhtin, M. (1981). *The dialogic imagination*, M. Holquist (Ed.), C. Emerson & M. Holquist (Trans.). Austin, TX: University of Texas Press.

Bourdieu, P. (1991). *Language and symbolic power*. Cambridge, MA: Harvard University Press.

Ching, L. (2001). *Becoming "Japanese": Colonial Taiwan and the politics of identity formation*. Berkeley: University of California Press.

Chomsky, N. (1965). *Aspects of the theory of syntax*. Cambridge, MA: MIT Press.

Davies, B., & Harre, R. (1990). Positioning: The discursive construction of selves. *Journal for the Theory of Social Behaviour, 20*, 43–63.

De Fina, A., Schiffrin, D., & Bamberg, M. (2006). *Discourse and identity*. New York: Cambridge University Press.

Dimitriadis, G. (2008). Series editor introduction. In N. Dolby & F. Fizvi (Eds.), *Youth moves: Identities and education in global perspective* (pp. ix–x). New York: Routledge.

Dolby, N., & Rizvi, F. (2008). Introduction: Youth, mobility, and identity. In N. Dolby & F. Rizvi (Eds.), *Youth moves: Identities and education in global perspective* (pp. 1–14). New York: Routledge.

Fine, M., & Weis, L. (2005). Introduction. In L. Weis & M. Fine (Eds.), *Beyond silenced voices: Class, race, and gender in United States schools* (pp. xi–xiv). Albany, NY: SUNY Press.

Gal, S. (1989). Language and political economy. *Annual Review of Anthropology, 18*(1), 345–367.

Goffman, E. (1979). Footing. *Semiotica, 25*, 1–29.

Huang, C.-H. (2003). The transformation of Taiwanese attitudes toward Japan in the post-colonial period. In N. Li & R. Cribb (Eds.), *Imperial Japan and national identities in Asia, 1895–1945* (pp. 296–314). London: Routledge.

Huang, C.-H. (2010). Zhong hua min guo zai tai wan (1945–1987): zhi min tong zhi yu qian zhan zhe guo jia shuo zhi jian tao. [Republic of China in Taiwan (1945–1987): A study on colonialism and settler state.] In *zhong hua min guo liu wang tai wan liu shi nian ji zhan hou tai wan guo ji chu jing* [Sixty years of Republic of China in Taiwan and Taiwan's postwar international status] (pp. 161–192). Taipei, Taiwan: Qian wei.

Huang, S. (1993). *Yuyan shehui yu zuqun yishi: Taiwan yuyan shehuixue de yanjiu* [Language, society and ethnic consciousness: The study of Taiwan's languages and societies]. Taipei, Taiwan: Crane.

Huang, S. (2000). Language, identity and conflict: A Taiwanese study. *International Journal of the Sociology of Language, 143*, 139–149.

Ikels, C. (2004). Introduction. In C. Ikels (Ed.), *Filial piety: Practice and discourse in contemporary East Asia* (pp. 1–15). Stanford, CA: Stanford University Press.

Irvine, J. T., & Gal, S. (2000). Language ideology and linguistic differentiation. In P.V. Kroskrity (Ed.), *Regimes of language: Ideologies, politics, and identities* (pp. 35–84). Santa Fe, NM: School of American Research Press.

Kerr, G. H. (1965). *Formosa betrayed*. Boston, MA: Houghton Mifflin.

Koven, M. (2007). *Selves in two languages: Bilinguals' verbal enactments of identity in French and Portuguese*. Philadelphia, PA: Benjamins.

Kroskrity , P. V. (Ed.). (2000). *Regimes of language: Ideologies, politics, and identities*. Santa Fe, NM: School of American Research Press.

Kuo, L.-Y. (Director). (2006). *Emerald horizon: Shonenko's stories*. Taipei, Taiwan Yuan-Liou Publishing.

Lee, M.-T. (2004). *Qin ri de qing jie jie gou* [Pro-Japan affinity and Japanophilia: A study on intergenerational politics of identity]. Paper presented at the 2004 Annual Meeting of the Taiwanese Sociology Association, Taipei, Taiwan.

Lin, S. (2009a). How listening is silenced: A monolingual Taiwanese elder constructs identity through television viewing. *Language in Society, 38*, 311–337.

Lin, S. (2009b). *Education at last! Taiwanese grandmothers "go to school."* (Unpublished doctoral dissertation). University of Illinois, Urbana, IL.

Liu, C.-Y. (2007, September 4). *Pi kai ha ri chou ri de xi jie* [Untying the knot of loving Japan and hating Japan]. *China Times*. Retrieved November 1, 2007, from http://news.chinatimes.com/

Miller, P. J., Fung, H., & Mintz, J. (1996). Self-construction through narrative practices: A Chinese and American comparison of early socialization. *Ethos, 24*, 237–280.

Ochs, E., & Capps, L. (2001). *Living narrative: Creating lives in everyday storytelling*. Cambridge, MA: Harvard University Press.

Philips, S. U. (2004). Language and social inequality. In A. Duranti (Ed.), *A companion to linguistic anthropology* (pp. 474–495). Malden, MA: Blackwell.

Sandel, T. L. (2003). Linguistic capital in Taiwan: The KMT's Mandarin language policy and its perceived impact on language practices of bilingual Mandarin and Tai-gi speakers. *Language in Society, 32*, 523–551.

Somers, M. R. (1994). The narrative constitution of identity: A relational and network approach. *Theory and Society, 23*, 605–649.

Su, H.-Y. (2008). What does it mean to be a girl with *qizhi*?: Refinement, gender and language ideologies in contemporary Taiwan. *Journal of Sociolinguistics, 12*, 334–358.

Tsurumi, E. P. (1979). Education and assimilation in Taiwan under Japanese rule, 1895–945. *Modern Asian Studies, 13*(4), 617–641.

Wei, T.-S. (Writer/Director). (2008). *Cape No. 7* [Motion Picture]. Taiwan: ARS Film Production.

Weis, L. (1990). *Working class without work: High school students in a de-industrializing economy*. New York: Routledge.

Weis, L. (2004). *Class reunion: The remaking of the American white working class*. New York: Routledge.

Wortham, S. (2001). *Narrative in action*. New York: Teachers College Press.

鈴木滿男. (Ling Mu Man Nan). (2002). *Ri ben ren zai tai wan zuo le she mo*. [What did Japan do in Taiwan] (E.-L. Ca, Trans.). Taipei, Taiwan: Qienwei.

5

PRODUCING CLASS AND ETHNIC IDENTITIES AMONG TURKISH YOUTH IN WORKING- AND MIDDLE-CLASS SCHOOLS IN GERMANY

Daniel Faas

Introduction

This chapter discusses the relationships between race, ethnicity, and class among 15-year-old Turkish youth educated in Germany. It argues that ethnic identities are stronger in working-class schools, especially in contexts of conflict, whilst political identities are more pronounced in middle-class schools. As a result of their schooling, community experience, and socioeconomic background, Turkish youth develop different forms of identities relative to their European and ethnic identifications. Although there are overlaps: I consider political identities to constitute a sense of belonging at the local, regional, national, or supranational citizenship level (such as Stuttgart or Europe), whereas ethnic identities are mainly linked to common ancestry, customs and traditions, and language and dialects (such as Swabian or Turkish). Discussions are largely based upon insights obtained from extensive fieldwork in German working-class (Tannberg Hauptschule) and middle-class (Goethe Gymnasium) schools in Stuttgart, supplemented by an analysis of the wider macropolitical background and its impact on schooling and youth identity formations.

Germany needed workers to fill labor needs and to rebuild the country's traditional economy (Bade, 2000), especially after the influx of refugees from the East ceased with the construction of the Berlin Wall in 1961. Turkish "guest workers" (*Gastarbeiter*), many of whom originated from the economically underdeveloped rural southeast Anatolia region bordering Syria and Iraq, were recruited to work in Germany, and were greeted enthusiastically. The October 31, 1961 bilateral agreement between Germany and Turkey, which Şen and Goldberg (1994, p. 10) referred to as "one of the most important milestones in the history of German-Turkish relations," stated that Turkish workers should return to their home country within 2 years. However, because of the need for Turkish (and other) guest workers beyond the initially agreed date, many of these young men continued to stay in Germany and were joined by their families. By 1980, the Turks formed the largest minority ethnic community in Germany and, because of family reunification, their number had increased to 2.6 million by the late 1990s (Statistisches Bundesamt, 2008). Most 15-year-old Turkish residents of Germany belong to the second-generation.

German politicians and policymakers have struggled to include minority ethnic communities like the Turks into its "Europeanized concept of nationhood" (Faas, 2010). Following World War II, successive governments employed the concept of Europe as an identity and developed an idealistic relationship with Europe (see Katzenstein, 1997; Risse & Engelmann-Martin, 2002). Integrating "guest worker children" into the German school system while preparing them for a possible return to their country of origin, known as "foreigner pedagogy" (*Ausländerpädagogik*), became the guiding principle of education, particularly in the 1960s and early 1970s (see Hoff, 1995; Luchtenberg, 1997). After the 1973 oil crisis and the end of foreign labor recruitment, the image of immigrants was transformed from being a welcome pool of cheap labor into unwanted "foreigners." Throughout the 1980s and 1990s, Europe became a focal point for national political identities in German schools. In 1998, the Social Democrat government under Gerhard Schröder broke with the mantra repeated since the 1970s that Germany was not "a country of immigration" (Bade, 2007; Martin, 1994), reformed the citizenship law (Schiffauer, 2006), and passed the country's first immigration law in 2005. There is now broad consensus on the need to promote integration, and the grand-coalition government, under Angela Merkel (since 2005), has hosted three integration summits to discuss German language learning, education, and job opportunities.[1] Several Islam conferences have focused on the interactions between the national majority and Muslim minorities, addressing religious topics, German law and values, and employment policies. Federal states have begun providing Islamic religious education in German for students of Muslim origin alongside the Protestant and Catholic religions. German schools are mediating these debates in rather different ways. In turn, these differing approaches impact the identities of Turkish youth.

Although I argue that schooling is a prime factor affecting identity formation, this does not imply that class and other factors such as gender are to be ignored—quite the contrary.[2] To get an idea of the socioeconomic status of each of the schools, I looked at the percentages of pupils eligible for free school meals, compared the achievement levels, and, most importantly, asked students to classify their parents' occupations. These were coded into four family class types: (a) families with at least one parent who is a middle-class professional, (b) families with two parents who do nonmanual work, (c) a transitional category comprised of one parent who does nonmanual work and the other skilled work, and (d) families where one parent is a skilled worker and the other an unskilled manual worker. Categories (a) to (c) were taken to represent the middle class and category (d), the working class. A majority of German and Turkish interviewees at Tannberg Hauptschule in Stuttgart (57%) had working-class parents, whereas more than half of all 15-year-olds at the Goethe Gymnasium (54%) had middle-class parents who were professionals. However, more than one-quarter of Turkish students at Goethe (29%) had working-class parents compared with just 1 in 10 of German students at Goethe. This indicates that the Turkish sample at Goethe is somewhat "less middle class" than the ethnic majority; it is very important to bear this point in mind because it adds to the complexity of contemporary youth identity formations. Not only were Turkish student backgrounds more similar across the schools in this study, but students also mixed well in both working- and middle-class localities in Germany. Clearly, however, social class matters with regard to developing a European identity. The privileged backgrounds of some of my respondents allowed them to take part in European school exchanges and to travel across Europe. Despite a similar curriculum input on Europe across German schools, clear differences emerged with regard to European identification across institutions which were not solely the result of inclusive European or Eurocentric policies. I return to this point below.

After a brief note on methodology, I discuss how socioeconomic background, race, and ethnicity intersect in a working- and a middle-class school in Stuttgart and what the implications are for the identity formation of Turkish youth.

A Note on Methodology

This chapter draws on data from fieldwork carried out in 2004 which investigated how socioeconomically and geographically different groups of young people in Germany and England negotiated their identities (Faas, 2010). Since the responsibility for implementing European and multicultural educational initiatives rests primarily with the 16 federal states (*Bundesländer*) in Germany, I selected two boroughs in Stuttgart with a similar interest in European and multicultural issues. My choices were also driven by pragmatic considerations, including proximity to my hometown of Pforzheim. I then formally approached schools and met with the liaisons prior to fieldwork.

Tannberg Hauptschule has a population of 320 students, 191 (62%) of whom come from minority ethnic communities. Turkish youth form the largest group (54 students, 18%), followed by Italians (30 students), those from Serbia and Montenegro (24 students), Croatians (18 students), and Greeks (14 students). Ethnicity did not play a major role in terms of the grades students received. German students had the same average as Turkish students (2.9), and the Italians (2.8) and Croatians (3.0) were only marginally above or below their German classmates. In contrast, only 135 (24%) of the 564 students who were attending Goethe Gymnasium during the study came from minority ethnic communities; the Italians (31 students, 5.5%) formed the largest group, followed by Turkish youth (26 students). Ethnicity played more of a role in terms of the grades students received. The sample of German students had an average grade of 2.6 and achieved half a grade better than Turkish students (3.1), who had the lowest score.[3] This underscores that, in both schools, Turkish students not only occupied minority status relative to their German peers but also in relation to the overall number of minority ethnic students.

The main data collection methodology consisted of a questionnaire as well as focus groups (six per school) and semistructured interviews with 15-year-old Turkish and ethnic majority students (eight per school). The main reason for choosing 15-year-olds was due to my experience as a secondary school teacher, which suggested that students of that age are able to develop personal opinions on a range of issues and challenge the opinions of those around them. In addition, I was trying to avoid age groups involved in, or nearing, examinations. Purposeful sampling was used in an effort to ensure a gender and ethnic balance. Additional interviews with the school principal, the citizenship coordinator, the head of the geography department, and the head of religious education were conducted in each school to gain insights into the role schools play in forming identities. All interviews were tape-recorded, transcribed, and then analyzed using a broadly inductive approach whereby the thematic categories and findings emerged from the deconstruction of the meanings of these transcripts.

Although I had some a priori codes based on the interview schedules, I gradually adapted the thematic categories while reading through the transcripts. I looked at the ways in which students responded to questions and positioned themselves within particular discourses. When I tried to deconstruct the multiple meanings of these narratives I was guided by approaches from poststructuralist theories of identity. Specifically, this work was informed by MacLure (2003), who argued that one of the most common ways that people stitch together texts is through the setting up of binary oppositions (e.g., "us" and "them"). "One 'side' comes to meaning through its difference with respect to a constructed 'other,' which is always lacking, lesser or derivative in some respect" (MacLure, 2003, p. 10). The space opened up by discourse, she argues, is an ambivalent one; it is both productive and disabling. Without distance, we would not be able to imagine others as distinct from ourselves: "It's the spacing, the difference that makes it possible for us to think truth, self, nature, etc. in the first place" (MacLure, 2003, p. 165). However, my analysis can only provide an account of my own reading(s). Other researchers might put together truths in different ways.

The interviewer, the author of this chapter, is a native German speaker and is fluent in English. I am also relatively young, which, in terms of age at least, resulted in fairly balanced power relations during interviews. The strategies I used to be a nonthreatening "other" included introducing myself as someone who would like to learn more about other cultures and ways of thinking about people and society. I also decided not to dress too formally so that students were not put off by the image of having a teacherlike adult in the room. Despite these strategies, there was a possibility that the respondents constructed their identities in response to my own identity (e.g., adult, German, middle-class, Christian) and the questions I was asking of them. It was difficult of course to determine the extent to which my own identity may or may not have interacted with the interviewees' self-perceptions. Theories of identity suggest that identities are constructed through dialectical processes of negotiation between people and the larger social categories within which they live (e.g., nation-states). It is especially fascinating to explore the shifting identities of Turkish youth during a period when Turkey is getting politically closer to Europe. Nowhere are these questions more relevant than in Germany, home to the largest Turkish community outside of Turkey.

The Identities of Turkish Youth in Two German Schools

Tannberg Hauptschule, a vocational-track school, is located in a residential area on a hill on the edge of an inner-city, multiethnic, mainly working-class borough in Stuttgart. Because of the predominantly working-class background of its students and the limited financial resources for travel, Tannberg Hauptschule has no European exchanges or partnerships. The school mediated national citizenship agendas through a dominantly European and arguably, at times, Eurocentric approach. The teachers I interviewed claimed that the school aimed to create self-confident, critical, tolerant, and informed citizens. However, the school was a "flashpoint school" (*Brennpunktschule*), meaning one with a substantial "at-risk" student population because of its location within a low-income neighborhood and the associated problems of poverty and neglect. Teachers believed students had linguistic difficulties and a lack of social skills. As a result, in the view of Mr. Müller, the deputy principal, it was difficult to put into practice theoretical conceptualizations, such as the notion of an informed and active citizen. The teachers admitted that they frequently had to address extracurricular concerns before meaningful learning and teaching could take place. According to Mr. Müller, only about half of the prescribed curriculum could be taught, whereas the remaining time was spent on improving students' social and civic skills, including the ability to live together in peace and develop feelings of mutuality and problem-solving strategies.

Despite some intercultural teaching, the teachers I interviewed seemed to struggle to combine the notion of multiculturalism with the dominant European agenda. Mr. Koch, the citizenship coordinator, maintained that there was no alternative to the European dimension and that it was essential to deal with Europe in school. While eating with the students in the canteen, I witnessed cultural insensitivity among some Tannberg Hauptschule teachers toward

Turkish Muslim students. On that particular day, there was pork and beef sauce available for the students and the teachers on duty told a male German student who wanted to help himself to some beef sauce that this is "Muslim sauce" (*Moslemsoße*) and that instead, he should take some "non-Muslim sauce." When the German student asked why he shouldn't eat beef sauce the supervising teacher replied, "You will get impotent from that." Besides this lunchtime remark, I sat in on some lessons where teachers occasionally spoke German with a foreign accent (*Ausländerdeutsch*), and thus, either intentionally or unintentionally ridiculed some minority ethnic students in class. These examples indicate the ways in which some teachers marginalized and oppressed minority ethnic students.

Although there was no obvious hostility toward Turkish youth at Tannberg Hauptschule, there were other suggestions that Turkish people were still considered strangers and not part of the European project. For example, Miss Klein (the head of religious education) referred to the White Christian roots of Germany and Europe and established a racial/religious hierarchy which privileged cross over hijab. Arguably, such a Eurocentric approach and ethos made it very difficult for the Turkish students to identify with the concept of Europe/European citizenship. The Turkish students I interviewed mostly adopted a German perspective when talking about the possibility of a Turkish EU membership, which was not only suggestive of their familiarity with national sociopolitical debates but also indicated the ways in which they brought together ethnic identities with national identities. The Social Democratic-Green coalition government (1998–2005) argued in favor of full Turkish EU membership, whereas senior members of the current ruling Christian Democrats preferred a "privileged partnership" (see İçener, 2007). A similarly distant approach was adopted by both Sema and Zerrin, who thought of Turkey as a largely backward country and not only distanced themselves from those Turkish people who live in Turkey and who, according to them, know little about life in Germany, but also rejected some of the customs associated with the Muslim religion:

DF: How do you feel about Turkey joining the EU?
Sema: I don't want Turkey to join the EU.
Zerrin: Me neither.
Sema: Germany, Turkey is bankrupt anyway. What do they want in the EU? In Turkey, they think that everything is fine in Germany. There, Turkish people approach me and ask me where I was from and when I say "from Germany" they...
Zerrin: (interrupting) They want to marry you, want to follow you to Germany and lead a better life here. That was the case with my brother-in-law too. Well some things are better here....
Sema: Some Germans also think that the Muslim religion is a bit stupid. I find it stupid too. The fact that you can't eat pork or have a boyfriend, which is the case amongst Turks, I mean you are only allowed to have a boyfriend when you're engaged. That's just nonsense.

In contrast, some Turkish boys in Tannberg who are part of the study were either neutral or in favor of their country of origin joining the EU, which may be a result of their stronger Turkish identity. There was a tendency among the group of 15-year-old boys at Tannberg to consider their ethnic background as more important than their German identity, while the group of Turkish girls identified with Germany and Turkey to an equivalent extent. Bülent says that it would be good for Turkey to share the knowledge of the European community whereas Tamer maintains that it would be financially beneficial for Turkey to join the EU:

Bülent: Well, I would say if more Turkish people come to Germany it wouldn't be good, I mean, there are advantages and disadvantages. It's good if Turkey joins because it's a community and the others know a lot; that's good.... I think that the human rights situation has changed a lot, not everything but many things.

Tamer: I find it quite ok, but also not. I wouldn't find it good if lots of people come from Turkey to Germany. But many want to improve their social position and that's good.... Turkey would get support if they joined the EU and then it would perhaps be better for the country than now.

Given the country's decade-long commitment to Europe and European politics, it was not surprising that nearly all 15-year-old Turkish youth I interviewed in the Tannberg Hauptschule thought that Germany should get closer to Europe. For example, Tamer claims that "Germany belongs to Europe." "We are the EU, Europe, I think," whereas Cari was slightly less emphatic in saying that "the US is fierce." "I think it's OK the way it is right now." Tamer used the inclusive first person plural form ("we") to describe Germany's relationship with Europe, thus revealing his level of integration and the extent to which he has adapted to the German way of life and thinking. While none of the Turkish 15-year-olds at Tannberg saw themselves as European, most Turkish interviewees seemed to identify with Germany, claiming that Germany was more important than Turkey. It was fascinating to listen to the ways in which the group of Turkish girls balanced their hybrid identities. Hybridization produced a third space that allowed other identities to emerge (e.g., Turkish German, Swabian German). However, there is some evidence in this data that "the language of binary oppositions" (i.e., German or Turk; Hall, 1992) has evolved into one of tertiary oppositions (i.e., German or Turk or German Turk) which also constructs, for instance, the German Turks as "Other." The following quotation shows an example of the dilemma Sema and Zerrin face as a result of their ethnonational (i.e., Turkish German) identities. In Germany, they are positioned as "foreigners" and in Turkey people refer to them as Germans, which is precisely what Boos-Nünning (1986) calls a "reference group problem" and what Auernheimer (1990) refers to as individuals acquiring a marginal identity in relation to both cultures of reference:

DF: Where do you feel you belong to?

Sema: As a citizen I feel I belong to Germany. But when people ask me, I mean, when I am here then people call me "foreigner." When I go to Turkey, they call me "German" there.

Zerrin: Yes, I don't feel I belong to anything. I don't think that I am German and I don't think that I am Turkish. I don't know. When I go to Turkey, then they say "Oh, look at the German;" and here I am a foreigner. Great. So, who am I? Where do I belong to?

Sema: As a citizen, I can say I belong to Germany.

Zerrin: I can say that I'm a German citizen but I'm not German. German citizen, I think, means that I have to adapt to this country, I try to adapt myself, and then I think about the laws and everything. I know a lot more about Germany so that I am a German citizen, but I'm not German. But, I'm not Turkish either if you see what I mean.

Sema: I know Germany better than Turkey. I could never ever imagine living in Turkey.

Zerrin's questions that ask "Who am I?" and "Where do I belong?" highlight the ongoing process of identity formation and the struggle between "being a German citizen" which is based on residence, and "being German" which is based on blood and race. During the course of the conversation, Sema further justified her feelings, saying that she could not speak Turkish that well and that she did not have any friends back in Turkey. Also, she preferred the freedom of Western societies to dress however you want and distanced herself from those "typically Turkish women who just sit around all day long not doing much apart from knitting and gossiping about others." Clearly, Sema, but also Zerrin and others from cities such as Antalya or Istanbul, rejected this traditional Muslim image of women, which is particularly strong in the rural villages of the southeast Anatolia region bordering on Syria and Iraq. This partly accounts for why Sema and Zerrin did not strongly identify with Turkey.

Other Turkish students I interviewed also had hybrid identities. For example, a group of Turkish boys argued that they felt slightly more Turkish than German because "although we were born in Germany, our origin and family background is in Turkey." However, their struggle for social acceptance was also highlighted in their experiences. "Here [in Germany] we're foreigners and in Turkey we are also foreigners, basically we're foreigners everywhere." Arguably, the tendency that some boys identified more strongly with Turkey than girls did might have to do with their different roles in Turkish society where women often have a more domestic role while men carry on their family name, and thus their honor and identity. This could also have to do with girls wanting and seeking out the freedoms for women allowed in German society.

In contrast, Goethe Gymnasium, a university-track school in a more middle-class neighborhood within the same borough of Stuttgart, was established in 1818 as a single-sex school for girls. Like Tannberg Hauptschule, the school promoted European values, but did so alongside multicultural values, rather than replacing them altogether. Sociocultural and ethnic differences were mediated in this school through notions of tolerance, liberalism, and a strong sense of community. The teachers I interviewed had a deeply ambivalent relationship toward German national identity and referred to Germany's Europeanized national identity. This submerged national identity was reflected in the school's approach which emphasized Europe as a common bond but, at the same time, allowed individuals to keep their cultural and ethnic identities. The European dimension of Goethe Gymnasium is not only visible in the teaching of French and English as compulsory modern foreign languages for all students, but also in the range of exchange programs with France, Italy, and Poland. The school's European and international profile is a result of its particular location and local community. Although there is no mother tongue in teaching, the school values the fact that ethnic minority students have an additional language and regards this as an asset. In religious education, for instance, students visit synagogues, mosques, and churches alike and the school also has contacts with a Buddhist teacher who is frequently invited to discuss her religion with students. These initiatives were aimed at promoting intercultural tolerance, mutual respect, and a sense of community.

Unlike at Tannberg Hauptschule, community studies (or civic education) only played a minor role in promoting the multicultural and European values of Goethe Gymnasium. Some teachers at Goethe admitted that it is difficult to "teach" a sense of European identity, arguing that traveling, school partnerships and exchanges, as well as modern foreign language learning, also help students develop a sense of European identity. While young people at Goethe Gymnasium had access to these European activities because of their privileged socioeconomic backgrounds, students at Tannberg Hauptschule were largely deprived of such opportunities. However, the fact that Goethe Gymnasium mediated ethnoreligious and cultural differences through notions of tolerance, liberalism, and a strong sense of community helped students to learn more about other cultures and connect with students from different backgrounds. Personality was more important than ethnicity when choosing friends. Nearly all 15-year-olds said that, on the whole, they felt "comfortable and safe" in Germany. A number of reasons emerged in the discussions I had with a group of four Turkish boys. The reasons they gave for their "comfort" were revealing. They consisted of a familiarity with the local area, a degree of adaptation to the German way of life, the generally good life in Germany, which was associated with social class, contacts, and friendships with other people, civil rights, and the view that Germany is a free country:

DF: How comfortable would you say you generally feel in Germany?

Zafer: I like it here 'cos you can live a very good life here as a foreigner, also 'cos there are many others but, erm, yes.

Yener: I feel very comfortable here. I've adapted and I couldn't, well, Turkey is my origin but in Turkey I couldn't live like I live here, particularly 'cos I've got everything here.

Sevilin: Here, you've got many chances to climb up in society as a foreigner, I think.

Irem: I couldn't imagine life elsewhere. I'm talking about Stuttgart, not Germany. I'm familiar with the area. I grew up here. Loads of people know me although I'm in Turkey six weeks during the summer. And when I'm there I think "just imagine another six weeks; that would already be too much."

Zafer: You just have your rights here and in other countries, I think, that's not the case. You won't be suppressed much as a minority here, when you have another religion. It's just a free country with a good welfare system.

Although the four Turkish boys were aware of their advantaged backgrounds, they were unable to empathize with socially deprived students. Ali maintained that "Germany is relatively safe although you can't be totally safe everywhere today 'cos of terrorism." Clearly, these statements were influenced by the memories of the September 11 terrorist attacks on the United States and the Madrid train bombings in March 2004, which took place 2 weeks before these interviews. The fact that none of the respondents referred to the presence of ethnic minority communities suggests the importance of social class over ethnicity. Social class becomes a unifying factor here and contributes to the societal well-being and identity formation processes of these 15-year-old youth.

In addition to socioeconomic background, parental encouragement and educational motivation contributed to students' sense of belonging. Several interviewees mentioned that their parents cared a great deal about their education. Parental support was not dependent on ethnicity or gender. For example, Andreas argued, "my mum always looks [to see] that I am studying, she controls me." Fatima, a Turkish girl, maintained that "my parents want me to do A-levels, to study at university and to have a good job. And they support me; they're willing to spend money as long as it's for school." Ali, a Turkish boy, argued that "they give me everything; I have everything, everything I want. [I have] tutors and so on, books. My parents demand a lot from me." Both Fatima's and Ali's remarks show a liberal, open-minded, and supportive attitude on the part of these Turkish parents who did not favor boys over girls with regard to education.

The Goethe Gymnasium's interpretation of "Europeanness" included multiculturalism, which encouraged Turkish students to relate positively to Europe and to construct a European political identity. This is in contrast to the findings at Tannberg where students were not happy to talk about supranational entities as separate (European/global) identities:

DF: To what extent do you see yourself as European?

Ali: Erm, of course I'm European. Europe is very big and is getting bigger and bigger. And when Turkey joins the EU it'll be even bigger. Europe is getting more and more important to me 'cos of Turkey.... Mariam: I feel European because of the euro. The euro impacts on your life. I mean, in the newspaper they always talk about the euro, Eurozone, Europe and so and I've noticed that the countries are getting closer and closer and not every country has its own policy. And the economy has grown together too. And you can travel to other countries without any problems at the borders.

While Europe was *part* of young people's identities at Goethe, the majority of Turkish youth I interviewed emphasized their German identities over and above Turkishness. They based their national identification on notions of birth and residence. Zeynep, a Turkish girl, thought, "I'd say [I'm] more German than Turkish. My dad works here, I plan to study here after school and work here as well." Nilgün, another Turkish girl, also prioritized her German identity saying that "I was born here and that's why I feel more German." Other 15-year-olds also distinguished between the "traditional Turk," who was described as wearing a headscarf, and the "westernized liberal Turk." The latter was more the type of Turkish student I encountered at Goethe Gymnasium as none of the girls wore the hijab and all dressed in a very western way, wearing jeans and trainers. Only one Turkish boy (Zafer), who described himself as a German Turk, signaled his Turkishness by wearing red sweaters and a necklace in the shape of the crescent moon and star on the Turkish flag. In the following quotation from a discussion with a group of four Turkish boys, Sevelin felt alienated from Turkey (which he viewed as a holiday destination) as a result of being born in Germany; Yener saw a new Turkish German subculture emerging from the Turkish influence from his parents and the German influence on the streets; and Irem referred to a possible loss of identity and the emergence of a single German identity amongst third- and fourth-generation Turkish Muslims in Germany:

DF: Where do you feel you belong to?

Zafer: Stuttgart.

Yener: Me too.

Sevilin: For me, this is my home and when I go on holiday to Turkey, I mean, I go there as a tourist although it's my country of origin. And when I go to the village my parents come from, they call me "the relative from Germany" and Stuttgart has become my home. And I don't think that I'd feel part of any other city.

Irem: In Turkey, I wouldn't feel as comfortable as here although my parents come from there. But I was born here and live here....

Yener: I'd say I'm German but the problem perhaps is to have the Turkish influence of my parents at home, 'cos they grew up in Turkey, and the German culture on the streets; that together is really a new culture for me and the foreigners are perhaps a new culture here....

Irem: I mean it's already difficult for my parents to pass on all the Turkish culture to me and when I pass it on to my children it will be even less and at some point nothing might be left. And eventually, the generation after us or so will say "We're Germans" just like the Black people in America say they're Americans.

The Turkish interviewees, all of whom were born in Stuttgart, did not identify with the regional Baden-Württemberg level (which is similar to what we saw in Tannberg Hauptschule) or the global level. For example, the boys and girls in the mixed-sex Turkish group referred to blood (e.g., ancestors) and family (e.g., home) to distance themselves from Swabia as a political and ethnic identity. Melik remarks in the following excerpt that he feels like a Turkish Stuttgarter, a German-European Turk, or a Turkish German, suggesting the multidimensional and hybrid nature of identities at Goethe:

DF: To what extent do you see yourself as Swabian or German?

Melik: I feel as a Turkish Stuttgarter so to speak, a German-European Turk or a Turkish German, but not Swabian. I don't know the Swabian culture and, I think, I'd have to be German for that with my ancestors being Swabians too.

Nurhan: You'd have to experience the culture at home but we can only see our Turkish culture and, I mean, I wouldn't want to lose that. I don't really know the Swabian way of life. Sometimes, teachers make Swabian jokes and stuff.

Ismet: (imitating the Swabian dialect) Gel.

Nurhan: We don't really know much Swabian stuff.

Ismet: I'd like to add that I don't see myself as a Swabian either, more as a Stuttgarter. It's also easier to get to know the German culture, just here generally by living here, but the Swabian culture is more at home and I'm not around that. Sometimes I don't really know whether something is particularly Swabian.

Nurhan: Perhaps Stuttgart is the Swabian world and it appears to me like a German world but maybe I don't fully grasp the contrast; I should go to Berlin or so for a while and see what the differences are.

Time and again, Turkish students such as Nurhan also spoke of being afraid of losing their Turkish identities as a result of integrating (or assimilating) into German society. Their Europeanized German identities had become so prevalent in the lives of these Turkish boys and girls that they felt their Turkishness was marginalized.

Discussion and Conclusions

The Turkish youth in this study had no singular identity but employed hybrid ethnonational, ethnolocal, and national-European identities as a result of their schooling and social class positioning rather than migration histories. Young people in the Gymnasium benefited to a greater extent from their privileged environment than their counterparts at Tannberg. The labor market opportunities for those students at Tannberg are likely to be much worse due to their relatively lower educational qualification (Hauptschule) compared to Goethe students. Because of their socioethnic marginalization, 15-year-olds in predominantly working-class schools are more likely to be caught up in ethnic tensions (though not necessarily inside the school premises). The ways in which social class worked within these different school contexts could also be seen in the extent to which students related positively to the political dimensions of the concept of hybridity, including Europe, rather than the ethnic dimensions. Turkish youth at the Goethe Gymnasium in Stuttgart, which promoted European and multicultural values, had the best opportunities of relating to Europe as a political identity. Their privileged socioeconomic background allowed them to take part in European school exchanges and to travel across Europe, thus benefiting from the opportunities associated with the European knowledge society. In contrast, as a result of their predominantly working-class backgrounds, Turkish youth at Tannberg Hauptschule did not seem to gain access to the same opportunities associated with the European knowledge society as their peers at Goethe, despite a similar curricular emphasis upon Europe.

The discussions in this chapter further underscore that when schools constructed an inclusive multiethnic concept of Europe, as the Goethe Gymnasium did, Turkish youth engaged with Europe as a political identity and developed national-European identities. If, however, Europe is conceptualized as an exclusionary monocultural (i.e., White, Christian) concept, as it was at the Tannberg Hauptschule, then Turkish students will struggle to relate positively to Europe as a political identity and emphasize their ethnic identities. It was the middle-class locale that appeared to respond to its multiethnic student populations by promoting inclusive citizenship models and, in so doing, allied the concept of diversity with social cohesion, or rather, what I call "multicultural Europeanness" in the Goethe Gymnasium. Similarly, ethnic identities were also stronger in working-class schools in other European societies whilst political identities were more pronounced in middle-class contexts, often as a result of "reethnicization" processes in working-class educational institutions (see Faas, 2010).

Germany has seen a wave of familial disputes not only between first-generation parents (representing the traditional Turks) and second-generation liberal Turks (mostly girls), but also intragenerational conflict between more conservative young Turkish males and more westernized young Turkish females. For example, between October 2004 and June 2005, eight Turkish women who broke with their family traditions and lived according to Western values (e.g., nonmarital sex, own living quarters, relationships, combined job and family life) were killed by male family members who felt that their *namus* (honor and dignity) and *seref* (reputation and prestige of the family) had been compromised (Banse & Laninger, 2005). Since 1996, more than 40 girls and women of Turkish or Middle Eastern origin who had lived in Germany for all, or most, of their lives were murdered for the same "crime." Many of these so-called honor killings were largely ignored by the media until 23-year-old Hatun Sürücü, born in Berlin, was shot dead in the open street on February 7, 2005 by three of her brothers who felt that she had brought dishonor to her family (Peil & Ernst, 2005). Officially she became the sixth victim among Berlin's 200,000-strong Turkish community. Her killing not only intensified the debate about integration (e.g., German language courses in kindergarten and primary school), but also sparked a new discussion about the necessity of introducing compulsory lessons on morals and ethics, following approval of the killing by several Turkish youth at a local school (Beckmann, 2005).

Despite these controversies, there is general recognition and valuing of the Turkish subculture that has emerged in Germany. This is particularly the case amongst the large Turkish community which has combined a commitment to their ethnic and cultural identity with an openness to German society. A thriving and colorful literary and cinematic Turkish-German subculture has sprung up, with over a thousand works written in Turkish and dealing with Sunni and Alevi experiences in Germany (Riemann & Harassowitz, 1990). In 2004, the German-Turkish film *Head-On* (*Gegen die Wand*), which tells the story of a marriage of convenience between two Turkish Muslims in Hamburg, won the Berlinale Golden Bear and was awarded Best European Film. There are also an increasing number of elected politicians and candidates with an immigrant background. However, there exists little published research on this development. In 2007, the journalist Mely Kiyak published a book *10 for Germany* (*10 für Deutschland*), which has portraits of 10 Turkish-origin elected politicians from all the major German parties. The most prominent of her interviewees is Çem Özdemir, who was first elected to parliament for the Green party in 1994 and subsequently held a seat in the European Parliament. In November 2008, Özdemir was elected one of two chairpersons of the party. Despite the upward social mobility of several individuals, the educational performance gap between Turkish and German students is still greater than that of any other migrant group in Germany (see Organisation for Economic Cooperation and Development [OECD], 2006) while the Vietnamese outperform German students (Beuchling, 2003).

The production of class and ethnic identity is thus a complex myriad. The extent to which migrant communities such as the Turks "(re)-ethnicize" also strongly depends upon personal and group discrimination within schools and societies at large, as well as the level of schooling (see Skrobanek, 2009).

Improving educational experiences and tackling socioethnic marginalization, especially within working-class contexts, has the potential to lead to more inclusive identities and stronger social cohesion, not only within the nation-state, but also within larger supranational entities.

Acknowledgments

I would like to thank Lois Weis and Nadine Dolby for taking the time to edit this volume and for inviting me to contribute. Thank you to previous publishers of my work: Parts of this chapter originally appeared in the Routledge Taylor & Francis journal *European Societies* (9[4], 573–599), and my monograph *Negotiating Political Identities: Multiethnic Schools and Youth in Europe* (Farnham, England: Ashgate).

Notes

1 The German debate about integration was further fueled by controversial comments by former German Federal Bank governor, Thilo Sarrazin, who argued that Muslim immigrants across Europe were neither willing nor capable of integrating into Western societies due to the different culture of Islam. He further claimed that (Turkish) immigrants make German society "dumber" because they are less educated but have more children than ethnic Germans (Sarrazin, 2010).

2 Although differences also emerged along gender lines, these are more fully discussed in Faas (2010). Male Turkish students argued that their country of origin is more important than Germany while female Turkish students claimed Germany was more important than Turkey. This gendered dimension might have to do with their different roles in the relatively patriarchal Turkish society where women have a more domestic role and men carry on their family honor.

3 In the German marking systme, a grade of 1.0 is the highest and 6.0 is the lowest.

References

Auernheimer, G. (1990). How black are the German Turks? Ethnicity, marginality and interethnic relations for young people of Turkish origin in the FRG. In L. Chisholm, P. Büchner, H- H. Krüger, & P. Brown (Eds.), *Childhood, youth, and social change: A comparative perspective* (pp. 197–212). Basingstoke, England: Falmer Press.

Bade, K. J. (2000). The German hub: Migration in history and the present. *Deutschland Magazine on Politics, Culture, Business and Science, 6*, 38–43.

Bade, K. J. (2007). Versäumte Integrationschancen und nachholende Integrationspolitik [Missed integration opportunities and catch-up integration policy]. In H.-G. Hiesserich (Eds.), *Nachholende Integrationspolitik und Gestaltungsperspektiven der Integrationspraxis* [Catch-up integration and perspectives of integration practice] (pp. 21–95). Göttingen, Germany: V&R unipress.

Banse, D. & Laninger, T. (2005). Mordmotiv: Blut für die Ehre [Murder motive: blood and honor]. *Die Welt.* Retrieved from http://www.welt.de/data/2005/02/16/464432.html

Beckmann, C. (2005). Özcan Mutlu: Alle haben versagt [Özcan Mutlu: We have all failed]. *Die Welt.* Retrieved from http://www.welt.de/data/2005/02/21/517683.html

Beuchling. O. (2003). *Vom Bootsflüchtling zum Bundesbürger. Migration, Integration und schulischer Erfolg in einer vietnamesischen Exilgemeinschaft* [From boat people to citizens: Migration, integration and educational success in a Vietnamese exile community]. Münster, Germany: Waxmann.

Boos-Nünning, U. (1986). Die schulische Situation der zweiten Generation [The student situation in the second generation]. In W. Meys & F. Şen (Eds.), *Zukunft in der Bundesrepublik oder Zukunft in der Türkei: Eine Bilanz der 25-jährigen Migration von Türken* [The future in Germany or Turkey: 25 years of Turkish migration] (pp. 131–155). Frankfurt, Germany: Dagyeli.

Faas, D. (2010). *Negotiating political identities: Multiethnic schools and youth in Europe.* Farnham, England: Ashgate.

Hall, S. (1992). New ethnicities. In J. Donald & A. Rattansi (Eds.), *"Race," culture and difference* (pp. 252–259). London: Sage.

Hoff, G. R. (1995). Multicultural education in Germany: Historical development and current status. In J. A. Banks (Ed.), *Handbook of research on multicultural education* (pp. 821–838). New York: Macmillan.

İçener, E. (2007). Privileged partnership: An alternative final destination for Turkey's integration with the European Union? *Perspectives on European Politics and Society, 8*(4), 415–438.

Katzenstein, P. J. (1997). United Germany in an integrating Europe. In P. J. Katzenstein (Ed.), *Tamed power: Germany in Europe* (pp. 1–48). Ithaca, NY: Cornell University Press.

Luchtenberg, S. (1997). Stages in multicultural theory and practice in Germany. In R. J. Watts & J. Jerzy (Eds.), *Cultural democracy and ethnic pluralism: Multicultural and multilingual policies in education* (pp. 125–148). Bern, Switzerland: Lang.

MacLure, M. (2003). *Discourse in educational and social research.* Maidenhead, England: Open University Press.

Martin, P. L. (1994). Germany: Reluctant land of immigration. In W. A. Cornelius, P. L. Martin, & J. F. Hollifield (Eds.), *Controlling immigration: A global perspective* (pp. 189–226). Stanford, CA: Stanford University Press.

Organisation for Economic Co-operation and Development (OECD). (2006). *Where immigrant students succeed: A comparative review of performance and engagement in PISA 2003.* Paris, France: Author.

Peil, F., & Ernst, S. (2005). Mord an junger Türkin [Young Turkish woman murdered]. *Spiegel Online.* Retrieved from http://www.spiegel.de/panorama/0,1518,342484,00.html

Riemann, W., & Harrassowitz, O. (1990). *Über das Leben in Bitterland: Bibliographie zur türkischen Deutschlandliteratur und zur türkischen Literatur in Deutschland* [Life in bitterland: Bibliography of German literature in Turkish and Turkish literature in Germany]. Wiesbaden, Germany: Harrassowitz.

Risse, T., & Engelmann-Martin, D. (2002). Identity politics and European integration: The case of Germany. In A. Pagden (Ed.), *The idea of Europe: From antiquity to the European Union* (pp. 287–316). Cambridge, England: Cambridge University Press.

Sarrazin, T. (2010). *Deutschland schafft sich ab: Wie wir unser Land aufs Spiel setzen* [Germany abolishes itself: How we are gambling with our country]. Munich, Germany: Deutsche Verlagsanstalt.

Schiffauer, W. (2006). Enemies within the gates: The debate about the citizenship of Muslims in Germany. In T. Modood, A. Triandafyllidou, & R. Zapata- Barrero (Eds.), *Multiculturalism, Muslims and citizenship: A European approach* (pp. 94–116). London: Routledge.

Şen, F. & Goldberg, A. (1994). *Türken in Deutschland: Leben zwischen zwei Kulturen* [Turks in Germany: Life between two cultures]. Munich, Germany: C. H. Beck.

Skrobanek, J. (2009). Perceived discrimination, ethnic identity and the (re-)ethnicization of youth with a Turkish ethnic background in Germany. *Journal of Ethnic and Migration Studies, 35*(4), 535–554.

Statistisches Bundesamt. (2008). *Ausländische Bevölkerung* [Foreign population]. Wiesbaden, Germany: Statistisches Bundesamt.

6

TRANSNATIONAL LATIN AMERICAN FAMILIES IN THE UNITED STATES

Parenting and Schooling in the "Neither Here Nor There"

Catalina Crespo-Sancho

Introduction

Globalization and changes in migration patterns have had a profound effect on how we understand contemporary society. As groups of people continue to move and develop cross-border relations, perceptions of space and place, social class dynamics, and educational matters are undeniably altered. These important global changes have led scholars to attempt to deterritorialize their research and consider processes that transcend national boundaries (Appadurai, 1991). This chapter is concerned with deterritorialized and multiterritorialized processes and the impact of social class on such processes. More specifically, this chapter looks at transnational and transcultural encounters within a Latino middle-class immigrant family and how multiple belongings affect parenting and schooling.

While there is much debate around the term *transnationalism*, it provides the possibility of an alternative conceptualization of cultural and ethnic studies. The chapter's focus on transnationalism allows highlighting questions about identity and education from a different perspective. This perspective does not view identity solely in terms of here or there, but also allows for spaces in between. A postmodern approach is used to investigate how alternative notions of the transnational help to reshape the family's understanding of social class, family, and education as both cultural constructs and means of deconstruction. This study seeks to understand the complex processes of incorporation, trans-nationalization, and education in the context of massive changes in the global economy.

This chapter provides an overview of how one middle-class transnational Latino family uses agency, influenced by experiences in their home country, to secure educational advantages for their children in the host country. In inter-viewing and observing a middle-class immigrant family, my goal was to under-stand the effects of transnational migration on the parenting and schooling of their children. My aim was to unravel the mechanisms by which immigrant families navigate the American educational system while negotiating home and host country social and cultural expectations.

I utilize the term *transnationalism* as "a process by which migrants, through their daily life activities and social, economic, and political relations, create social fields that cross national boundaries" (Basch, Glick Schiller, & Szanton Blanc, 2003, p. 22). Moreover, Bourdieu's notion of cultural capital is used to explain how the family draws upon class-related cultural factors in order to simultaneously adapt to two different places (1977a, 1986). I start from the premise that cultures, like individuals and families, cannot be fixed to a specific place (Gupta & Ferguson, 2002), as the experience of the family in this study shows. Transnational migrants construct an identity based on home and host country influences; constant negotiation between these influences is essential in the reconfiguration of how migrants perceive and are perceived by others. The story of the Latino family portrayed in this chapter allows us to understand the lives of people that overlap two worlds. The family's story emphasizes the man-ner in which migrant families are able to exercise their agency in the process of simultaneously belonging to multiple spaces and places.

The chapter is organized into four sections. In the first section, I provide an overview of my approach to social stratification and the value of using social class analysis in this study. I review literature about social stratification, includ-ing school and family structure formation as well as the effects of social class on educational attainment. In addition, I review theories on how contemporary migration is changing the social landscape of nations. In the second section I provide a description of the methodology used in this study, including a descrip-tion of the research setting, participants, methods, and data analysis. In the third section I examine the narratives and experiences of the Denegris, the middle-class Latino family studied here. In particular, I look at how parenting practices, in the form of settling patterns and neighborhood choice, influence children's education. This section includes findings on the connections of home and host country expectations and signifiers that affect transnational migrants' choices on where to live. In addition, I illustrate how these choices shape their children's schooling experience. The final section provides a discussion of the findings.

Theoretical Background

Social Stratification

The reproduction of society is a controversial topic in social science. Rather than a coherent system of indicators, as earlier theorists of social stratification have argued, social class can be better described as a collection of resources. In this study, I see social class broadly as the range of resources—cultural, economic, and social (Bourdieu, 1977a)—that individuals and families use to make sense of their lives, as well as the links these meanings and resources have to specific strategies of action. Resources are generally viewed in more measurable terms, such as income, education, or occupation. In this work I take into consideration terms such as income, educational attainment, and neighborhood location to assist with the social class classification of the family. My main interpretation of social stratification joins with that of other scholars who bring the importance of nonmaterial resources to the surface, revealing the ways in which resources, including friendships, ways of behaving, and networking, act to allow different means of access into society (Bourdieu, 1986; Lareau & Horvat, 1999).

Bourdieu (1977a) suggests that a family's social origin influences children's educational attainment by providing different cultural and social resources. Bourdieu and Passeron (1977) found that academic standards, believed to be neutral, are filled with specific cultural resources and requirements acquired within the family setting. Furthermore, the authors recognize that cultural experiences lived in the home facilitate children's adjustment to school, thereby transforming cultural resources into cultural capital. Bourdieu (1977a) draws on the concept of capital in understanding the objective of human activity in the social world. The definition of capital is not strictly economic; rather, "capital, defined as attributes, possessions, or qualities of a person or a position exchangeable for goods, services, or esteem, exists in many forms-symbolic, cultural, social, or linguistic, as well as economic" (DiMaggio, 1979, p. 1463).

With respect to schools, Bourdieu (1977a, 1977b) argues that these are not neutral spaces; rather, they reproduce and legitimate class structure by guaranteeing the success of students who are familiar with the valued capital. He states that families from different socioeconomic backgrounds teach their children cultural experiences that facilitate or impede their adjustment to school, thus transforming cultural resources into cultural capital. These resources, taught primarily in the family, include behaviors such as modes of use and relationship to language (Bernstein, 1971), relationship to authority, perceptions and disposition toward education, preferences, behaviors, and goods. Lareau (2002) argues that disparity in types of cultural capital provide children with different resources that affect their future outcome and reproduce inequalities.

The majority of research conducted on education and cultural capital centers on the relationship to educational attainment. In existing studies, cultural capital adopts a "highbrow" reductionist approach (De Graaf, De Graaf, & Kraaykamp, 2000; DiMaggio, 1982). However, the argument related to cultural capital in America is much more complex than just class. Other fundamental factors such as culture, ethnicity, race, and national background should also be considered. Many authors have used Bourdieu's concept of cultural capital in order to explain phenomena that include the relation to the reproduction of social inequality (Giroux, 1983; Weis, 2004), the impact of family background on educational attainment (De Graaf, et al., 2000; Lareau, 1987), and the influence of race in students' education (Lareau, 2002). Still, little research has been conducted on how cultural capital is expressed differently in diverse cultural and ethnic groups. Moreover, there has not been sufficient research conducted on how capital is expressed and reproduced by families that simultaneously participate in two societies. This study addresses this gap and looks at the effects of cultural and social capital in the parenting and schooling practices of a Latino transnational family.

In this work, I show that individuals simultaneously act on and are acted upon by multiple societies. By broadening our understanding of social class as a multidimensional term, which looks at material and nonmaterial factors, I argue that we must also understand class as a subjective concept that is lived differently in different parts of the world. My empirical observations led me to a view of social class that is not totally dependent on the context. Understanding the different contexts in which social class is malleable (through analyzing and comparing home and host land class signifiers) helps us to examine how families coming from other countries, with different social structures, might develop unique ways of using and developing social class schemas to create their identities in the host land.

Transnational Migration

It was traditionally believed by migration scholars that for the most part immigrants would cut off ties with their home countries while assimilating into their host countries (Gordon, 1964; Park & Burgess, 1969). However, recent research suggests that some immigrants sustain strong ties to their home country while simultaneously being integrated into the host country (Levitt, DeWind, & Vertovec, 2003). The notion of transnational relations is not a new concept. Studies on early 20th century migrants, such as Russian Jews and Italians, suggest that these communities sustained sociocultural, economic, and political ties to their home countries (Foner, 2001). Nonetheless, advances in technology, travel, and communications have been pointed out as essential explanations for the increasing numbers of contemporary transnational migrants (Appadurai, 2002; Hollifield, 2007). The continuous and simultaneous ties between home and host societies have led scholars to discuss transnational migration as it relates to contemporary migration (Basch, Glick Schiller, & Szanton Blanc, 1997; Portes, 1996).

Scholars focusing on transnational migration have centered their research on three main areas of connection between migrants and their country of origin. Scholars looking at the relationship of transnational migration to the economy have looked at remittances (Mooney, 2003; Roberts & Morris, 2003) and entrepreneurship (Levitt, 2001; Zhou, 2004). Researchers studying the connections of transnationalism and politics have centered on trans-state political activities (Levitt & de la Dehesa, 2003; Ostergaard-Nielsen, 2003) and citizenship (Croucher, 2004). Finally, researchers focused on understanding the sociocultural life of transnational migrants have looked at religion (Ebaugh, 2004; Levitt, 2004), identity (Chaunhuri, 2005; Thapan, 2005), and belonging (Al-Ali & Koser, 2002).

Despite the diversity of social class backgrounds among transnational migrants, scholars of both immigration and social stratification have tended to neglect the role of social class in the process of transnational migration. Some exceptions are the work of Wallerstein (2000) and Li (2008). Wallerstein (2000) looks at the effects of social class on migration and distinguishes between migrants from the top of the occupation scale and those in the lower part. Li (2008) utilizes social class analysis to understand migration. Both Wallerstein and Li agree that migration is a phenomenon that is experienced very differently depending upon one's social class background. However, these studies have not analyzed the effects of home and host society influences on educational issues such as parenting and schooling.

Multiple studies have explored the different ways in which migrants locate themselves and create cross-border connections. Rouse (2002) studied the experiences of migrant communities that cut across multiple national spaces, and found that the circulation of people, money, goods, and information has closely connected the communities across national boundaries. Continuing to explore the lives of transnational migrants, Chaudhuri's (2005) ethnographic work with migrant women's identity is negotiated between the host land's legal expectations and their homeland's social order and culture. Like Rouse (2002), Chaudhuri suggests that culture is not fixed to a specific place or nation, and thus has become deterritorialized. In addition, Appadurai (2002) notes that deterritorialization is one of the main forces of the current global setting. He argues that the creation of a new type of citizen and society is developing under these circumstances "in which money, commodities, and persons are involved in ceaselessly chasing each other around the world" (p. 54). Although Rouse, Chaudhuri, and Appadurai agree that the social landscape is being changed by multiple belongings, they do not conjecture about the mechanisms by which transnational migrants introduce new ways of educating children. As transnational families educate their children within multiple social systems, I argue that these children are being raised, not as traditional citizens who feel they belong to one country, but as citizens of multiple territories.[1]

Methodology

This chapter draws on a larger ethnographic study that compared the experiences of transnational Latino families of varying social class (Crespo-Sancho,

2009). Over a 12-month period, from June 2006 to July 2007, I conducted in-depth ethnographic case studies of four Latino families of varying nationalities and social class, two families from low socioeconomic and two from middle-class backgrounds. This study explored the ways in which first generation Latino migrant families, living in the United States, reconceptualize notions of belonging and social class while ascertaining their ethnic identity in the context of vast changes in the global structure. In addition, I compared the experiences of these transnational families and described how issues such as social class, belonging, identity formation, children's schooling, and parenting differed for these groups. I focused in particular on their everyday family life and how these daily practices, in both home and host land, influenced their transnational experience.

For the purposes of this chapter, I use data collected from one of the middle-class families. In particular I highlight the parenting and schooling experiences of the Denegri family.[2] In addition, I center my attention on the focus child, who was of elementary school age, and who was observed intensively at home and at school. Although the home and the school were the primary research sites, other sites including church services, visits to relatives, and medical appointments were also observed. The study took place in Buffalo, NY; the Denegris reside in one of its suburbs.

The family was chosen based on criteria which included the following: Parents are first generation migrants; living in the United States for at least 3 years; and having at least one child attending elementary school. The social class selection of the middle-class family was based on having an income above $40,000 per year, college education, neighborhood location, and self-described social class in the home country. The Denegri parents are first generation Latinos from Peru. In Peru, Ana was a teacher and Rodrigo a college professor. They moved to the United States in 1999 in pursuit of their PhD degrees; their future plans include settling permanently in the United States. They have only one child, 7-year-old Rosita. The Denegris describe their social background in Peru as upper class; both have graduate degrees; have jobs at the university; and in the United States live in a predominately White, middle-class neighborhood. The Denegris are full-time students; thus their income situation is temporary. They receive a combined annual income of $40,000, along with economic support from their families back in Peru of an additional $12,000 for a total of $52,000 per year.

The research design included interviews with all family members and the child's homeroom teacher, home and school observations, and field notes. I visited the Denegris's home four times a week for a little over a month. There were a total of 12 weekday home observations, and five weekend home observations. During the weekday observations, I was at their home when their child arrived from school and stayed until she went to bed. During weekend observations, I arrived at their home before noon and stayed until 6:00 p.m.

in the evening. During the home observations, I accompanied the family on their daily routine, which sometimes included grocery shopping, cleaning, and visits to friends. Interviews were utilized as a critical method to collect specific details on previous observations. Between the second or third week of observations, I interviewed all the family members individually for a period of 1 hour each; first the adults then the child. At the end of the observations, I conducted a 1-hour follow-up interview with the mother. The school was the second setting observed. Bowles and Gintis's (1976) reproduction theory stresses the importance of family, work, and schooling as the main reproducers of social class. Schools are sites where academic and social learning takes place. Many authors have researched the school as a site to gain understanding on the relationship between home and education (Anyon, 1980; Lareau, 1989; Rist, 1970). My objective in entering the school was to gain knowledge on how family living practices relate to educational engagement. I visited the school four times including a field trip and a school presentation. I followed the child throughout her school activities for the day and observed how she interacted with the lesson being taught, her peers, teachers, and other school personnel, and vice versa.

My approach for data analysis follows Miles and Huberman's (1984) three major stages of data organization: data reduction, data display, and conclusion drawing/verification. All interviews were audiotaped and later transcribed. All the interviews were in Spanish and therefore needed to be translated. All data were manually coded and organized using N-Vivo software, which groups similar narratives into codes. A start list of codes was developed based on the interviews and the theoretical framework. In addition, a second level of codes was established based on field notes and observations.

Settling Patterns and Their Effects on Education

Neighborhood, Race, Ethnicity, and Class

Even though families' everyday living practices are known to influence children's life chances, little is known about the mechanisms through which families transmit these advantages or disadvantages. A significant body of research documents the importance of family influence on increasing children's educational success (Epstein, 1987; Henderson & Berla, 1994; Olmstead & Rubin, 1983). Some researchers look at the influence of family structure and children's educational attainment (Biblarz & Raftery, 1999; Boggess, 1998). Others have concentrated on questions related to time, including how many hours parents spend at work (Hertz & Marshall, 2001; Jacobs & Gerson, 1998). However, not enough work has been conducted on how parenting practices in the form of settling patterns, especially in transnational populations, affect children's educational and schooling experience.

Work on the influence of neighborhood context on families has been increasingly popular since 1990 (Ainsworth, 2002; Burton, Price-Spratlen, & Beale Spenser, 1997; Leventhal & Brooks-Gunn, 2003). These studies conclude that family and neighborhood characteristics have a significant effect on children's life outcomes. According to Fischer and Kmec (2004), there are three key findings about the ways neighborhoods influence youth development and educational attainment processes: exposure to social networks, existence of sources of social control to monitor and control behaviors, and as providers of contacts with institutional resources such as schools, cultural centers, and churches. Furthermore, Fustenberg and Hughes (1997) argue that "social class differences mark the character of neighborhood organization and culture" (p. 28).

In order to understand the settling experiences of the Denegris one cannot look only at their experience in the United States, but it is essential that the analysis adopts a transnational, rather than a national, standpoint. An essential component of a Latino family's move to the host land is the possibility of finding a neighborhood with social and racial characteristics similar to the place where they lived in their home country. For the Denegris, the neighborhood choice in the United States is a product of their experience in Peru. The Denegris, who refer to their class position in Peru as belonging to "the rich," lived in the best neighborhoods in Lima. Upper-class neighborhoods in Peru tend to be mostly populated by Whites and segregated from the majority indigenous population. Rodrigo and Ana Denegri attended prestigious private schools, went to top tier universities, and their social network included politicians, professionals, and other prominent Peruvians. Back in Peru, they perceived their identity in terms of social class first and skin color or race second. Ana explains the dynamics of identification in Peru as:

> First, you see people in terms of rich or poor. Then, of course, because we have such a big indigenous population, then you look at their skin color. If they are short and have darker skin, we know that they are *cholos* [indigenous people] and that they're poor.

For Rodrigo and Ana, moving to the United States meant keeping their identity and social distinctions intact. When they came to the United States, their main concern was finding a place to live where there were good schools and where most of the people were White and middle class. Thus, they settled in a majority White middle-class neighborhood close to their university. Skin color plays an important role in class distinction in Peru. The Denegris use this criterion, learned in their home country and reinforced by frequent travel, as a settlement tool in the host country. Ana explains the relation of skin color to class in both countries:

> In the majority of cases [back in Peru] if you are White, it means that you come from a good social class; not necessarily upper class, but you

will never be in the low class.... Usually upper class neighborhoods are safer, cleaner, and just in general nicer.... When we moved here [in the United States] we wanted the same type of neighborhood ... we mainly looked for good schools, safety, and although it sounds bad, we wanted the majority of the people that lived there to be White.

The Denegris not only want to live in White middle-class neighborhoods because it is what they are used to in their home country, but also, because they believe that this type of neighborhood can give their daughter better access to resources and social networks. Rodrigo explains, "most of our neighbors are professionals; most of them have a college education ... we want Rosita to relate to other kids that have parents of good background." The concept of having a "good background" came up several times in the interviews with both parents and in conversations that I observed between Rodrigo and Rosita and Rodrigo and Ana. However, this concept took a different meaning depending on the occasion. For example, a "good background" could mean a good financial, educational, or racial background. During a conversation between Rodrigo and Ana, she was explaining that Rosita got invited to a classmate's house. Ana describes the parents: "She [classmate] comes from a good background. Her father is a lawyer and the mom stays at home with the kids; she is very involved at the school." During a conversation between Rodrigo and Rosita about a school play, Rodrigo refers to the importance of race; he jokingly said: "Rosita someday you will find a nice man, with a good background to marry. Oh and he should be White."

Bourdieu (1984) points out that the upper class performs a continuous reinvention of superiority in order to retain power. Brantlinger (2003) finds that "[t]he sense of worthiness of one group is based on confirming the unworthiness of Others" (p. 39). Because of the transnational nature of the Denegris's living conditions, in order to be able to confirm the unworthiness of Others,[3] the family constantly redefines who these Others are, how they look, behave, and live. Ana illustrates: "When I first came to Buffalo, I was afraid of Black people. I think it was because of TV. In Peru we don't have a large Black population; we don't mix.... Now, I am more used to Black people, I am not afraid anymore; my TV stereotypes are gone." Although her perceptions have changed mainly because of her experiences in the United States, there is a transnational component that affects her racial beliefs. Ana explains: "I would not like Rosita to marry a Black man. My family, especially my mother, would have a heart attack...although we live here and multiracial couples are more common, Rosita has to think about her family's [extended family] expectations back in Peru."

When immigrants move to the United States, they find that racial and ethnic dynamics are different from those in their home country. Several scholars have looked at identity issues within the United States. In their work with African Americans, Whites, and Latinos/as, Fine and Weis (1998) describe how these groups look for an Other in order to define themselves. For example, the authors illustrate how working-class White males construct an unpleasant Black "Other" against which to see themselves as superior. Work by Stacy Lee (2005) on race dynamics in the United States shows how discussions on race are based on a White and Black dichotomy, in which Whiteness is seen as the normative "good" and Blackness as the undesirable "Other." Thus, immigrants who want to achieve the American Dream and aspire towards upward mobility, "often interpret the racial conditions to mean that they must simultaneously embrace whiteness and reject blackness" (Lee, 2005, p. 4). There is an attempt by the Denegris to create their own space within American society; a space that is shaped by defining a distinction between themselves and Others. Not surprisingly, racial segregation surfaced as a deliberate choice in both home and host country. Ana volunteered:

> In Peru, the people with darker skin, the *cholos* are usually Indians [indigenous people] and mostly poor. Here in the States, skin color is also important. Black people are usually considered violent and poor. I have never had a bad encounter with a Black person, but when we moved here, one of the things we were looking for was a neighborhood that didn't have many Black people.

Clearly class, racial, and ethnic segregation is a deliberate choice, one that is based on home country experiences. However, it also includes American stereotypes in relation to minorities such as African Americans and Latinos. The Denegris's physical aspect is important to mention. All three family members have fair skin; Ana has brown eyes and light brown hair. Rodrigo and Rosita both have blonde hair and blue eyes. The Denegris not only draw on their skin color and social class to set differences, but also make use of their national origin to make distinctions from other Latinos/as as well. For example, they explain the importance of race and ethnicity on choosing a place to live: "We didn't want a neighborhood where there were a lot of Black people or Puerto Ricans. It's not that I'm racist; it's just the reality of things. Black and Latino neighborhoods are dangerous and poor; we don't want to live there." American society tends to see Latinos/as as a homogeneous group; however, the Denegris resist this pan-ethnic notion by emphasizing their nationality. What is interesting about the Denegris is that they perceive both African Americans and Puerto Ricans as negative Others. They identify being Puerto Rican as what they described as "low class." Thus they are careful to distance themselves from Puerto Ricans and identify themselves with their country of origin; they identify themselves as Peruvian. Rodrigo elaborates: "It seems that the majority of Latinos in Buffalo are Puerto Rican, and yes, definitely they are mostly poor. If one goes downtown where the Puerto Rican community lives, you can tell that their neighborhoods are very poor."

When families describe themselves in terms of their country of origin, they are saying as much or more about who they are as about who they are not. These families are not rejecting all values associated with being Latino. Rather, they are rejecting the negative stigmas, such as being poor, violent, government dependent, and illegal. Rodrigo explains: "If you speak Spanish you are either Mexican or Puerto Rican. Because of where we are [in Buffalo], people automatically think we are Puerto Rican. I guess I wouldn't mind so much, but the problem is that then people think we are lazy and living off welfare. That does bother me, because I am neither poor nor living off welfare." The Denegris embrace certain aspects associated with being Latino (e.g., Spanish language and familism) and consider them important characteristics of their culture. By describing their identity in terms of their nationality, the Denegris resist the dominant group stereotyping of Latino culture as unfavorable and otherwise problematic. By emphasizing their own nationality and differentiating themselves from African Americans and other Latino groups, they strategically develop an identity separate from what they construct as Others in hopes of aligning themselves to the White middle-class population.

In conclusion, the Denegris's parenting skills include strategies on choosing a neighborhood that would allow the family, in particular Rosita, to access resources and networks. The family's strategy is to use home country experience in helping them choose a home located in a neighborhood where most inhabitants are middle class and White. They believe that by staying away from minorities, including low socioeconomic Latinos, they will keep Rosita safe and away from bad influences. They also believe that Rosita can better develop her skills through relating to other children of similar social class background.

Accessing Opportunities through School Selection and Location

Settling patterns not only influence the type of neighborhoods Latino families live in, but also have significant effects on their children's schooling. My study that compared low socioeconomic and middle-class transnational Latino families (Crespo-Sancho, 2009) indicates that social class is an essential factor in determining the schooling experience of immigrant Latino children. In addition, the school's racial and ethnic composition also differed by class. Low socioeconomic class children attended schools populated mainly by African Americans and Latino/a students, while middle-class children attended schools mainly populated by White students. The Denegris's experience with their daughter's school illustrates this point. Over 65% of the students in Rosita's school are White, while only 3% are Latinos/as. Ana explains that the students "are mostly White kids with middle-class parents ... just like us." In Rosita's classroom, out of 18 children, there were only three students that were not White, two African Americans and one Latina. In addition to student's racial and class background, teachers' background was similar to that of the students. My observations at Rosita's school and informal conversations with the school administration show that the majority of the teachers were White and came from middle-class backgrounds. In addition, most teachers, including Rosita's homeroom teacher, lived in the same neighborhoods as the students, and their children attended the same school district. During the interviews with Rosita's teacher, Mrs. K shared: "I live close by, so that helps me to stay in contact and meet all the parents. I see my kids' [her students] parents at the supermarket, at the doctor's office."

Just as in the United States, schools in Peru are segregated by class and race. Public schools are mainly attended by indigenous and low socioeconomic class children, while private schools are mostly populated by middle- and upper-class White children. Because the Denegris went to predominantly high-income and racially segregated schools, they believe Rosita needs to attend a school that is also predominantly White. The Denegris believe that it would disadvantage their child to attend schools with predominately minority students. Ana explains: "we want our daughter to go to a good school.... White kids go to good schools." It is important to mention that in their discourse, the Denegris use the words "minority students" rather than low-income students due to the fact that they believe that race, just as in their home country, is one of the main predictors of social class belonging. For them, in the United States, Whiteness equals privilege while being Black or Latino is seen as inferior.

Added pressure to choose a good neighborhood and school comes from the sustained social interaction with their family and friends back in Peru. Instead of immigrating, cutting ties to the home country, and adapting to the American way of life, the Denegris have adopted a transnational way of living, and thus try to simultaneously negotiate expectations from both societies. On multiple occasions, Ana Denegri expressed the difficulty in fulfilling her family's educational expectations for Rosita. Ana constantly has to supplement Rosita's education, in particular with issues related to language; she explained that, "they [her in-laws] are always telling me that schools in Peru are better, that children there learn both languages perfect." Rosita's school does not provide any language instruction during the elementary years, so Ana tries to help her with learning spoken and written Spanish at home.

In addition to language issues, Rosita's schooling is constantly being compared to Rodrigo's nephews' and nieces' schooling in Peru. Rodrigo's nephews and nieces are close in age to Rosita and attend one of the most prominent private schools in Peru. Rodrigo, but in particular Ana, who is the one who talks more to her sisters-in-law, is continuously comparing Rosita's schooling in the United States to that in Peru. Details of the characteristics and quality of education in both settings are regular topics of discussion with family and friends in Peru. The most salient criticism of U.S. schools was the perception that American schools, in general, are not rigorous enough. An underlying worry apparent in the discussions with Rodrigo and Ana was that Rosita should have the same or better education than what upper-class children in Peru were receiving. "Rigor" and "discipline" seemed to be code words for choosing settings that promoted a high level of academic achievement. The Denegris trusted that choosing a neighborhood based on racial and class characteristics, would provide schools with a disciplined and rigorous academic environment.

Conclusions

Despite the differences in demographics and social class background, Latinos are nevertheless seen as a homogeneous group; one that is uniformly poor, lacking education, and in general perceived with hostility by American society. Explanations for this perception have historically focused on a cultural argument emphasizing pan-ethnic values in education, work ethic, family, and legal status (Tienda, 1989; Zambrana, 1995). While this cultural dimension is undoubtedly significant, it misses crucial differences between Latino groups. This dominant pan-ethnic argument fails to explain the full diversity in contemporary migration that includes amongst other factors, differences in social class background.

This chapter suggests that while there are middle-class Latino families living among us, they have been ascribed with invisibility. While most low socioeconomic Latino families live in highly segregated and poor neighborhoods, making them more perceptible to society, middle-class Latinos try to blend into White middle-class neighborhoods. Although this is not the case for all middle-class Latinos/as, for example Cubans in Miami, it is happening with many other Latino middle-class families. This study cautions against a single focus on migration and calls for a deeper analysis of the transnational experience. As migration moves people into new cultural, economic, and social environments, and transnational migration allows for a coexisting of the old with the new, it is essential to include in any analysis of transnational migration an understanding of how decisions and experiences are influenced by both home and host country.

This chapter has shown that the Denegris utilize cultural capital learned in the home country to negotiate their way in the United States. In trying to understand the experiences of transnational families and how they educate and school their children, it is essential to understand the basics of the migration process. These basics include who these families were and their experiences and perceptions of the social world in their home country. In addition, it is essential to understand the settling process, which includes neighborhood and school choice. Negotiating living location in order to access educational opportunities and resources that will benefit children is an important parenting skill. Like Lareau (2003), I am affirming that the family's class position influences the transmission of advantages or disadvantages to their children. Looking at the Latino middle-class family, we see that parents select their neighborhood based on school quality and racial and social class composition. However, their choices are influenced by their experience in the home country. In addition, they are in a constant state of duality where they feel they need to fulfill parenting and schooling expectations of two societies.

A striking point about schooling transnational Latino children is that there is, unlike the case in numerous previous studies, little evidence of a pan-ethnic identity. I agree with Norma Fuentes (2007) that "immigration type, race, and ethnic networks as well as household structures differentially affect the resources available" (pp. 95–96); furthermore, social class background is also a significant determinant of educational resources and opportunities. The Latino middle-class family, in fact, schools their children depending on their own socioeconomic background.

Notes

1   For a further discussion on issues of belonging and transnational migration see Catalina Crespo-Sancho (2009).
2   At the time of this study I was an international student from Costa Rica. Given that I am White and from an upper-middle class background, this particular family may have felt comfortable making statements about the relationship between race and class that they might not have made under different circumstances.
3   I utilize the capitalized version of Other to refer to a process of marginalization and segregation.

References

Ainsworth, J. W. (September 2002). Why does it take a village? The mediation of neighborhood effects on educational achievement. *Social Forces, 81*(1), 117–152.

Al-Ali, N., & Koser, K. (2002). Transnationalism, international migration and home. In N. Al-Ali & K. Koser (Eds.), *New approaches to migration? Transnational communities and the transformation of home* (pp. 1–14). New York: Routledge.

Anyon, J. (1980). Social class and the hidden curriculum of work. *Journal of Education, 1*(1), 67–92.

Appadurai, A. (1991). Global ethnoscapes: Notes and queries for a transnational anthropology. In R. G. Fox (Ed.), *Recapturing anthropology: Working in the present* (pp. 191–210). Santa Fe, NM: School of American Research.

Appadurai, A. (2002). Disjuncture and difference in the global cultural economy. In J. X. Inda & R. Rosaldo (Eds.), *The anthropology of globalization* (pp. 46–64). Malden, MA: Blackwell.

Basch, L., Glick Schiller, N., & Szanton Blanc, C. (1997). *Nations unbound: Transnational projects, postcolonial predicaments, and deterritorialized nation-states*. Amsterdam, the Netherlands: Gordon & Breach Science.

Basch, L., Glick Schiller, N., & Szanton Blanc, C. (2003). *Nations unbound: Transnational projects, postcolonial predicaments, and deterritorialized nation-states*. London: Routledge.

Bernstein, B. (1971). *Class, codes, and control*. Boston, MA: Routledge & Kegan Paul.

Biblarz, T., & Raftery, A. (1999). Family structure, educational attainment, and socioeconomic success: Rethinking the "pathology of matriarchy." *American Journal of Sociology, 105*(2), 321–365.

Boggess, S. (1998). Family structure, economic status, and educational attainment. *The Journal of Population Economics, 11*(2), 205–222.

Bourdieu, P. (1977a). Cultural reproduction and social reproduction. In J. Karabel & A. Halsey (Eds.), *Power and ideology in education* (pp. 487–511). New York: Oxford University Press.

Bourdieu, P. (1977b). *Outline of a theory of practice* (R. Nice, Trans.). Cambridge, England: Cambridge University Press.

Bourdieu, P. (1984). *Distinction: A social class critique of the judgment of taste* (R. Nice, Trans.). Cambridge, MA: Harvard University Press.

Bourdieu, P. (1986). The forms of capital. In J. Richardson (Ed.), *Handbook of theory and research for the sociology of education* (pp. 241–258). New York: Greenwood Press.

Bourdieu, P., & Passeron, J. (1977). *Reproduction in education, society and culture.* Beverly Hills, CA: Sage.

Bowles, S., & Gintis, H. (1976). *Schooling in capitalist America.* New York: Basic Books.

Brantlinger, E. (2003). *Dividing classes: How the middle class negotiates and rationalizes school advantage.* New York: Routledge Falmer.

Burton, L. M., Price-Spratlen, T., & Beale Spenser, M. (1997). On ways of thinking about measuring neighborhoods: Implications for studying context and developmental outcomes for children. In J. Brooks-Gunn, G. J. Duncan, & J. K. Aber (Eds.), *Neighborhood poverty: Policy implications in studying neighborhoods* (Vol. 2, pp. 132–144). New York: Russell Sage Foundation.

Chaudhuri, M. (2005). Betwixt the state and everyday life: Identity formation among Bengali migrants in a New Delhi slum. In M. Thapan (Ed.), *Transnational migration and the politics of identity* (pp. 284–311). New Delhi, India: Sage.

Crespo-Sancho, C. (2009). Migration in the age of globalization: Transnationalism, identiy, social class, and education of Latino Families. Retrieved from www.proquest.com

Croucher, S. L. (2004). *Globalization and belonging: The politics of identity in a changing world.* Lanham, MD: Rowman & Littlefield.

De Graaf, N., De Graaf, P., & Kraaykamp, G. (2000). Parental cultural capital and educational attainment in the Netherlands: A refinement of the cultural capital perspective. *Sociology of Education, 73*(2), 92–111.

DiMaggio, P. (1979). On Pierre Bourdieu. *The American Journal of Sociology, 84*(6), 1460–1474.

DiMaggio, P. (1982). Cultural capital and school success: The impact of status culture participation on the grades of U.S. high school students. *American Sociological Review, 47*(2), 189–201.

Ebaugh, H. R. (2004). Religion across borders: Transnational religious ties. *Asian Journal of Social Science, 32*(2), 216–231.

Epstein, J. (1987). Parent involvement: What research says to administrators. *Education and Urban Society, 19*(2), 119–136.

Fine, M., & Weis, L. (1998). *The unknown city: Lives of poor and working class adults.* Boston, MA: Beacon Press.

Fischer, M. J., & Kmec, J. A. (2004). Neighborhood socioeconomic conditions as moderators of family resource transmission: High school completion among at-risk youth. *Sociological Perspectives, 47*(4), 507–527.

Foner, N. (2001). Transnationalism then and now: New York immigrants today and at the turn of the twentieth century. In H. Cordero-Guzman, R. C. Smith & R. Grosfoguel (Eds.), *Migration, transnationalization, and race in a changing New York* (pp. 35–57). Philadelphia, PA: Temple University Press.

Fuentes, N. (2007). The immigrant experiences of Dominican and Mexican women in the 1990s. In C. B. Brettel (Ed.), *Constructing borders/crossing boundaries: Race, ethnicity, and immigration* (pp. 95–119). Lanham, MD: Lexington Books.

Furstenberg, F. F., & Hughes, M. E. (1997). The influence of neighborhoods on children's development: A theoretical perspective and a research agenda. In J. Brooks-Gunn, G. J. Duncan & J. L. Aber (Eds.), *Neighborhood poverty* (Vol. 2, pp. 23–47). New York: Russell Sage Foundation.

Giroux, H. (1983). *Theory and resistance in education.* South Hadley, MA: Bergin & Harvey.

Gordon, M. M. (1964). *Assimilation in American life: The role of race, religion, and national origins.* New York: Oxford University Press.

Gupta, A., & Ferguson, J. (2002). Beyond "culture": Space, identity, and the politics of difference. In J. X. Inda & R. Rosaldo (Eds.), *The anthropology of globalization: A reader* (pp. 65–80). Malden, MA: Blackwell.

Henderson, A. T., & Berla, N. (Eds.). (1994). *A new generation of evidence: The family is critical to student achievement*. Washington, DC: National Committee for Citizens in Education.

Hertz, R., & Marshall, N. (Eds.). (2001). *Working families: The transformation of the American home*. Berkeley: University of California Press.

Hollifield, J. (2007). The emerging migration state. In A. Portes & J. DeWind (Eds.), *Rethinking migration: New theoretical and empirical perspectives* (pp. 62–89). New York: Berghahn Books.

Jacobs, J., & Gerson, K. (1998). Who are the overworked Americans? *Review of Social Economy, 56*, 442–459.

Lareau, A. (1987). Social class differences in family-school relationships: The importance of cultural capital. *Sociology of Education, 60*(2), 73–85.

Lareau, A. (1989). *Home advantage: Social class and parental intervention in elementary education*. Philadelphia, PA: Falmer Press.

Lareau, A. (2002). Invisible inequality: Social class and childrearing in Black families and White families. *American Sociological Review, 67*(5), 747–776.

Lareau, A. (2003). *Unequal childhoods: Class, race, and family life*. Los Angeles: University of California Press.

Lareau, A., & Horvat, E. M. (1999). Moments of social inclusion and exclusion race, class, and cultural capital in family-school relationships. *Sociology of Education, 72*(1), 37–53.

Lee, S. (2005). *Up against whiteness: Race, school, and immigrant youth*. New York: Teachers College Press.

Leventhal, T., & Brooks-Gunn, J. (2003). Moving on up: Neighborhood effects on children and families. In M. H. Bornstein & R. H. Bradley (Eds.), *Socioeconomic status, parenting, and child development* (pp. 209–230). Mahwan, NJ: Erlbaum.

Levitt, P. (2001). *The transnational villagers*. Los Angeles: University of California Press.

Levitt, P. (2004). Redefining the boundaries of belonging: The institutional character of transnational religious life. *Sociology of Religion, 65*(1), 1–18.

Levitt, P., & de la Dehesa, R. (2003). Transnational migration and the redefinition of the state: Variations and explanations. *Ethnic and Racial Studies, 26*(4), 587–611.

Levitt, P., DeWind, J., & Vertovec, S. (2003). International perspectives on transnational migration: An introduction. *International Migration Review, 37*(3), 565–575.

Li, G. (2008). Parenting practices and schooling: The way class works for new immigrants. In L. Weis (Ed.), *The way class works: Readings on school, family, and the economy* (pp. 149–166). New York: Routledge.

Miles, M., & Huberman, M. (1984). *Qualitative data analysis: A sourcebook of new methods*. Newbury Park, CA: Sage.

Mooney, M. (2003). Migrant's social ties in the U.S. and investment in Mexico. *Social Forces, 81*(4), 1147–1170.

Olmstead, P. P., & Rubin, R. I. (1983). Linking parent behaviors to child achievement: Four evaluation studies from the parent education follow-through programs. *Studies in Educational Evaluation, 8*, 317–325.

Ostergaard-Nielsen, E. (2003). *Trans-state loyalties and policies: Turks and Kurds in Germany*. New York: Routledge.

Park, R. E., & Burgess, E. (1969). *Introduction to the science of sociology*. Chicago, IL: University of Chicago Press.

Portes, A. (1996). Transnational communities: Their emergence and significance in the contemporary world-system. In R. P. Korzeniewicz & W. C. Smith (Eds.), *Latin America in the world economy* (pp. 151–168). Westport, CT: Greenwood Press.

Rist, R. (1970). Student social class and teacher expectations. *Harvard Educational Review*, 411–451.

Roberts, K., & Morris, M. (2003). Fortune, risk, and remittances: An application of option theory to participation in village-based migration networks. *International Migration Review, 37*(4), 1252–1281.

Rouse, R. (2002). Mexican migration and social space of postmodernism. In J. X. Inda & R. Rosaldo (Eds.), *The anthropology of globalization* (pp. 157–171). Malden, MA: Blackwell.

Thapan, M. (Ed.). (2005). *Transnational migration and the politics of identity* (Vol. 1). New Delhi, India: Sage.

Tienda, M. (1989). *Immigration and Hispanic educational attainment: Challenges for the 1990s.* Madison: Institute for Research on Poverty, University of Wisconsin-Madison.

Wallerstein, I. (2000). The national and the universal: Can there be such a thing as world culture? In A. D. King (Ed.), *Culture, globalization and the world-system: Contemporary conditions for the representation of identity* (3rd ed., pp. 91–106). Minneapolis: University of Minnesota Press.

Weis, L. (2004). *Class reunion: The remaking of the American White working class.* New York: Routledge.

Zambrana, R. (Ed.). (1995). *Understanding Latino families: Scholarship, policy, and practice.* Thousand Oaks, CA: Sage.

Zhou, M. (2004). Revisiting ethnic entrepreneurship: Convergencies, controversies, and conceptual advancements. *International Migration Review, 38,* 1040–1074.

7

AFRICAN MIGRANT YOUTH, SCHOOLING, AND SOCIAL CLASS IN CAPE TOWN

Caroline Foubister and Azeem Badroodien

Introduction

In cities throughout Africa, both citizens and immigrant communities are forced daily to negotiate new globally inflected spaces, alongside the myriad of challenges and hardships that have long characterized life in contemporary urban Africa (Adepoju, 2006, Lekogo, 2006).[1]

In this chapter, we focus on the educational experiences of a group of African migrant students in Cape Town, drawing on a qualitative research study of 20 African migrant students at Mountain View High School (a pseudonym) in 2009 and 2010. We explore how social class and education is lived in the everyday lives of the African migrant youth, focusing on how migrant students organize and make meaning of the multiple spaces of their lives, particularly family, friendships, religion, and school. These spaces are not fixed and stable categories. Rather they are part of an amalgam of ways that youth make meaning for themselves in a fluid, often dangerous situation, where the future is very uncertain.

In an urban space where a wide variety of poor communities have very limited prospects of improving their circumstances or livelihoods, we argue that youth were particularly concerned to invest in what Bourdieu (1990; Bourdieu & Wacquant, 1992) has referred to as the "game" or the ability to draw on one's capital and habitus. We show that such dispositions of African migrant youth were not developed solely in relation to the school but were reproduced via a complex combination of objects, spaces, people, and practices that span multiple sites (Simone, 2008).

We use the term *African*—as do Landau (2009), Hemson (in press), and Nyamnjoh (2010)—to refer to a broad category of refugees, asylum seekers, and immigrants in South Africa who have in common that they are foreign and from elsewhere in Africa. We make no distinction as to whether or not they have applied for citizenship or whether or not they are legally in the country. We utilize the general term *guardian* later in the text to refer to all parents, siblings, family members, and friends that have legal guardianship over the African migrant students in their new living contexts. Many of the interviewed African migrant students lived with brothers, sisters, uncles, aunts, and family friends in Cape Town.

Finally, at certain points in the chapter we use terms that *formally* emerged under apartheid as "racial" classifications; namely, the description of South Africans as African, Indian, coloured, and white. We use the terms here both for their utility purpose and to remind the reader about the ongoing, decidedly structural and historical form of such identities in contemporary South Africa (see Bray, Gooskens, Kahn, Moses, & Seekings, 2010; Soudien, 2007).

African Immigration and South Africa

African migrants arrive in South Africa fueled by dreams of opportunity and possibility. However, as they settle in a variety of mostly urban spaces, their dreams quickly begin to fade as they encounter enormous anxiety, desperation, and increasing hostility toward them as outsiders. This is largely because the South African government continues to struggle with redressing a deeply unjust past and responding appropriately to the needs of millions of impoverished citizens. Bray et al. (2010) note,

> Massive unemployment in South Africa sentences many to chronic poverty, mitigated only to the extent that people receive financial support from the state through old-age pensions, child-support grants or other social assistance programmes. In many respects, class has replaced race as the foundation of deep social cleavages in post-apartheid society.
>
> *(p. 23)*

Statistics South Africa reported that in 2008 the proportion of South Africans living below the poverty line (defined as R593 or $80 per capita per month) was 47% and that of those designated as poor in South Africa 93% were African, 6% were coloured, 0.4% were Indian, and 0.1% were white (cited in Swartz, 2010, pp. 26, 195). Thus, while South Africa may well allow large numbers of African migrants over its borders daily, its policies make daily life and even basic survival very difficult. As Gordon (2010) and Peberdy (2008) note, South Africa's immigration policies have become stronger since 2002. Furthermore, migrants are only allowed to (legally) work and stay in South Africa if they apply for temporary work permits (sometimes 4–5 times a year) with permanent residency being a near impossibility for most of them. Thus, African migrants (especially refugees and asylum seekers) are powerless to find suitable work or a stable existence in South Africa. This inevitably means that most of them are barely able to make ends meet. At the economic level, refugees find themselves in direct competition with millions of local South Africans also trying to make some kind of living and gain access to very limited economic and social resources.

Migrants face discrimination in almost every society. However, in 2008 the local context of high rates of migration into South Africa and high levels of poverty and unemployment led to a particularly dire situation in South Africa, when intense xenophobic attacks led to large numbers of African migrants being hurt, displaced, and killed. The *Cape Argus*, a leading Cape Town newspaper reported that local inhabitants were going "on the rampage, tearing down homes and shelters and accusing migrants of stealing their jobs" (Prince, 2009, p. 1). Living side by side with the poorest South Africans and competing for resources and available jobs, African migrants were met by a wave of anti-foreigner sentiments in June 2008 that led to 50 people dead and thousands displaced, homeless, and penniless (Human Sciences Research Council [HSRC], 2008). These kinds of sentiments and attacks against African migrants have continued since 2008 albeit on a smaller scale.

Husseini, 19 years old and from Burundi, summed up life as an African migrant in Cape Town in the following way,

> We work, even though these jobs foreigners get is not compared to his qualifications. That's why I don't understand why African South Africans hate other African foreigners. For what? For us taking the security guard jobs? Is this a job for someone who is really educated? I don't think so and they shouldn't think so, because security jobs aren't for human beings who have potential. Foreigners work as parking guards because we don't have anything—to expect to survive in this world especially in South Africa without jobs you'll be homeless and we as foreigners wouldn't let that happen to us.

Social Class and Schooling in South Africa

While education is invariably touted as the key mechanism for social mobility and the means by which to climb out of poverty, schooling in 21st century South Africa has taken on a decidedly narrow and overall (middle) social class orientation which is repeatedly at odds with the lives of both local (South African) and migrant students. This reality has led to a particularly fractured experience of schooling in South Africa. Crain Soudien (2007) asserts that,

> There are few countries where growing up requires so much "headwork" as in South Africa, especially (but not only) for black people. African adolescents carry the double burden of poverty and cultural alienation. They are being exposed to a culture which is traditionally not their own ... and

they have to work out what dominant middle class culture wants from them. This culture provides education with its content throughout the world. Middle class culture is now the aspiration of people everywhere. It is the primary medium in which cultural systems (such as schools, families and media) want their young to interact.

(p. 1)

As Swartz (2010) argues, youth derive their concept of what it means to have "successful lives" through both popular culture and media, and the luxury that youth see in the rich suburbs of urban areas throughout South Africa. She suggests that youth continue to covet such social forms and lives no matter how much they are confronted by the inevitable prospect of long-term unemployment and poverty. In this regard, Eder (1993) suggests that the *dream* of social class success has been preserved within most modern societies via a probabilistic vocabulary of attainment, accessibility, hard work, and planning. In the above scenario attainment has remained the sole proxy and signal of success and is invariably the key driver for students, even for those whose actual life circumstances are desperate, and who live on the margins of society.

Schooling in Cape Town and the Allure of Social Success

Since 1994, the majority of students at Mountain View High School have come from the city's African population. These South African students live predominantly in areas defined as informal settlements, which are located more than 25 km away from the city center. Indeed, more than 90% of this section of the school population migrate daily (using public transport) across the city to attend school.[2] A teacher at the school noted that because Mountain View High School started off as a "white school" during the apartheid years, African parents living in the townships believe that the school will provide their children with a better life and social class trajectory than other schools in their more immediate vicinity. Since 2002, larger numbers of African migrants have entered the school. Parents of migrant students noted that they were attracted to the school due to its low school fees, its proximity to areas where African migrant communities were mainly settling in Cape Town at the time, and the school's reputation for readily enrolling African migrant students. By 2010, 20% of the 1,000 students at Mountain View were categorized as foreign. The participants in this study were 20 students at the school (10 male, 10 female) between the ages of 14 and 19 in grades 8 through 11. The sample included a number of students that came from Zimbabwe and the Democratic Republic of Congo (DRC) as well as from Congo-Brazzaville, Rwanda, Burundi, Ethiopia, and Malawi.[3] At least nine of the students lived in fairly middle-class surroundings in their countries of birth before having to leave (with their guardians being mostly either educators or politicians). While the other 11 students lived in poor social conditions in their countries of birth, most reported that they had access to appropriate education. As a result of war, persecution, and poor employment opportunities they migrated to South Africa and Cape Town, where all of the learners now live in abject social conditions, surrounded by poverty, in overcrowded accommodation, with few job opportunities, and some in physically dangerous township and suburban spaces.

Frank, a 15-year-old student from an educated Zimbabwean family, reflects,

> Mountain View High School is a good school because lots of foreigners are schooling there and so for the first time it is going to be easy there, as you have got a lot of friends you can speak to for the first time and they can teach you what is going on there. It is a little bit easier now for the newcomers. There are also many people from our own belief and religion and that ask ," Where do you really come from in your rural area or urban area?" So it's really good for me.

For parents and students, "choosing the right school" is critical, and often viewed as the most significant decision in their quest for social class mobility. For African migrant students, getting access to Mountain View High School was sometimes regarded as an end in itself. Many African migrant students noted that the main reason for them attending the school was not as much about what they thought they could learn or gain from formal schooling, but about acquiring a variety of attitudes, temperaments, attributes, work skills, and individual ambitions that would ensure that their dreams of success were kept alive. Many pointed to the number of obstacles, both official and informal, that made it unlikely that they would progress further (in educational terms) beyond high school. Attending school and doing well was then more about the ability to "continue dreaming" and with acquiring the tropes of knowledge, particular attitudes, and values that would not lock them (as in township schools) into the worlds of poverty prevalent amongst the predominant underclasses of post-apartheid South Africa (Seekings & Nattrass, 2005). In the following sections, we examine the three areas of students' lives that allow them to succeed at Mountain View, despite their life circumstances.

Family, Cultural Capital, and Social Class

Many African migrant students reflected that, notwithstanding the challenges of what they would do once they completed their schooling, their focus on achieving some level of success at Mountain View High was built on a combined effort between them and their guardians and siblings. These support systems provided them with key lessons about the best ways to learn, how to develop various reading dispositions, and how to embed a core work ethic within their everyday practices. Despite their lack of economic capital within the present context of their lives, parents and guardians drew on their social and cultural capital from their more middle-class pasts to provide their children with these resources. Many guardians read regularly to and with their children and some even developed individualized study programs for their children to painstakingly follow. Others focused on providing the intellectual and emotional spaces at home to support their children with their schoolwork. This included an emphasis on learning, practicing, and speaking English at home to ensure that students carried some of the nuances of the language with them into school. Many guardians and their children were quite adept at understanding what was required vis-à-vis schooling, and had social and cultural capital often equal to that of the teachers and administrators at Mountain View: yet because of their migrant status they felt a constant pressure to demonstrate their value and worth. In providing educational assistance to their children, guardians and siblings invariably focused on how best to help them integrate into the urban school, and provided them with the skills that allowed them to manage their school lives and develop some sense of belonging within the school.

Students often noted that their mothers provided them with key sources of support and buffering at important moments in their lives (see Reay, 2004). For example, Gideon, 16 years old and from the Democratic Republic of Congo, reflected that his mother's daily encouragement was the only thing that got him to attend school,

> She would say, Gideon, if you don't learn at school then you will land up like most South Africans. You will then never understand what life can bring to you. You must go on no matter what with education.

For Jean-Paul, like Gideon 16 years old and from the Democratic Republic of Congo, his mother's encouragement often made him euphoric and motivated him to do better. He commented,

> I remember the one day I wrote a maths test and it was out of 175 and I got 101. Hey! My mother was so proud. They told us to take it home and show it to our guardians. Hey, the marks were not that good, but she was proud of me! I cannot express the happiness I felt that day.

Kenneth, 17 and from Zimbabwe, recalled that whenever he thought of doing bad things all he needed to do was remember his mother: "I never want to see my mother cry. So I just think of her and I stay out of trouble."

Students also asserted that an important source of support (and protector of their social class aspirations) came from the strict rules and boundaries of many African migrant households. John, 18 and also from Zimbabwe, noted that,

> We are not allowed to go out. No parties at all. My father is not a democratic father and he goes strictly according to the word of the Lord. My father is the one who says when I am watching TV, "Read your book!"

Other guardians placed severe restrictions on the movement of their children because of the high hopes and dreams that they had for them. Many students regarded this as important to keeping them on the straight and narrow and ensuring that they achieved their goals. Jean-Paul noted that their guardians not only wanted to ensure that they focus on their school work but also wanted them to stay at home to avoid the bad influences and dangers associated with being friends with other young people. Thus, a critical element of students' social class understandings lay in the emotional value attached to what was deemed success. Steinbach (2010) refers to this as the deeply embedded emotional and psychological aspects of cultural knowledge that communities carry with them and use at appropriate times. She notes that the key purpose of such knowledge was to prepare their children for the world beyond the family, and to provide them with the cultural intuitions and memories (like manners and social etiquettes) that could inform their "emotional, moral, and occupational consciousness at school" (Yosso, 2005, p. 79). Bourdieu (1986) refers to this as institutionalized cultural capital, where the embodied cultural dispositions of guardians and siblings get readily transferred to children via what happens at home. These dispositions also empowered migrant children to be able to recognize when they were in danger of being sidetracked. Jonatha is 16 and originally from Rwanda. He has been in South Africa since age 6, having left Rwanda at age 1 at the height of the genocide, strapped to his mother's back. Despite having lived in South Africa for 10 years, he is still considered an asylum-seeker. He remarks,

> My father always says, "You can't soar with eagles if you are flying with ducks." So, I try to analyze people and to see what this guy is all about, if he won't drag me down from my vision that I have or if he will improve me.

Indeed, a key element in migrant students being able to recognize when "fellow students were dragging them down" was the formation of social networks or friendships through which African migrant families were able to retain and reinforce the core values and attributes that they felt their children needed to uphold. Bourdieu (1986) argues that it was through such networks that particular forms of social capital are created and underpin the social class thinking of individuals.

Friendships and Social Capital

In an uncertain and very mobile world, friendships are another main navigational tool that youth rely on in the urban world (Weeks, Donovan, & Heaphy, 1999). Youth invariably turn to friendships to provide security and support. It is in the kinds of friends they make that social class forms take on particular meaning and shape. Devine (2009) notes that youth both choose friends and get chosen to be friends through forms of recognition, depending on the individual's ability to be seen as competent and having the mutual dispositions of the governing social group. Putnam (2000) refers to this as bonding, where youth choose friends based on a shared (often social class) origin, a sense of comfort and social connectedness, and the kinds of behavior exhibited by the various individuals (Reynolds, 2007).

Unsurprisingly, most African migrant students at Mountain View High School tended to stick together. Most either traveled home together, spent time together during breaks, or ensured that they were on the same project teams during class. Students reflected that their friendship choices were based on the protection of their collective goals at school, particularly instilling and protecting values and attitudes that they believed would facilitate various achievements. For example, Frank noted that he had formed a close friendship with Kenneth and John not only because they were Zimbabwean, but because "they did not smoke or drink, they were not nasty, and most importantly they were generous people." Jean-Paul lamented that his preference to associate with other African migrant students from his home country of the Democratic Republic of Congo was based mainly on his father's constant reminder that if he did not apply his mind critically to everything he did at school then the only job he would get on leaving school would be on construction sites,

> My father always reminds me to work. He says that you may be clever at school but a lot of other people are clever too but they are still suffering. So he tells us to have goals and to remain focused on what we want to do. He says that if my mind is weak and I allow myself to be misled then I will suffer. So every time I think about who my friends are and what I am doing I think about what he says, because I don't want to suffer later in life.

While most of the African migrant students shared a common and tenuous social position within the city, it is notable that the language of social class was ever-present in the social networks that African migrant youths developed in Cape Town, especially in their shared affinities, familiarities, empathies, and common languages (Reynolds, 2007). For these youth it was about identifying friends that could be confided in: friends who would protect them and offer good advice and support at the required times. These were typically exclusionary practices, often formed in defensive spaces where students struggled to make sense of their lives. Reynolds (2007) refers to these kinships as "buffers and support mechanisms in the face of social exclusion and racial discrimination" (p. 385). For many African migrant students, these social networks were a critical component of both their social stability and mobility. For example, Kenneth spoke about his friendship with Frank in the following way,

> We share everything. We talk about everything. We protect each other. When we go to break we will put our money together and buy something.

> There is other stuff like when there is someone who wants to tease Frank, I will say, "No, you must not do that! If you do that you will make me angry." Then they will stop.

Friendship offered migrant students a sense of self while allowing them to express important aspects of their personalities (Reynolds, 2007, p. 386). Paul noted in this regard that he had been able to pluck up the courage to perform on stage because "my friends had encouraged me and even inspired me to get into music."

Religion as a Form of Resistant Capital

The increased role of religion in the lives of displaced communities is a fairly common phenomenon across history. Given that (most) migrants invariably lose both their physical possessions and their previous social and economic standing when they enter new locations, religion offers them a clear sense of place, dignity, and belonging when they move and also provides access to the internal and external support of a given community. Religion is also regarded as an unconditional safe space or place of belonging, offering individuals a sense of respectability (Foner & Alba, 2008) which "is particularly important for those who are denied social recognition or have suffered downward mobility as a result of migration" (p. 362). Indeed, "being a good Christian, Muslim or Buddhist brings respect within given religious communities as within such religious groups there remain typical opportunities for leadership and service that brings prestige" (Foner &Alba 2008, p. 362). Such moments of recognition invariably provide migrants and their children with confidence boosts that assist their meaning making and their learning in the city. Blom Hansen (Blom Hansen, Jeannerat, & Sadouni, 2009) argues that religion provides ways of claiming "respect and recognition as a 'proper' person by the surrounding society" (p. 193) and often provides African migrants with what Yosso (2005) calls a form of "resistant capital" that is critical in keeping them positive and moving forward on their journeys to social acceptability and survival.

By serving as an important entry point at which individuals can be incorporated into mainstream society, religious spaces provide important and "rich resources for the reproduction of cultural norms and friendships within a distinctive cultural/ethnic tradition" (Devine, 2009, p. 526). Important relationships and support structures are also developed within local churches. These help African migrant students cope and adapt to urban life and develop dispositions that allow them to overcome obstacles and to succeed at both life and school. This is particularly important with regard to the support individuals within the church provide to students who struggle educationally and emotionally.

The church provided a further sanctuary that offered African migrant students a place where particular meaning could be ascribed to what they sought to achieve in life. Various African migrant students noted that religion brought particular meaning to their lives and shaped how they perceived social success. For Jonatha, for example, living as a refugee in Cape Town and facing an uncertain future, religion provided him with a crucial crutch and a source of stability and meaning in life. He explained that,

> Well … I would say that my church is my home. I don't really feel comfortable out of my church. Even if I were to stay there for a month, I could stay there. It would not be a problem. When I am in my church I feel comfortable because I am more in my nature. I feel like I can do things because of my religion. Without God I feel like a stray dog wandering the street, but when you know God, you feel proud like you belong to the one who is omnipotent.

For Paul, religion brought him some sense of respectability, which was important given his extreme feelings of loss, alienation, and loneliness in Cape Town. Religion offered him support both in and out of school in practical and emotional ways. Yosso (2005) observes that while "family consciousness can be fostered within and between families, it is mainly through sports, school, community, and religious gatherings" that isolation can really be reduced as "families become connected with others around common issues" and realize that "they are not alone in dealing with their problems" (p. 79).

Migrant African Students at Mountain View High School

Drawing on these three external sources of support and strength (family, friendships, and religion) allows African migrant students to succeed at Mountain View, despite their limited economic capital. Thus, teachers and administrators noted substantial differences in attitudes and dispositions between African migrant students and local (South African) students. Mr. Safradien, a teacher at Mountain View, claimed that there was a close correlation between the attainment of students at the school and the various situations that they had previously found themselves in: this was reflected in the "good control" of African migrant students "over themselves in terms of behavior and attitude, and their willingness to do things and progress."

There are numerous cross-cutting dynamics that complicate African migrant students' experiences at Mountain View, and significant tensions between African migrant and South African students. Though this is not surprising given the larger cultural and social milieu of xenophobia, there are also particular ways that these dynamics play out in a school environment. As the quote from Mr. Safradien suggests, educators also tend to treat African migrant learners as having better academic ability (and support at home), given their different educational contexts, upbringing, and culture, and this further fuels tension and aggravation between African migrant students and South African students. The use of the English language as a medium for teaching and learning also causes tensions. Given the diversity of home languages spoken by African migrant students, they prefer to communicate in English. In contrast, local South African students still predominantly speak and converse in their home language, isiXhosa, outside the classroom. Thus, the inherent hierarchies built into the schooling system, and the limited (or nonexistent) capacity of the mostly white teachers to speak isiXhosa, give the African migrant students a higher status within the school.[4] Divisions are deep, and are reflected in the perspectives of African migrant students. Dorothy, a 16-year-old student from Rwanda, suggested that "bad attitudes" among local South African students stemmed from them not knowing why they were at school. She commented that,

> The children, they are wasting some people's time. Like, they are lazy and they are just making noise. They are wasting the time of those who want to work. Sometimes you ask, why do you come here? Did you come here to play and then some of them say, I come here because my mommy says I must go to school. I don't know what I am doing here.

Jonatha summed up the attitudes of most African migrant students to schooling in his comment that "if you don't really know where you are going then any road could take you there." He suggested,

> It's messed up. You know the [local South African] students, most of them don't have a vision. Here when I talk to the students in my class and ask them what they want to do after matric they say, "Ah, this and that I don't know. Maybe I am going to sit at home." So, too many students don't know where they are going and it causes them to have disinterest and then you are not going to work to the best of your ability.

Flourishing or succeeding at school thus required a particular temperament and attitude, and a keen understanding of what was needed to succeed. For African migrant students, that means drawing on the three sources of capital that sustain them: family, friendships, and religion, and resisting the temptations of the larger South African society. Godwill, from Zimbabwe, pointed out,

> I just remember the reason why I am here, how I got here and why I got here. That makes me pull through and to know my goals and what I want to do in the future. I just mind my own business, because if you see other things in the South African culture you might start to like them and to change and then you will change who you are.

Indeed, most African migrant students attributed their supposedly more focused dispositions to the various hardships, collective memories of what they had been through, and their ongoing encounters with immigration authorities in South Africa, which spurred them on to work harder. Given what they had left behind in their home countries, these memories and hardships served as "a set of inner resources, social competencies and cultural strategies" that permitted them to "not only survive, recover or even thrive after stressful events, but also to draw from the experience to enhance subsequent functioning" (Salazar and Spina cited in Yosso, 2005, p. 80). It also served as a constant reminder, as Philippe, 18 and from the Democratic Republic of Congo, explained, that they had been the lucky ones to have "made it out of refugee camps" and that they had a responsibility to those left behind to "send them monies, to work hard, and not to fail." Philippe noted that "my brother took me, at least one child, to come here and study and get a job, so I can also help the family. Schooling was thus not about individual success but about fulfilling my responsibility to my family."

Schools are undoubtedly culturally textured spaces where the life chances of students are shaped in quite profound and determined ways. However, given the particular socioeconomic and migratory statuses of African migrant students in Cape Town, it would have been expected that there would be some misrecognition between the home habitus of students and the habitus implicit in the curriculum and in dominant pedagogies of schooling. This proved not to be the case with the African migrant youth in the study given that the migrant students carried valuable social capital with them into the school that they then used to navigate their way through the educational system.

It should be noted, however, that students tended to use this social capital not to enhance their school achievements (for economic gain or educational success) but to refine the variety of attitudes, attributes, dispositions, work skills, and available aspirations in ways that kept the possibility of success alive, despite the odds. In that regard, their key goal was not necessarily to gain clarity and direction on where they were going, but rather ensuring that they remain on course and in the game.

Conclusion: African Migrant Students and New Local/Global Realities

Paul Willis (2005) has described young people as the "unconscious foot soldiers on the long front of modernity," noting that while they invariably "respond to global changes in disorganised and chaotic ways, they do so to the best of their abilities and often with relevance to the actual possibilities in their lives as they see, live, and embody them" (p. 461). As Willis (2005) points out, "schools are one of the principal sites for the dialectical playing out of the apparent disjunctions and contradictions in changing societies, which underlie some of the most urgent education debates" (p. 462). Bourdieu (1990, p. 63) has further noted that it is the dispositions of students toward their individual schooling spaces that predispose them to particular ways of behaving and responding. He is mindful, however, that such dispositions derive their key power from a "feel of the game" and "a mastery of its logic" (Reay, 2004, p. 433).

In order to negotiate the social and academic space of Mountain View High School, African migrant students derive strength and the capacity to persevere from the dispositions they have acquired (and continue to solidify) from their families, friendships, and religious practices. African migrant students generally characterized themselves (whether true or not) as hardworking, disciplined, focused on learning, well mannered, and deeply respectful. It is not a surprise that these are the attributes normally associated with success (and a feel for the game) in current middle-class education systems worldwide. Students also both absorbed and reflected other beliefs resonant with middle-class culture, such as the individual's responsibility for him- or herself. For example, Jonatha asserted that education could not be expected to solely provide the dispositions, attitudes, and impetuses for social success. That, he argued, lay within individuals, and the onus was thus on individuals to draw together their variety of practices to make better sense of their worlds. He reflected,

> They say that education is the great engine to social development. It's through education that the daughter of the peasant can become a doctor or the child of a farmer can become the president of a great nation. But it is what we make of what we have, not what we are given, that will always separate one person from another.

When asked about what motivated him to achieve educationally in an urban environment with such limited access to employment and other opportunities, Jonatha observed,

> I can't recall a time in my life when I have not had to be brave. From the minute I learnt how to think I knew that my life was not going to be easy. It would be up to me to change that. So I face my fears, each and every one of them. Sometimes it takes one confrontation and some I am still fighting with. But I know in my inner self that I will never solve them by going into my shell. When I look into the mirror I see a warrior at war with his fears. My weapon is courage and my ammunition is perseverance. I won't stop fighting until I have killed the very last of them. In schools you have to be brave in doing your work because it's difficult to get opportunities in South Africa. You have got to be brave in the sense that you must know that even if you finish, there may be something coming next that you don't want. That is why you must focus on what you can develop for yourself.

The current influx of African migrant youth into the South African school system and their struggles to find a home within such schooling spaces, is a reminder that the social ecology of the South African schooling system has become significantly more complex in the 21st century, echoing trends around the globe. This chapter has highlighted how these students, despite their limited opportunities and futures, use social and cultural capital to keep themselves in a "game" that is no longer solely local or national, but is global in nature. Furthermore, this chapter has explored how the previously static category of "class" in South African society has been opened up and challenged by African migrant students (and their families), as they seek to negotiate their everyday lives on rapidly changing terrain.

Notes

1   See Foubister (2011) for a more detailed discussion about the nature and scale of migration worldwide.

2   See Foubister (2011) for a more detailed description of the school and its environs.

3   Male students are overrepresented in the direct quotations chosen for this chapter. This is not a reflection of their actual percentage at Mountain View. See Foubister (2011) for complete discussion and analysis.

4   Given the scope of the chapter and the kinds of arguments that are made there is a danger that we have created a stereotypical, one-dimensional portrait of the South African students, and not acknowledged the extent to which local South African students have been structurally caricatured within the school environment and hierarchy as lower-performing students, behaviorally difficult students, and disinterested and problem children; a conceptual box from whence there is no escape. The complexity of the dynamics between South African and African migrant youth can be at least partially explained through John Ogbu's notion of voluntary and involuntary minorities and his cultural–ecological theory of minority school performance (Ogbu & Simons, 1998). The importance of this insight is crucial, and is suggestive of possible future research trajectories in South African schools, as the African migrant student population grows.

References

Adepoju, A. (2006). Internal and international migration within Africa. In P. Kok, D. Gelderblom, J. Oucho, & J. van Zyl (Eds.), *Migration in South and Southern Africa: Dynamics and determinants* (pp. 26–45). Cape Town, SA: HSRC Press.

Blom Hansen, T., Jeannerat, C., & Sadouni, S. (2009). Introduction to portable spirits and itinerant people: Religion and migration in South Africa in a comparative perspective. *African Studies, 68*(2), 187–196.

Bourdieu, P. (1986). The forms of capital. In J. Richardson (Ed.), *Handbook of theory and research for the sociology of education* (pp. 15–29). Westport, CT: Greenwood.

Bourdieu, P. (1990). *In other words: Essays towards a reflexive sociology.* Stanford, CA: Stanford University Press.

Bourdieu, P., & Wacquant, L. (1992). *An invitation to reflexive sociology.* Chicago, IL: University of Chicago Press.

Bray, R., Gooskens, I., Kahn, L., Moses, S., & Seekings, J. (2010). *Growing up in the New South Africa: Childhood and adolescence in post-apartheid Cape Town.* Cape Town, SA: HSRC Press.

Devine, D. (2009). Mobilising capitals? Migrant children's negotiation of their everyday lives in school. *British Journal of Sociology of Education, 30*(5), 521–535.

Eder, K. (1993). *The new politics of class.* London: Sage.

Foner, N., & Alba, R. (2008). Immigrant religion in the U.S. and Western Europe: Bridge or barrier to inclusion? *International Migration Review, 42*(2), 360–392.

Foubister, C. (2011). *Navigating their way: African migrant youth and their experiences of schooling in Cape Town* (Unpublished master's thesis). Stellenbosch University, South Africa.

Gordon, S. (2010). Migrants in a "State of exception." *Transcience Journal, 1*(1), 1–19.

Hemson, C. (in press). Fresh grounds: African migrants in a South African primary school. *South African Review of Education, 17*(1).

Human Sciences Research Council. (2008). *Citizenship, violence and xenophobia in South Africa: Perceptions from South African communities.* Cape Town, SA: HSRC Press.

Landau, L. (2009). Living within and beyond Johannesburg: Exclusion, religion and emerging forms of being. *African Studies, 68*(2), 197–214.

Lekogo, R. (2006). Francophone Africans in Cape Town: A failed migration? In C. Cross, D. Gelderblom, N. Roux, & J. Mafukidze (Eds.), *Views on migration in Sub-Saharan Africa: Proceedings from an African Migration Alliance Workshop* (pp. 207–219). Cape Town, SA: HSRC Press.

Nyamnjoh, F. B. (2010). Racism, ethnicity and the media in Africa: Reflections inspired by studies of xenophobia in Cameroon and South Africa. *Africa Spectrum, 45*(1), 57–93.

Ogbu, J., & Simons, H. (1998). Voluntary and involuntary minorities: A cultural-ecological theory of school performance with some implications for education. *Anthropology & Education Quarterly, 29*(2), 155–188.

Peberdy, S. (2008). *Selecting immigrants: National identity and South Africa's immigration policies, 1910–2008.* Johannesburg, SA: Wits University Press.

Prince, N. (2009, November 18). Bid for peace as 2500 refugees forced out of homes. *Cape Argus,* p. 1.

Putnam, R. (2000). *Bowling alone: The collapse and revival of American community.* New York: Simon & Schuster.

Reay, D. (2004). "It's all becoming a habitus": Beyond the habitual use of habitus in educational research. *British Journal of Sociology of Education, 25*(4), 431–444.

Reynolds, T. (2007). Friendship networks, social capital and ethnic identity: Researching the perspectives of Caribbean young people in Britain. *Journal of Youth Studies, 10*(4), 383–398.

Seekings, J., & Nattrass, N. (2005). *Class, race and inequality in South Africa.* New Haven, CT: Yale University Press.

Simone, A. (2008). People as infrastructure. In A. Mbembe & S. Nuttall (Eds.), *Johannesburg: The elusive metropolis* (pp. 68–90). Johannesburg, SA: Wits University Press.

Soudien, C. (2007). *Youth identity in contemporary South Africa: Race, culture and schooling.* Claremont, SA: New Africa Books.

Steinbach, M. (2010). "Quand je sors d'accueil": Linguistic integration of immigrant adolescents in Quebec secondary schools. *Language, Culture and Curriculum, 23*(2), 1–27.

Swartz, S. (2010). *iKasi: The moral ecology of South Africa's township youth.* Johannesburg, SA: Wits University Press.

Willis, P. (2005). Afterword: Foot soldiers of modernity: The dialectics of cultural consumption and the 21st-century school. In C. McCarthy, W., Crichlow, G. Dimitriadis, & N. Dolby (Eds.), *Race, identity, and representation in education* (2nd ed., pp. 461–479). New York: Routledge.

Weeks, J., Donovan, C., & Heaphy, B. (1999). Everyday experiments: narratives of non-heteral sexual relationships. In E. Silva & C. Smart (Eds.), *The new family* (pp. 113–126). London: Sage.

Yosso, T. (2005). Whose culture has capital? A critical race theory discussion of community cultural wealth. *Race, Ethnicity and Education, 8*(1), 69–91.

Class and the Changing Global Educational Context

8

GLOBAL SCAPES OF ABJECTION

The Contemporary Dynamics of Some Intersecting Injustices[1]

Jane Kenway and Anna Hickey-Moody

Introduction

In globalizing times, the ways certain places and populations are produced as abject is changing. Localized processes of abjection intersect with abjectifying global flows of people, ideas and images. Together, these cultural movements bring about contemporary inflections of longstanding social and cultural prejudices. In what ways do global scapes of abjection fold in to produce local processes of spatial abjection? How are social processes of local abjection necessarily spatial? What generative possibilities are held within the abject space? The space that Kristeva (1982) suggests 'be-seeches, worries, and fascinates desire it wrench(es) bodies, nights and discourse' (p. 10). Such spaces are generative, yet maligned.

This paper addresses these questions drawing on a wider study of the intersections between the changing social and cultural base of nonmetropolitan Australian places and identities as they are increasingly caught up in, and also attempt to stand apart from, globalizing flows.[2] The methodology for this wider study involved what we call 'place-based global ethnographies' (2006).[3] The specific focus here is on mobility and stasis in such places and their implications for unequal social and cultural relationships.[4] We focus on three Australian localities: Eden (a coastal fishing and logging town); Morwell (a coal mining and power generation town); and Coober Pedy (a tourist and opal mining desert town). The most economically and culturally marginalized and stigmatized are the welfare poor and Aboriginal people. Our purpose here is to analyse the composite processes of abjection that these groups are subjected to and through which they are produced. Our other purposes are, first, to develop the concept 'scapes of abjection'[5] and second to illustrate the manner in which place based global ethnography enhances understandings of the complex contemporary spatial dynamics of intersecting injustices.

Scapes of Abjection

In globalizing circumstances conventional notions of material and cultural injustice are usefully complemented by ideas associated with the global politics of scapes, mobility and affect. Appadurai (1996, 2000) considers global cultural mobility through his notion of scapes. 'Ethnoscapes are: scapes of persons who constitute the shifting world in which we live: tourists, immigrants, refugees, exiles, guest workers, and other moving groups and individuals' (2000, p. 95).

Lived cultures of ethnoscapes are reconfigured in global ideoscapes (moving political ideas) and mediascapes (moving electronic images). These 'scapes' come together to form imagined worlds. Such worlds are 'multiple [and] constituted by the historically situated imaginations of persons and groups spread around the global' (1996, p. 2). According to Appadurai the politics associated with these scapes are disjunctive. In some circumstances they can also be highly noxious. We add a political and affective edge to Appadurai's scapes and imagined worlds through taking up the ideas of Bauman and Kristeva.

Bauman (1998a, 1998b) talks of 'global hierarchies of mobility' and identifies two main typologies. First, he focuses on those who are constantly on the move by choice, usually the 'time poor' but asset rich winners of globalization, those who float free from grounded injustices and any responsibility for their amelioration (Bauman, 2000). Bauman also points to the difficulties and anxieties that arise for those who are forced to move, and for those others who are forced to stay put. The former, he says, are 'pushed from behind' and 'not welcome when they stop' (1998a, pp. 92–93). The latter find themselves in a situation of 'enforced localization'; they are tied to space in a period when the freedom to act is increasingly tied to the freedom to move (1998a, p. 70). These people are 'bound to bear passively whatever change may be visited on the locality they are tied to'. Bauman stresses that these various meanings of mobility are linked and that 'Freedom of choice for capital descends as a cruel fate for others' (1998a, p. 93).

One of the ways these hierarchical ethnoscapes are linked, is through global ideo and mediascapes of abjection. In the early 1980s, Kristeva (1982) theorized the corporeal, psychological and social processes associated with the abject. Drawing on Douglas' (1966) work on pollution and taboo, she identified three main forms of abjection associated with food, waste and sexual difference. The abject has since come to be associated with those bodily fluids, people, objects and places that are couched as unclean, impure and even immoral. The abject disturbs 'identity, system, order' (Kristeva, 1982, p. 4) and provokes the desire to expel the unclean to an outside, to create boundaries in order to establish the certainty of the self. It involves the production of social taboos and individual and group psychic defences. Insofar as the abject challenges notions of identity and social order it 'must' be cast out. Indeed, the production of identity and social order necessitates processes of abjection because abjection involves naming and reviling certain people and places, and endorsing the belief that they are only to be repelled and resisted. But the 'abject' does not respect such expulsions and boundaries and so constantly threatens to move across them and contaminate. It is thus understood as a threat to 'the pure and the proper'. Grosz (1989) observes that the abject 'can never be fully obliterated but hovers at the borders of our existence, threatening the apparently settled unity of the subject with disruption and possible dissolution' (p. 71).

Scapes of abjection circulate globally and seep into national and local geometries of power and affect. As we will show, they reproduce things such as the ugly history of colonization and the geopolitical relationships between the metropolis and its othered spaces. They justify injustice, draw attention away from social suffering and thus deny the social reality of the marginalized. They are woven through neoliberal economic and social ideologies and help to legitimate the more insidious aspects of global economic restructuring. They provide a justification for the diminishment of state welfare support for those who suffer the economic and cultural consequences of the noxious politics of mobility. The associated social tensions come to be expressed in the language of disgust and it becomes accepted that certain social groups, the Black and White welfare poor particularly, can justifiably be treated as trash. Scapes of abjection can also be entangled with the long chains of commodification associated with global ethnoscapes. In such cases, we go on to explain, the processes of abjection take on an even more complex configuration as culture is navigated for profit.

Animating Animosity

Amongst those who suffer the burden of the noxious politics of mobility are the increasing numbers of 'new poor' (Bauman, 1998b). In 'developed' Western nations, these include the working poor and the unemployed. Given its declining economic power and tax base and the escalating demands upon it, the nation-state is increasingly unwilling to meet the needs of these so-called losers of globalization. It thus finds it convenient to rearticulate ideoscapes of abjection into the national and local vernacular.

The situation of the new poor in Eden and Morwell involves denial and demonization, not only of the poor by those who are not, but also of the welfare poor by the working poor. Both Eden and Morwell once enjoyed periods of relative economic and cultural stability and predictability. For Morwell this came about during the 'golden years' of the state-owned power industry, when workers enjoyed a higher than state average of disposable income and jobs were secure, often for life. The affluent times for Eden occurred prior to the regulation of the fishing and logging industries, before environmental controls were put into place. But both localities have experienced dramatic economic change and along with this, rising numbers of 'new poor' in the locality. Bauman (1998a) argues that '[t]he mark of the socially excluded in an era of time/space compression is immobility and immobilization' (p. 86). In Eden and Morwell, the excluded include both those who have been 'left behind', constrained by space, and also those who have had no choice but to move *into* each township. These economically barren contexts with their emotional climate of vulnerability, uncertainty and anxiety have provided the perfect breeding grounds for the toxic emotional dynamics of abjection. The unemployed on welfare support have been marginalized economically and stigmatized culturally.

For the most part, those receiving unemployment benefits, especially those enduring long-term unemployment, are written off as lazy 'wasters' and 'bludgers'. Such views are quite widespread, even amongst those who might be considered the working poor. In short, the view is that '[t]he work is out there if people will get out and look for it' (Beau Knox, p. 14). Opinions such as these draw on neoliberal economic and social policy ideoscapes circulated globally by such international organizations as the Organisation of Economic Co-operation and Development (OECD) and the International Monetary Fund (IMF) and nationally by many 'developed' nation-states. These mobilize discourses of derision to justify the reduction and privatization of welfare support and reframe and shame those who receive it (Mendes, 2003). They construct unemployment as an individual problem that is due mainly to an individual's attitude to work and refusal to move to look for it. The logical conclusion to this proposition is that those in this predicament are there by personal choice. Bauman (1998b) argues that by constructing unemployed people as choosing not to extradite themselves from poverty, the state specifically and society more generally are absolved from any responsibility in the creation and resolution of this problem, thus negating the globalized economy's reconfiguration of the economies of place. But the derision has deepened to also suggest that accompanying the 'choice' to be unemployed is the compulsion to cheat and defraud the system. Disadvantage and dishonesty have become somewhat fused.

The unemployed are understood as exploiting the system and by implication their neighbours, getting their daily needs met by the state rather than from their own work. Unemployed parents are blamed for cultivating cultures of laziness. Certain local residents worry that this declining work ethic is what Jones and Novak (1999, p. 27) describe as 'cancerous'. Such expressions of intolerance give local life to the global ideoscape that state welfare creates poverty and dishonesty by reducing individuals' motivation to work and by encouraging them to cheat (Mendes, 2003, pp. 42–43). And, Peel points out that such ideoscapes have become popular mediascapes; what he calls 'poverty news', which relishes threat, fraud, helplessness and incapacity (2003, p. 31). In Australia, when recipients of welfare appear, to some, to be better off than the working poor, a politics of anxiety and aversion emerges. Deleuze (1992) describes the interpersonal dynamics of such contagious, sad affects with insight. He states: 'affections rooted in sadness are linked to one another in exercising our capacity to be affected, and this in such a way that our power of action is further and further diminished, tending towards its lowest degree' (p. 243). Sorrow and fear are self-perpetuating emotions. This negative cycle of sad affect is fuelled by the media's 'amplification of affect'; 'intensifying rage (and outrage), magnifying fear, and, not coincidentally, inciting hatred' (Gibbs, 2001). One consequence of this is widespread public support for more stringent welfare regulation and onerous eligibility criteria and more intense policing of entitlements (Mendes, 2003). In carefully crafted processes of blame shifting, systems of welfare support are redefined as systems of welfare dependency that actually create dependency, irresponsibility and dishonesty. Social injustice is redefined as individual fault. What is left of the welfare state is blamed; the need for 'mutual obligation' policies is proclaimed and such policies are introduced (Mendes, 2003). Economic globalization is not usually blamed; it is too vast, intangible and intractable. Rather, ideoscapes of abjection help to do its ideological work.

This process has notably masculine overtones. Unemployment and immobility are associated with laziness, weakness and submissiveness—in fact, with a lack of masculinity. Masculinity, 'breadwinning' and mobility are linked, as are dependency, immobility and femininity. To bludge (scrounge, scavenge) 'off your mates', even if indirectly via the tax system, is to sink beneath contempt in terms of historical working-class norms of male propriety. The bludger is akin to the strike-breaking 'scab'. The scab is the sign of the pustule or wound and symbolizes the body's unending battle against offensive residues. The 'scab' and the 'bludger' have very different origins in terms of the working class. The former arises from the organized working-class worker (Fox, 2000) and the latter from government discourses of derision with regard to those on welfare. However, they both signify the humiliated, defiled male who 'beckons the subject ever closer to its edge' (Grosz, 1989, p. 73), and who highlights the 'abyss at the borders of the subject's existence, a hole into which the subject may fall when its identity is put into question' (Grosz, 1989, p. 72). The economic and existential uncertainties associated with economic globalization have caused deep divisions among those who have been most disadvantaged by the global economy in 'developed' Western world countries. Those who fear becoming unemployed and dependent vilify those who are already. People's anxieties about their own vulnerability are displaced onto those whose positions they fear, and such fear is converted into revulsion and rejection. As Kristeva (1982) says, 'abjection is above all ambiguity. Because, while releasing a hold, it does not radically cut off the subject from what threatens it—on the contrary, abjection acknowledges it to be in perpetual danger' (p. 9).

Spaces of Deprivation and Denigration

The notion of the underclass entered the popular imaginary in the 1990s and its dominant discursive inflection is infused by ideoscapes of abjection. These encourage the social 'mainstream' to view 'underclass' culture as a pathology (often racial), as dysfunctional, to deride its behaviours, values and survival strategies (Bullen & Kenway, 2004). Such cultural pathological constructions have seeped into public consciousness and morphed into 'contagious feelings' of disgust (Gibbs, 2001). Underclass groupings are seen as a form of 'social pollution' that contaminates the proper local order and brings about moral and social decline and decay. Containing the 'underclass' discursively and spatially and rejecting them emotionally are some of the mechanisms of abjection whereby their social exclusion and polarization occur in Morwell with regard to a government housing trust area, which the locals call the 'Bronx'.

The Bronx is a space of abjection, which brings to mind Kristeva's links between abjection and waste and the lengths to which people go to externalize aspects of the abject. The Bronx is described by some of the local boys as 'a bum area where all the no-hopers live' (Mark Thinley); as 'disgusting'. The young people who come from the Bronx are commonly described as 'Rats'. 'Rats have bad hair, look scruffy and don't wear deodorant. Rats are normally poor people' (Jed Duda, age 13). 'Rats wear grotty clothes, have grotty hair, and they stink' (Deanna Marginson, age 15). The children of the local poor are associated with dirt, bad smells and the defilements associated with unclean bodily residues. They disgust their peers. Sibley (1995) observes that the rat is a particularly potent abject symbol. Rats, he says,

> are associated with residues—food waste, human waste with spaces which border civilized society, particularly subterranean spaces like sewers. The potency of the rat as an abject symbol is heightened through its role as a carrier of disease, its occasional tendency to violate boundaries by entering people's homes, and its prolific breeding.
>
> *(p. 28)*

We return to the matter of 'prolific breeding' shortly. Nayak's (2003) discussion of the 'Charver Kids' subculture in urban Britain also identifies the anthropomorphic qualities of the abject. Via the symbol of the rat, race, class and place are articulated together in popular British imaginaries, as being anthropomorphically embodied in the rodent-like 'Charver Kids'. These 'Kids' are youth of North East England, represented by the figure of the 'Rat Boy', a character who is 'very UnBritish, once alien but now increasingly familiar' (p. 92; Collier cited in Nayak, 2003, p. 83). Popular discourse in Australia is populated with similar comparisons between the welfare poor and 'Un-Australian' behaviour. Nayak notes that such conflation of nationality, race and class is a contemporary performance of colonial ideals, a tradition of abjection in which the rat features prominently as a symbol of the poor:

> The idea that poverty-stricken people 'poured' and 'streamed' into English cities was … evoked in the 1980's with New Right discourses which appealed to an imagined sense of British decency to acknowledge that 'immigrants' were now 'swamping' the nation. [The] poor are seen as 'dense black masses' and vividly compared with rats. The surreptitious representation of the urban poor as alien, teeming hordes, carrying all manner of disease, was secured in the hated symbol of the rat. Indeed, the rat can be said to signify the defiled, 'polluted' Other which was ritually segregated from the 'purified' spaces of the bourgeoisie and marked as taboo.
>
> *(1993, p. 84)*

The Bronx in Morwell is similarly constructed as the taboo, defiled 'polluted' space of the Other, beset with rough, dangerous and deviant rodent-people.

The main street that runs through the Bronx is Beady Crescent. One local service provider, Gary Silva, describes crime as part of the lifestyle in that area; 'Unemployed, on the benefit, drugs, thieving and manipulative'. Many young people who live outside the Bronx are not allowed in the area by their parents. It is considered unsafe. To the young, Beady Crescent has an alluring aura of danger. Stories about its horrors abound, and become quite fanciful. Such fantasies of expulsion are illustrated by the following young man's story:

> There is always the police down there, a few years back mum told me that there was a big massacre down there or something, and six people got their heads chopped off with a machete or something. Someone shot himself in the head.
>
> *(Frank Chigetto, 15)*

Mobilizing such fictions of depravity and constructing prohibitions around them are among the rituals deployed by the 'pure' to defend themselves against the impure. Across the generations they reproduce the dynamics of abjection.

'Degenerate' Mothers and Fatherless Boys

Many of the single mothers in our study are an example of the people Bauman terms 'vagabonds', those who have no choice but to move and are unwelcome when they arrive; the 'waste of the world' (Bauman, 1998a, pp. 92–93). The common view is that the high cost of living in major cities and government housing policies mean that increasing numbers of city 'single mums and unemployed' are 'being dumped' into low cost rural housing. Single mothers on the move are seen as city waste draining out from the metropolis to contaminate the country. Their abjection powerfully disturbs *local* 'identity, system, order' (Kristeva, 1982, p. 4).

Like all those on welfare support, single mothers are thoroughly resented and despised for their state dependency and are castigated as welfare freeloaders. They are seen to get pregnant in order to secure an income and a home and to avoid working. Further, the state is seen to encourage their 'promiscuity'. Such views were expressed in our Community Focus Group discussion in Morwell:

Woman: A young girl came in, she had two babies. It was obvious that she was having another one. Her mother came in and said 'Oh well, when she has this one, she goes to the top of the list to get a Commission home'. So it seemed you had an extra baby and you were actually rewarded. I know girls that have married and had three children and their husbands are just on a production line or a low wage and they are actually worse off money wise than their sisters who haven't married and have had three or four kids.

Man: I've heard the term used 'Oh, she's due in about three months. She'll get a pay rise.

Clearly the mother with the working husband is pure while the single mother on welfare is impure, scheming, manipulative and untrustworthy. Somewhat similar views are expressed by some of the young men in Eden about young single mothers. Such girls are variously described as 'dead shits' and 'the used and abused'—in a sense as disposable female waste—who have failed to subscribe to dominant local standards of respectable femininity and in so doing are implicitly seen as a threat to the local gender order.

Teenage and single mothers have been central figures in global ideoscapes of abjection and malevolent underclass discourses for some time (Bullen & Kenway, 2004, 2005). The single mother not only challenges notions of the proper family and respectable femininity; by her very existence she defies and defiles the view that women need men. Her abject fecund maternal body disturbs phallocentric forms of thought. Jones and Novak (1999) note that conservative social commentators actually blame the declining work ethic on the breakdown of the nuclear family, which they claim has taken away men's motivation to work. Furthermore, single mothers are seen to be instrumental in effecting this process of disintegration. To the usual range of antisocial behaviours associated with the underclass (crime, drugs, violence) the single mother may add 'illegitimacy'.

A particular focus of this ideoscape of abjection is on the corrosive social consequences of 'illegitimacy' and 'fatherlessness' for young males. Commenting on the work of Charles Murray (1990, 1999), a global propagandist of this view, Bullen and Kenway (2005) argue:

The key indicators which Murray selects to track the growth of the underclass: [are] illegitimacy, criminality and unemployed young men. Criminality and unemployment among young men are an outcome of illegitimacy since the masculine role model for unfathered boys 'is the unconnected male for whom success is defined by sexual conquests and who sees the responsibilities of parenthood as a trap for chumps' (Murray 1999). Clearly, all roads lead back to the single mother's door.

(p. 50)

Within this mindset, the particular 'illegitimacy' to which she is party, constitutes the single mother as the 'abject womb' to borrow Creed's (1993, p. 43) terminology. She is seen to 'prolifically breed' the next generation of 'rats' and underclass social scavengers.

Abjectifying Aboriginality

The various processes whereby the abject is expelled, restricted to 'abject zones' (McClintock, 1995, p. 71), and returns to 'haunt' are all evident in the complex history of the abjection of Aboriginal Australians. These processes of abjection are integral to Australia's colonial and neocolonial history and have been rearticulated in recent discourses of 'downward' envy associated with the abject positioning of Aboriginal welfare recipients. They have also been rearticulated in the ideoscapes and mediascapes related to the tourist industry.

The noxious politics of mobility and associated processes of abjection are a characteristic of the treatment of Australia's original inhabitants by the British occupying power in the 18th and 19th century. Cast out and treated as nonhuman contaminants, Aboriginal Australians were dispossessed of their land, denied their laws and customs, refused citizenship and usually treated brutally and exploited by White settlers (Broome, 2001; Reynolds, 1999). Australia's colonial history involves the dispossession, denial, and exploitation of Aboriginal peoples who continue to experience well-documented, indisputable economic injustice and widespread social exclusion, cultural denial and denigration. Such injustices are integral to their mobility, which has included not just voluntary movement but also being forcibly moved (Haebich, 2001).

More than any other group in Australia today, Aboriginal people experience social deprivation in terms of housing, health, education and employment. Various forms of government welfare support seem little able to alter this situation and, equally, various approaches to reconciliation seem unable to end racist sentiment. Interwoven with this situation is a racialized version of the abjection processes we have already discussed with regard to the welfare poor, although in this instance the White working poor and the White welfare poor join forces to abjectify Aboriginal people who come to be seen as privileged, undeserving and ungrateful: 'out of sadness is born a desire which is hate. This desire is linked with other desires, other passions: antipathy, derision, contempt, envy, anger and so on' (Deleuze, 1992, p. 243). Through scapes of abjection, the production of race becomes enmeshed in affective economy of sadness, derision and resentment.

There is quite a common belief in Coober Pedy that Aboriginal people get it easy because of the government subsidies and allowances allotted to them. This provision of government benefits is a feature of the local white residents' abjectification of local Aboriginal people. Stefani Moulder, age 14, holds this dominant view.

> When school camps come up, we had to pay $200 and the Aboriginals only had to pay $20. That is because the government pays for them, and I think that is stupid. They [Aboriginal people] think that they own this place but they don't.

Stefani's logic is that everyone in financial difficulty should be entitled to the same financial subsidies and allowances. The common view is that the locally poor Whites are more in need and deserving of assistance than Aboriginal people. Further, Stefani's comment that 'They think that they own this place but they don't' is a rather poignant reminder that while they once did 'own the land' they now do not. Welfare benefits seem little compensation for the loss of their land and independence and the attacks on their identities and pride. Stefani's view is also that Aboriginal people should not be so 'pushy', should not act as if 'they own the place'.

Such 'pushy' assertions of Aboriginality have been 'shaped within a long-standing, but now vigorously contested subordination' (Cowlishaw, 2004, p.11). They include an assertion of self-respect and a denial of an 'ever-abject state of being'. This state of being is implied in the 'permanent victim status' associated with a politics whose 'central motif' is 'injured and suffering Aboriginal people' (Cowlishaw, 2004, p. 52). Who represents whom, how and with regard to what are highly contentious questions within and beyond Aboriginal communities and come to the fore in relation to the Indigenous tourist industry.

The Tourist Glaze

The cultural and economic dynamics of abjectifying Indigenous peoples now feature prominently in global tourist ideoscapes and mediascapes. Bauman calls people who are on the move by choice and who accept few territorial responsibilities as they travel, 'tourists'. 'They stay and move at their heart's desire. They abandon a site when new untried opportunities beckon elsewhere' (1998a, p. 92). Bauman's notions of the tourist is one of many 'metaphors of mobility' (Urry, 2000, p. 27) in current social thought and his tourist metaphor is applied largely to the mobile winners of globalization, 'the global businessman, global culture managers, or global academics' for instance, those who are 'emancipated from space' (Bauman, 1998a, pp. 89–93) because of the resources at their disposal. Amongst Bauman's 'tourists' are actual tourists—those who combine leisure and travel in search of 'experience' (MacCannell, 1999).

Tourism has become a key economic renewal strategy among many non-urban communities around the world. It involves branding place. It is about the identification and promotion of difference, where differentiation marks a place as unique. It is also about the construction and promotion of marketable differences within places. Aboriginal culture has become a highly marketable feature of the Australian tourist industry, particularly to those sorts of tourists whom Cohen and Kennedy (2000, p. 219) call 'alternative tourists' (as opposed to mass tourists). These people require adventure, contact with nature, spiritual renewal or experiences of authenticity. As Cohen and Kennedy (2000, p. 221) observe, they yearn to 'sample exotic cultures', seek the 'curative properties of wilderness, remote regions', the 'off beat and unusual'. They 'are disposed to interact directly with locals and show interest in traditional culture'.

The contemporary ideoscapes and mediascapes that frame our discussion are certain global, national, state and local tourist texts constructed to tantalize the palate of such tourists. These texts and some of their associated spatial practices involve complex abjection processes of selective recognition and erasure. Aboriginality with all its complexity (Cowlishaw, 2004) is denied and instead spilt in two; certain aspects become cultural embellishments to the tourist industry while other aspects are expunged. Denials and erasures occur when features of Aboriginality are found lacking in market value or when they detract from the image of place. These are eliminated to abject zones beyond the 'tourist gaze' (Urry, 1990). Alternatively, marketable aspects of Aboriginal identity become tourist 'zirconia': culturally fabricated gems—the tourist glaze.

Aboriginal Australians have their own disparate and evolving cultures and histories, which continue to be significant despite past and present injustices. But only highly select aspects of Aboriginal culture and history have become Australia's cultural tourist zirconia. These aspects are the 'acceptable' and commodifiable parts of the abject split. Included here are Aboriginal cultural knowledge, ancient art, connections to the land and experiences of spirituality. These are allocated a tourist patina. Such processes of commodification and exoticization can be understood as contemporary examples of Aboriginal abjection. They involve a stage-managed set of comfortable images that white populations want to see. As culturally objectified zirconias, Aboriginal identities become bound to a colonial past and a neocolonial present.

In appealing to the tourist demographic noted above, marketing Australian places beyond the metropolis often involves the historical and spatial fixing of Aboriginal Australian people. They may thus, for instance, be conflated with Australian bush scapes; as if that's all there is to contemporary Aboriginal Australians. They may be used to make nonmetropolitan places seem especially interesting and significant. The consumer-driven psychology here is that tourists will feel there is something exciting, almost sensual, about Aboriginal histories. In order to relate to such ancient powers, one must travel and get close to the land, as the soil holds traces of such mythical peoples. Subtly implied within these ideoscapes are particular tropes of Aboriginal masculinity. 'Authentic' Aboriginal masculinity is sutured to timeless ideas of the wise tribal elder, the purveyor of spiritual wisdom, the skilful hunter and tracker with spears or sticks in hand, the pensive player of the didgeridoo, the semi-naked, body-decorated and scarified ceremonial dancer. Many examples of such temporal and spatial fixity and exotic imagining can be found in online tourist mediascapes. The examples to follow are collectively emblematic of abject splitting processes.

Texts produced by The Lonely Planet publishers are a significant feature of contemporary global tourist mediascapes and ideoscapes and have important implications for out of the way places around the world. They support 'adventure on demand' (Friend, 2005, p. 20). *Journeys to Authentic Australia* is written as a guide to what the Lonely Planet suggests is 'Authentic Australia'. The Lonely Planet has declared the left hand side of Australia is its 'authentic' region. Indeed, according to their advice, travelling this land is a way of 'accessing Australia's heart and soul' (The Lonely Planet Online, 2005). A key aspect of this 'authenticated' Australia is ancient Aboriginal culture, which lends the land particular desirability.

> Away from Australia's eastern seaboard lies a treasure-trove of superb beaches, mind-blowing natural features, authentic outback experiences, world-class wines and gourmet fare, ancient Aboriginal cultures, rare and precious fauna, and, of course, the resilient and welcoming people who have made this part of Australia the intriguing and unforgettable place that it is.
>
> *(The Lonely Planet Online, 2005)*

Through the use of the word *ancient*, Aboriginal culture is positioned as temporally distinct from 'the resilient and intriguing people' (some of whom are Aboriginal) 'who have made this part of Australia the intriguing and unforgettable place that it is'. Here, ideoscapes of abjection deploy what McClintock (1995, p. 37), drawing on Foucault, calls 'panoptical time'. Panoptical time is an 'image of global history consumed—at a glance—in a single spectacle from a point of privileged invisibility' (McClintock, 1995, p. 37). Panoptical time makes invisible the full history of colonized peoples but also makes hypervisible, indeed turns into a tourist spectacle, those historical features that can be exoticized.

Increasingly since the 1970s and 80s, as part of a more general refusal of the 'ever abject' images that batter them, Aboriginal people have been taking charge of their own representations and rekindling their own language, stories and customs—a 'cultural renaissance'. For instance, many dance companies have been founded which recognize 'culture as the touchstone of Indigenous well-being' and which aim to 'promote a strong sense of heritage and identity amongst Indigenous populations' (Australian Dance Council, 2005), in part through traditional/contemporary fusions.

Sadly, such Aboriginal sensibilities do not play a major role in most tourist constructions of Aboriginal Australia. They certainly do not resonate with Coober Pedy's construction of itself as a tourist destination. Coober Pedy's District Council's promotional online site is aimed at showcasing Coober Pedy to a 'World Wide' audience. The District Council invokes a selective past tense notion of Aboriginal people that imagines them only in relation to landscape. Indeed, the following quote is one of three past-tense references made to Aboriginal people or communities on this particular page of the website. There are no present tense references to Aboriginal peoples on this page. It reads:

> For thousands of years Aboriginal people walked across this area. Because of the desert environment, these people were nomadic hunters and gatherers who travelled constantly in search of food and water supplies as well as to attend traditional ceremonies.
>
> *(District Council of Coober Pedy Online 2005)*

According to this website, the land around Coober Pedy is steeped with the sacred significance of ancient nomadic knowledges of Aboriginal people. But no connection is made between these 'nomadic hunters and gatherers' and the existing, large Aboriginal population in Coober Pedy. By focusing only on the past, it is easier to erase them from the present.

Alongside the construction of Aboriginal people as spirits that infuse the landscape with qualities of desirability, they are positioned as culturally manufactured gems, charming zirconias, to be consumed alongside fine local produce, live art and scenic tours. For instance, the South Australian Tourist Commission (STAC) suggests that tourists with 'special interests' in backpacking or four-wheel driving may like to sample some Indigenous Culture. The backpackers' page of the South Australian Tourist Commission's website (2005) features images of didgeridoos and a link to the Commission's page on Indigenous Culture, which also discusses Aboriginal people mainly in historical terms, or positions them as the special ingredient that makes the Australian landscape worthy of tourist consumption. This retrospective/consumed by landscape discursive continuum is broken by a single reference to seeing the 'city through the eyes of the Kaurna people' and learning to play the didgeridoo. Interestingly, none of the Commission's 'special interest' tourist groups are Aboriginal people, nor are there images of Aboriginal people in representations of 'special interest' groups, which include 'Family, Gay & Lesbian, with Pets, Disability, Backpacker and Self-Drive'.

Erasure and Spatial Purification

Another example in which historicized imaginings of Aboriginal Australians are deployed to market place can be found in the media corporation Fairfax Digital's international tourist website. This website is called the *Walkabout Australian Travel Guide* (2005). 'Walkabout' is the name given to the nomadic wanderings of Aboriginal people and has deep cultural resonance. However, in relation to Coober Pedy, the *Walkabout Australian Travel Guide* textually erases the town's Aboriginal people. It does so via a discussion of the town's multi-cultural population.

> At the moment there are about 4000 people living in and around the town and over 45 nationalities are represented. The majority of the population is Greek, Yugoslav and Italian (the town has a remarkable similarity to a dusty Mediterranean village) with many Chinese buyers of opals.
>
> *(Fairfax Digital Online 2005)*

Aboriginal people are not mentioned here even though they constitute 11.8% of the total population of Coober Pedy (ABS, 2001). This is a notably higher percentage than the Greek population (4.0%; ABS, 2003) and the Yugoslav (2.8%; ABS, 2003) population. Only 1.4 % of Coober Pedy residents were born in China. The Italian population of Coober Pedy is so small that it is not listed by the Australian Bureau of Statistics.

As this example suggests, tourism results in the development of what we call artificial authenticities. These conceal those things that are seen to detract from 'best face', including place-based divisions, stratifications and conflicts. The packaging and selling of place by the tourist industry is not just about mobilizing marketable differences but also about willing away certain unpalatable differences. In Coober Pedy such willing-away has involved a form of 'spatial purification', an attempt to provide a 'clean space' for tourists (Sibley, 1995, p. 77). Here many local Aboriginal people are made invisible in order to attract tourists.

The development of the Coober Pedy tourist industry has resulted in an increased focus on the image of the town. Pailin Rieflin, age 13, observes 'They [Aboriginal people] make the place look messy. The street is ruined by the drunken Aboriginals'. Chuck Clinton, age 14, agrees: 'They look like flies hanging around [and make] Coober Pedy look bad'. Like rats, flies are also an abject symbol. Aboriginal people in the street are marked as dirty and dangerous. Their public alcohol consumption is seen as a particular issue. Indeed, Aboriginal people are often constructed as a constantly drunk public spectacle. 'It is not really something you want to see or you want your children seeing everyday', says Mario Ciccone, age 16. Steps have been taken to remove them from the main street; to create a 'clean space' for the tourist gaze.

Kristeva explains, 'that word, "fear" no sooner has it cropped up than it shades off like a mirage and permeates all…with a hallucinatory ghostly glimmer' (1982, p. 6). The deployment of abject splitting keeps Aboriginal identity and culture both erasable and marketable. But it also means that the tourist industry constantly 'shades off' into a 'hallucinatory ghostly glimmer' of fear that the erased will return to 'haunt' the industry. A particular fear is associated with what we call 'abject agency' (drawing on Cowlishaw, 2004). Such agency arises from 'chronic discontent' and 'continuing and unresolved rage and resentment which has resulted from past injustices' (Cowlishaw, 2004, pp. 75, 189). It is derived from the derogatory symbolic codes used to abjectify the group in the first place. Abject agency involves 'taking up an abject position' (Cowlishaw, 2004, p. 158), mocking and exaggerating it through defiance and disrespect, and hurling it back at the original perpetrator. Cowlishaw talks of the ways in which some young Aboriginal men participate in this process. As a result, say, of being noisy or fighting in the street or throwing stones at shop windows, or drinking or chroming (sniffing petrol), many come into direct contact with the White legal system. She explains how

> Anger and abjection are performed in the court and in the street, using language which confounds, disconcerts and embarrasses the white audience [and] seem to confirm the grotesque images of deformed Aboriginality.
>
> *(2004, p. 74)*

'Experiences and actions that whites despise can be displayed as triumphant defeat of attempted humiliation' (Cowlishaw, 2004, p. 192), and as a consequence, such young men may be treated 'like champions' with cries of 'Good on you brother'. This form of 'desperate excess' (Cowlishaw, 2004, p. 163) is designed to evoke extreme discomfort, disgust or dismay in the dominant White population. It can thus be argued that 'spatial purification' for the tourist gaze may create precisely the sorts of behaviours it seeks to hide. Kristeva explains:

> abjection is elaborated by a failure to recognize its kin hence before they are signifiable—[the subject in question] drives them out and constitutes his own territory edged by the abject. Fear cements his compound.
>
> *(1982, p. 6)*

The splitting of abject Aboriginal people and culture into 'compounds' of the desirable and the undesirable can be read in Kristeva's (1982, p. 6) terms as a refusal to let a population solidify and become fully recognizable to itself and to others; to be understood and to understand itself in all its complexity and ambiguity. So, for Aboriginal boys growing up in Coober Pedy, tourism has a range of different significances, not the least being its abject refusal of their full selfhood.

Conclusion

We have added spatial, political and affective density to Appadurai's global 'scapes', showing how these scapes intersect with local geometries of poverty, gender and race. Apparently minor mobilities and immobilities within the nation-state are, we have argued, modulated through noxious global ideoscapes and mediascapes of abjection. Further, we have illustrated how ethno- and mediascapes abjectify 'local' populations in contradictory ways. We developed the notion of 'scapes of abjection' to show how affect and abjection work on and in the imagination. They have flow-on effects on particular economically and culturally marginalized and stigmatized populations. Long-standing and intersecting injustices are rescripted and reinscribed through their links with contemporary scapes of abjection, highlighting the noxious politics of movement and stasis and the infectious ill-feelings they provoke.

Notes

1 We thank the Australian Research Council for funding this research and Palgrave for permission to use selections from Kenway, Kraack, and Hickey Moody (2006).
2 This wider study considers youthful masculinities and gender relations in marginalized, stigmatized but also sometimes romanticized and exoticized places beyond the metropolis in the so-called developed West. We call our approach to identifying, gathering and reading data, 'place-based global ethnography' (see Kenway et al., 2006). It draws from but adapts Burawoy et al. (2000, 2001) The ethnographic fieldwork in four locations involved in-depth semi-structured interviews with 36 young people. For 6 weeks, 24 males were each interviewed weekly and 12 females were interviewed fortnightly. Loosely structured focus and affinity group discussions were held with mothers, fathers, community members, teachers and youth and welfare service providers. Informal conversations were held with a wide range of local people. All participants have been anonymized. Field research also involved time at a variety of community and youth-specific locales (e.g., the school, beach and main street) and events (e.g., sporting matches, discos, local carnivals). Bringing these localized texts together with global media- and ideoscapes, we identified and analysed popular discourses about places and people beyond the metropolis in film, television, print media and internet media.
3 This methodology is being further developed in our current project *Elite Independent Schools in Globalising Circumstances: A Multi-Sited Global Ethnography* http://www.education.monash.edu.au/research/projects/elite-schools/index.html. See also Kenway (2010).
4 The implications of some of these ideas for curriculum are developed in Kenway (2008). Further, the implications of various global scapes for public pedagogy are explored in Hickey-Moody, Windle, and Savage (2010).
5 This is part of a wider project to conceptually and empirically develop the idea of 'global emoscapes'. For an example that focuses on contemporary global capitalism, class relations and the global financial crisis see Kenway and Fahey (2010).

References

Appadurai, A. (1996). *Modernity at large: Cultural dimensions of globalization*. Minneapolis: University of Minnesota Press.
Appadurai, A. (2000). Disjuncture and difference in the global cultural economy. In F. J. Lechner & J. Boli (Eds.), *The globalization reader* (pp. 322–330). Oxford, England: Blackwell.

Australian Bureau of Statistics. *The health and welfare of Australia's Aboriginal and Torres Strait Islander peoples* 4704.0, 2003. Retrieved from http://www.abs.gov.au/

Australian Bureau of Statistics. (2001). *Updated Coober Pedy stats 2001 census*. Retrieved December 2, 2005, from http://www.abs.gov.au/ `

Australian Bureau of Statistics. (2003) *The health and welfare of Australia's Aboriginal and Torres Strait Islander peoples* 4704.0. Retrieved November 8, 2005, from http://www.abs.gov.au/

Australian Dance Council. (2005). Indigenous dance: The place not the space. Retrieved from www.australiacouncil.gov.au/__data/assets/pdf.../03_aia_dance

Bauman, Z. (1998a). *Globalization: The human consequences*. Cambridge, England: Polity.

Bauman, Z. (1998b). *Work, consumerism and the new poor*. Buckingham, England: Open University Press.

Bauman, Z.(2000). *Liquid modernity*. Cambridge, England: Polity Press.

Bauman, Z. (2002). *Society under siege*. Cambridge, England: Polity Press.

Broome, R. (2001). *Aboriginal Australians: Black responses to white dominance, 1788–2001* (3rd ed.). St. Leonards, NSW: Allen & Unwin.

Bullen, E., & Kenway, J. (2004). Subcultural capital and the female "underclass"? A feminist response to an underclass discourse. *Journal of Youth Studies, 7*(2), 141–153.

Bullen, E., & Kenway, J. (2005). Bourdieu, subcultural capital and risky girlhood. *Theory & Research in Education, 3*(1) 47–61.

Burawoy, M., Blum, J. A., George, S., Gille, Z., Gowan, T., Haney, L., ... Thayer, M. (Eds.). (2001). *Global ethnography: Forces, connections, and imaginations in a postmodern world*. Berkeley: University of California Press.

Cohen, R., & Kennedy. P. (2000). *Global sociology*. New York: New York University Press.

Cowlishaw, G. (2004). *Blackfellas, whitefellas and hidden injuries of race*. Oxford, England: Blackwell.

Creed, B. (1993). *Monstrous feminine*. London: Routledge.

Deleuze, G.(1992). *Expressionism in philosophy: Spinoza*. New York: Zone Books.

District Council of Coober Pedy. (2005). Retrieved from http://www.opalcapitaloftheworld.com.au/history.asp

Douglas, M. (1966). *Purity and danger: An analysis of concepts of pollution and taboo*. London: Routledge.

Fairfax Digital. (2005). 'Coober Pedy' *Walkabout Australia travel guide*. Retrieved August 7, 2005 from http://walkabout.fairfax.com.au/theage/locations/SAcooberpedy.shtml

Fox, C. (2000). *Fighting back-the politics of the unemployed in victoria in the great depression*. Melbourne, Australia: Melbourne University Press.

Friend, T. (2005, August 13). "He's been everywhere, man." *The Good Weekend, The Age Magazine*, pp. 20–24.

Gibbs, A. (2001). Contagious feelings: Pauline Hanson and the epidemiology of affect. *Australian Humanities Review*. Retrieved August 7, 2005, from http://www.lib.latrobe.edu.au/AHR/archive/Issue-December-2001

Grosz, E. (1989). *Sexual subversions: Three French feminists*. Sydney, Australia: Allen & Unwin.

Haebich, A. (2001). *Broken circles: Fragmenting indigenous families 1800–2000*. Fremantle, Australia: FACP.

Hickey-Moody, A. C., Windle, J., & Savage, G. (Eds.). (2010). [Special issue, "Pedagogy Writ Large"]. *Critical Studies in Education, 51*(3).

Jones, C., & Novak, T. (1999). *Poverty, welfare and the disciplinary state*. New York: Routledge.

Kenway, J. (2008). Beyond conventional curriculum cartography via a global sense of place. In M. Summerville, K. Power, & P. de Carteret (Eds.), *Landscapes and learning: Place studies for a global world sense publishers* (pp. 195–207). Melbourne, Australia: Melbourne University Press.

Kenway J. (2010). *The education-social class nexus: Beyond methodological nationalism*. Paper presented at the invited symposium, Facing the Interface between Cultural Studies and the Sociology of Education, Australian Association for Research in Education Conference, Melbourne.

Kenway, J., & Fahey, J. (2010). Is greed still good? Was it ever? Exploring the emoscapes of the global financial crisis [Special Issue, "Education Policy and the New Capitalism"]. *Journal of Education Policy, 25*(6), 717–727.

Kenway, J., Kraack, A., & Hickey Moody, A. (2006). *Masculinity beyond the metropolis.* New York: Palgrave Macmillan.

Kristeva, J. (1982). *Powers of horror.* New York: Columbia University Press.

The Lonely Planet. (2005). *Journeys to authentic Australia.* Retrieved from http://www.lonely-planet.com

MacCannell, D. (1999). *The tourist: A new theory of the leisure class.* Berkeley: University of California Press.

Mendes, P. (2003). *Australia's welfare wars: The players, the politics and the ideologies.* Sydney, Australia: UNSW Press.

McClintock, A. (1995). *Imperial leather: Race, gender and sexuality in the colonial contest.* New York: Routledge.

Murray, C. (1990). *The emerging British underclass.* London: IEA Health and Welfare Unit.

Murray, C. (1999). *The underclass revisited.* Retrieved from http://www.aei.org/docLib/20021130_71317.pdf

Nayak, A. (2003). *Race, place and globalization: Youth cultures in a changing world.* Oxford, England: Berg.

Peel, M. (2003). *The lowest rung: Voices of Australian poverty.* Sydney, NSW: Cambridge University Press.

Reynolds, H. (1999). *Why weren't we told?: A personal search for the truth about our history.* Ringwood, Victoria: Penguin.

Sibley, D. (1995). *Geographies of exclusion: Society and difference in the West.* London: Routledge.

The South Australian Tourist Commission. (STAC). Retrieved from http://www.southaustralia.com

Urry, J. (1990). *The tourist gaze.* London: Sage.

Urry, J. (2000). *Sociology beyond societies: Mobilities for the twenty-first century.* New York: Routledge.

Walkabout Australian Travel Guide. (2005). Fairfax digital media. Retrieved from http://walkabout.com.au/index.shtml

9

"BEING MIDDLE CLASS IS NOT ENOUGH"

Social Class, Education, and School Choice in Spain

Antonio Olmedo and Luis Eduardo Santa Cruz

> Class is never more potent and damaging than when inequality is no
> longer explained in its terms, when classed policy is naturalised, becomes
> common sense—when class policy is simply good policy.
>
> *(Ball, 2003b, p. 3)*

This chapter focuses on the changing role of social class and the creation of
strategies of social closure and social segregation in the field of education, as a
result of the implementation of neoliberal policies in Western countries. We are
interested here in the intertwined changing nature of social equity and class,
in the ideological nature of the former and the changing character of the latter.
This traditional discussion within the field of the social sciences has regained
importance during the last two decades. On the one hand, some authors denied
the role of social class as an explanatory variable, viewing it as useful in the past,
but of decreasing relevance at present (Beck, 1992; Clark & Lipset, 1991; Lash
& Urry, 1994). On the other hand, an important body of research has focused
its efforts on showing how the concept still exerts a determining role in the
configuration of social dynamics (Bourdieu, 1986a; Wright, 2000), while suggesting the need for different methodological approaches in order to show the
new ways in which it is working (e.g., Bourdieu, 1986b; Wacquant, 1991). Our
interest rests within this second group and is based on the necessity to contex-
tualize the specific changes and characteristics of the present situation as a way
of unveiling the spheres in which the influence of social class can be detected.
Though we are aware of the need to broaden its definition, we do not pretend
to defend the idea that everything should be explained merely in class terms,
nor that it continues to operate as in the past.

Bourdieu's framework (1986b) is an original approach to the concept of class stressing its *relational* nature. He defines the classes, or the *class situation*, in terms of the proximity of the position of individuals within the *social space*, determined by the amount of accumulated capital (as the sum of different forms: economic, cultural, and social capital). In turn, different positions imply different ways of understanding the structure as a whole and the relations within it, defining different habitus that condition the possibilities for action and response of the individual faced with different situations and problems. Ball's definition sums it up succinctly:

> Class is not the membership of a category or the simple possession of certain capitals or assets. It is an activation of resources and social identities, or rather the interplay of such identities, in specific locations, for particular ends.
>
> *(Ball, 2003a, pp. 175–176)*

Defining class in these terms allows us to introduce new dimensions and ways to approach the chain of mechanisms, reasoning, and decisions that social actors develop, both individually and as a group, in their everyday relationship with the social world. This chapter deals with the strategies and discourses of one specific social group, middle-class families, in relation to their school choices, showing how class still exerts an important role in the functioning of contemporary capitalist societies. On the one hand, analyzing the way in which the "winners" organize and schedule their actions and pathways is important in order to fully understand broader social segregation dynamics. In this sense, our research is aligned with the postulates of positional conflict theory, which represent, as Brown suggests, "an attempt to extend the focus on the monopolistic 'rigging' powers of social elites to include an understanding of how individuals and social groups mobilise their cultural, economic, political or social assets in positional power struggles, whatever form they take" (2000, p. 638).

On the other hand, within the educational field, school choice constitutes one of those significant moments in which social class emerges from the "subterranean levels of meaning of the social world" (Parkin, 1979, p. 3), allowing the social researcher to trace and analyze its inner structure, configuration, and mechanisms. As noted above, the new configuration of Western societies establishes new parameters in the organization of the social structure based on the central role of knowledge, modifying its foundations and the nature of production (Castells, 2000; Morgenstern, 2003). This implies a new perspective from which education becomes a key *positional asset* in the differentiation of individuals (Brown, 2000), retranslating and framing old and new ways of understanding relations in society and defining social groups. Given the centrality of cultural capital as the main differentiating characteristic of this group, middle-class success is based on the use of education as an instrument to guarantee the perpetuation of their privileged position (Ball, 2003a; Van Zanten,

2005). In sum, the centrality of education in the explanation of class differences could be seen as resulting from the "transformation of the system of strategies of reproduction employed by those fractions of the upper and middle classes" (Bourdieu & Boltanski, 1978, p. 198).

Researching School Choice Dynamics at a Local Level: A Qualitative Approach

In Spain, different policies have been implemented progressively during the past 30 years that favor the creation of a neoliberal environment based on "freedom" and "choice." This has had had important effects on the way in which we understand education, redefining the meaning of concepts such as "participation" and "school community" (Olmedo, 2008a). School choice policies were first implemented in the 1980s, with important modifications since then.[1] The 1978 Constitution of Spain acknowledges the right of parents to choose the type of education that they consider most appropriate for their children according to their religious or moral convictions (art. 27.3). Furthermore, the Constitution declares the right of every individual or legal entity to open a school (art. 27.6), and orders the state to assist those public and private schools that meet the minimum requirements established by the legislation (art. 27.9). These constitutional principles provided the groundwork on which further legislation has been built, and form the actual base of the Spanish educational system. As a result, schools are divided into three groups according to their legal ownership and their funding sources. Besides the traditional differentiation between public (state schools) and private (independent) schools, a third type, which we call "subsidized-private schools," has been operating in Spain for more than 40 years. In this third case, the ownership is private, although the school receives the majority of its economic resources directly from the state, in order to develop compulsory and, occasionally, noncompulsory education. In order to be eligible to obtain state funding,[2] these schools have to follow the national curriculum and participate in the same enrolment plan as the public schools.

The regulation of school choice and enrolment criteria was first introduced by the socialist party in 1985. They created a system of scales to regulate school enrolment in all state-funded schools (both public and subsidized-private schools) in cases where the number of applicants exceeds the number of places available.[3] These scales have changed considerably during the past 25 years, and are now under the control of the regional governments, necessitating individual analysis in each of the 17 regions and two autonomous cities that constitute Spain. In broad terms, the national legislation sets the main criteria that all regional entities must follow: siblings/parents already enrolled/working in the school; proximity of the family home or the parents' workplace to the school; family annual income; and student disability or disability of any other family member. But, as mentioned above, every region may individually interpret the criteria, assign values to each item, or even include new ones.

Analysis of the evolution of the legislation developed by both the socialist and the conservative parties suggests that the state is becoming less active in its role of compensating for potential initial inequalities arising out of social, cultural, and economic differences in the population (Fernández Esquinas, 2004; Fernández Soria, 2007). For instance, the school enrolment scales initially favored those families with fewer resources, giving them priority of choice, whereas in subsequent legislation, this trend has given way to other variables, such as proximity to home or the workplace of either parent (Escardíbul & Villarroya, 2009). All the previous elements, together with a policy of extending the schools' catchment areas so as to widen families' potential choices, and the creation of information tools on the operation and results of the schools (standardized tests published in the media, awards for improved quality, etc.), constitute the foundations of the Spanish quasi-market in education (Calero, 1998).

This new situation transfers responsibility for the educational processes and results from the state to other actors, primarily the families, which take on greater responsibility for their children's progress. The change in the role of the state (Jessop, 2002) is a result of the introduction of new forms of governance; what Rose and Miller call "governing at a distance" (1992, p. 173) or what Rhodes defines as "governance without government" (1996, p. 658). This has led to a reappraisal of the nature of our study, situating the family at the center of the creation of social reproduction dynamics mentioned above.

In this chapter we analyze the strategies and discourses of a group of Spanish middle-class families in a local education market. Although our methodological design was mixed, comprising both quantitative and qualitative methods, the analysis and quotes given here are taken from a subgroup of 32 semistructured interviews from the whole sample.[4] The selected families fulfilled the following conditions: occupational group[5] and at least one of the parents having a university education. A twin-axis internal division was later generated with the aim of assisting during the process of analyzing the interviews. First, families were classified according to the types of school chosen for their children (public, independent-private, or subsidized-private schools). Second, we resituated both the educational and occupational levels of the parents. At this stage, the families were divided into three types: first, a group in which cultural capital is predominant, where both parents are professional people with a university education to degree level or beyond; the second group was composed of families with a predominance of economic capital, mainly administrative personnel and managers or professionals, where only one parent had a university education; finally, the third group was a mixed group with predominance of both types of capital, mainly consisting of managers or professionals with a university education.

In the next sections, we will focus on the importance given by these families to the process of school choice, and the ways in which it relates to the creation and mobilization of a number of social closure strategies developed by this group of parents with the aim of ensuring the reproduction of their social position.

Making the "Imagined Futures" Come True: Education, Education, Education

In the current landscape, school choice emerges as "a major new factor in maintaining and indeed reinforcing social-class divisions and inequalities" (Gerwirtz, Ball, & Bowe, 1995, p. 23). This apparently straightforward affirmation gains strength throughout the analysis of the middle-class parents' discourse in relation to their choices, which were carefully and scrupulously planned in all of our cases. In these middle-class households, school choice takes shape through the creation of strategies and constant control and monitoring of the children with one specific purpose: positioning them as best as possible to reproduce the social position of their parents. These families are aware that class privilege is not transmitted automatically (Lareau & McNamara, 1999), being equally conscious of the necessity for their intervention to maximize the possibilities of maintaining their class position (Allatt, 1993). As Ball puts it, they know that "being middle class is not an absolute guarantee of success" (2003a, p. 92), and, therefore, they are "forced" to find new ways of keeping their positional advantage, mobilizing their capital to "maximize" their children's opportunities in the educational field. Their actions could be seen as what Bourdieu and Boltanski defined as "strategies of reconversion"; that is, "the sum of the actions and reactions by which each group tries to maintain or change its position in the social structure or, more precisely, to maintain its position by changing" (1978, p. 220). This positional struggle situates education as a vital field for class reproduction and school choice as one of the key processes through which class strategies become visible.

The introduction of school choice policies redefines the concept of parenting itself. This is clear in the case of the middle-class families because they are forced to face new challenges and develop novel strategies, which leads to high anxiety levels (Lucey & Reay, 2002). As our interviewees explain, parenting nowadays implies an important responsibility, because their children's future depends to a great extent upon their decisions and strategies. Carolina, for instance, feels responsible both in personal and social terms because she believes that her children are meant to be the "future rulers of society":

> We feel responsible about having two children that you are going to let go out into this world. These children are going to be part of a generation that will rule the country, that will rule everything, isn't it? And I think

that it is our responsibility to contribute to this world by raising people that are the best prepared as possible in the widest sense (…) you need to give what for you is essential (…) the best possible education. (Carolina)

Achieving the highest educational level becomes the central objective. This is clear in the percentage of students in higher education in terms of their social background. According to Feito (2010), among young adults between 20 and 24 years old, 65% of the children of managerial and professional families attend university after compulsory education. The figures fall to 35% in the case of those from the intermediate classes, 20% of the qualified workforce, 14% of manual workers, and 9% of agricultural workers' children. Fully aware of the *positional* significance of education, these middle-class parents have no hesitation about the correct pathway that their children should follow:

> I want them to be something in this life, and it is very clear for them that their life as students is not only to go to school, but also to the university. We just want to take them to the position where they can choose later.… And, what is the best way for you to have a very good job in the future that allows you to choose the type of life that you want? A very good education! (Laura)

The effect of social class emerges in the definition and implementation of these "imagined futures" (Ball, Macrae, & Maguire, 1999), as these families make explicit the ideal that they both consciously and unconsciously have in mind. Their habitus defines the horizon of options and pathways, situating education as the door to future success and happiness. Maria's words below are a clear example of the distribution of social positions in the social space (Bourdieu, 1986a). She conceptualizes "being educated" as being able to make the "right choices":

> I think that education implies everything. It is mainly about knowing what to choose … I mean … choosing what to eat, choosing a good book, choosing your partner … you are not going to choose in the same way if you are one way or the other, do you? (…) So, it is everything and it is going … to … [affect] the rest of your life. (Maria)

Making the right choices has far-reaching consequences for establishing their children's middle-class identity. The effect of such personal choices configures an unconscious sense of natural closeness to specific individuals. These choices create "filters," based on everyday decisions and activities that help children to differentiate between their "equals" and "the others." The parents' discourse clearly shows their preoccupation with developing a singularity regarding their position. "Marking" their children as distinctive from "others" is as important as connecting them to their equals (described as "normal"). In order to do so, they are conscious of the need to explore and experience other social realities, but within calculated limits and avoiding the risks of possible misidentifications from either below or above:

> I want them to be with people like them, normal.... I want them to learn how to treat everybody, but I want them to be with people like them, with their same problems. This doesn't mean that I am not going to let them have friends or be with all kinds of people, but not eight hours in the school! I mean ... for example, I would never put my daughters in a public school in Almanjáyar [an impoverished area in the city], because they are not going to feel located ... because maybe their problems are not going to be the same as those ones that other children could have. These girls were lucky to be born in a family that can give them 5 and the other children were unlucky to be born in a family that only can give them 1. Well, the result is that my daughter shouldn't feel bad because she hasn't chosen it, but was born ... but anyway when they finish they will need to fight for what they want, you know? They are not going to inherit a big fortune ... but I am going to give them whatever I can now. But ... I don't want them also to go to the school of prince Felipe, you know? It is the same, the prince has 10 and mine 5, so I don't think that they need to be with children whose biggest hope is to ride a horse or to go to ski in Saint Moritz, because mine cannot do it. (Laura)

The strategies that Laura's words suggest, relate to the Weberian concept of social closure and are clear examples of what Parkin defined as "exclusionary closure"; that is, "a form of collective social action which, intentionally or otherwise, gives rise to a social category of ineligibles or outsiders" (1979, p. 45). These are "legal" strategies of "aggregation," social barriers, which contribute to the creation of "educational reservoirs" that contribute to broader social exclusion dynamics. Education constitutes the wall that separates their children from the children of others, and this is, in their opinion, the best heritage that their parents could pass on to them. It is an investment that can lead to all sorts of available capitals but one that guarantees profits:

> I am not thinking of buying a flat for my children. They should get it by themselves, in the same way that I did. But I am going to try hard for them to have a good education that would allow them to do it. It is like that advertisement that said: "if you give him a fish, he will eat just that day, show him how to fish!" I am going to teach them how to fish: "Do you need private classes? Take them. Do you need a tutor to pass math at the university? Here it is. But you have to do the rest of it. I mean, it is an expenditure, but, thanks to God, I get it back. (Julio)

Helping their children is synonymous with getting them a good education, which implies not only academic knowledge but also the development of certain capacities and competences that will be valued by future employers.

Although, because of space limitations, we are not dealing in depth here with internal differences between the subgroups within these middle-class families, the parents with higher cultural capital tend to emphasize more vigorously the relationship between educational success and future success in the labor market (Devine, 2004). The "person as a whole," as Carolina expressed it above, becomes the "entitled worker" for Jose:

> Somebody with a degree goes up. It doesn't matter if he is good or bad professionally; he has a degree. And this is what society demands today, "degree-itis." The private companies demand "degree-itis," and also experience. But, clearly, you are not going to have experience without the degree. So, to start working you need a degree ... a degree from the university. This was very clear for me. (Jose)

This father's discourse is clearly aligned with human capital theories. Moreover, school choice is for them an entangled mixture of personal feelings and rational calculation (Boudon, 2003). Though they face an active reflection process, the emotional dimension plays a very important role (Hatcher, 1998). The chosen school should fulfill some objective criteria, as explained in the next section, but, most importantly, it needs to feel good as Enrique and Marina suggest below. We compared elsewhere the process of choosing a school with that of "buying shoes for everyday use" (Olmedo, 2008b), where quality should guarantee a reasonable durability through time but also a minimum of comfort needed to be useful in consecutive and multiple everyday situations. Price is one indicator of such desired quality and comfort but not necessarily a guarantee. The parents know that paying at that specific school, though it might imply making substantial financial efforts, could assure success and prevent potential failure (Ball, 2003a), and, also, it adds a distinctive character to their choices. Enrique and Marina clearly exemplify this mixture of emotions, rational calculation, and imagined future and expectations that we have been relating above:

E: I think that we thought once about it [changing to a public school] for economic reasons, because we were economically overwhelmed and we couldn't ... we were very sad thinking that for economic reasons we couldn't. But, finally, we managed to tighten our belts and keep our children in the private school.

M: It is mainly that you choose between investing in a better car, better holidays, better house, or a second or third house, better trips ... or you invest in something that, for us, is the best investment that you can do for your children. I mean, you could leave them fifty millions in a current account ... but at the end it is just money. Otherwise, if you make an effort and invest in your kids, in an integrated education, I think that it is more valuable for them in the long run.... So when that person goes to the labor market, apart from all the knowledge, they are going to value all that. So, this is our investment. (Enrique and Marina)

It is important to point out the different emphasis given to that investment in relation to the predominant form of capital in specific families. In line with Van Zanten (2003), those parents who send their children to private schools tend to emphasize the economic character of their investment, while those who opt for public schools do so through their cultural capital, especially by helping their children themselves while they study at home. In the second case, the investment is seen as their main responsibility and implies taking some risks consciously and in a controlled way (Beck, 2002). The families that detect any trace of possible "failure" reinforce their current investment not only in economic terms but also in terms of their presence and dedication:

> Well! Knowing that the academic level was going to damage my daughters, I was always there, trying to help in everything I could. Look, we organized, for example, English lessons for all the children from the parents' association. I remember that we hired a native speaker teacher, well, he was already my English teacher at that time. (Ángel)

The success of this process of transmission of privileges depends on success at school, but also on control over and correct choice in other dimensions of their children's lives. While the parents can control some school conditions, it is more difficult for them to do so over the socialization process of their children. In this sense, social reproduction is not the absolute responsibility of the parents, nor can it be achieved by them alone. The school must also become involved in the process, helping the children to gradually acquire the skills necessary to complete the "reproduction cycle" (Allatt, 1993). In this sense, to consummate the privileged situation with which middle-class children start off, these parents will need to work together with the school for the children to become personally committed to their preconceived plan. Home is defined as "a second place for schooling" (Ball, 2003b), a place where Bernstein's "invisible pedagogies" ferment. For that reason, it will be crucial that the specific culture of the chosen school is attuned to the family project:

> And I thought: "they [the teachers] almost know my child better than I do" … then, with all the information that I got from them, and knowing his weak points, it is much easier. We are in constant communication and with small targets we are getting the most out of every child. (Maite)

> And that's how I'm bringing them up and, since I'm bringing them up like that, I want the education I'm giving them here [at home], to carry on in the other place, where they spend seven hours a day. Because if I'm giving them an education and at school it's different and then he gets something else from his friends, well the child gets all mixed up. What I want is the same both at home and at school…. As I told you before, we have laid down the foundations. And we wanted that foundation to carry on in the school we chose for our children. (Juan)

This necessary connection between the families and school in the creation and development of processes of social closure highlights the existing relationships between the individuals and institutions within the social structure. It raises interesting questions about the relation between agency and social reproduction, which, as suggested in the next section, takes shape in these families' decisions about the schooling process of their children.

Looking for the "Right School": The Role of Instrumental and Expressive Orders

The analysis of the tools and aspects that are valued when searching and choosing the desired school unveils hidden mechanisms of social reproduction. Given their accumulated level of cultural and social capital, middle-class parents are in a privileged position to make the right choices because they are better prepared and have more means with which to "work the system" (Ball et al., 1999). Finding the right school implies an intense process of calculation and, as Lucey and Reay put it, a "great deal of social, cultural and psychic work" (2002, p. 334). Working the system implies a significant degree of knowledge about its operation and organization on the formal and political levels (understanding the limits and possibilities in the legislation) and at the local level (information on specific schools). There are different sources of information that these parents are able to mobilize in order to inform their choices. On the one hand, they have access to different sources of official knowledge, which consists of government and school documents; for example, in the form of test scores, league tables, and publicity. This is what Ball and Vincent (1998) identified as "cold knowledge," a set of resources and data created to inform and give account of the progress of the educational system and the schools. To be processed and put into play, this type of knowledge requires certain specific skills, determined by the parents' level of cultural capital, and both the confidence and ability to deal with official institutions, which might not be accessible to families from less educated social classes:

> Then, well, I went to the Regional Government office in Granada to gather some information about the school: the percentage of passes and fails, etcetera.... And I found that it had even received awards! It had extraordinary prizes! All that made me make the decision. (Rocío)

On the other hand, the social networks in which these middle-class parents are involved give them access to a full body of additional information on the operation of the system and the schools that will be crucial in decision making. Each of these networks "works through and is animated by story-telling, rumour and gossip," and represents "a collective attempt to make sense of the locality and particular features within it (in this case, schools)" (Ball & Vincent, 1998, p. 379). The existence of "rumor circuits" formed around this group is crucial in the transmission of important information based on experience by other families with similar concerns. This is understood as "hot knowledge" (Ball & Vincent, 1998) and it is especially valued and useful when contextualizing the official information provided by the schools and institutions, which lacks the emotional component pursued by middle-class families. In this sense, the combination of cultural and social capital assets are crucial components in the elaboration of social closure dynamics that will help this group of parents maintain their advantage in the field.

> The information came from my colleagues. All of them, or almost all of them, were sending their children there. Then I asked if they were happy about it and they were! In general this is the information I gathered. I also knew some teachers, more as friends, right? I think they are serious people. That school had very hardworking teachers and the atmosphere is very good, which is also important. (Pilar)

The information that circulates through the grapevine helps the family to identify the connection between their own needs and the school's educational project. As Bourdieu and Passeron state (1977), the existence of such connections will ease their children's passage through the educational system and to a large extent guarantee their success. This requires the identification and evaluation of the schools around the *instrumental* and the *expressive orders* (Bernstein, 1977). The *instrumental* order relates to awareness of the importance of educational progress (discussed above) and obtaining the qualifications and credentials that permit access to further stages (Olmedo & Santa Cruz, 2008). Academic success is seen as a strategy developed by the middle classes as a defense against the uncertainty and anxieties generated by the functioning and the configuration of the system (Lucey & Reay, 2002). As Devine (2004) points out, these families know that their children are "well-equipped academically," but they still need an environment where they feel academically challenged and where teachers are successful in making them internalize those competitive values. It is at this point where the *expressive* order plays a decisive role (Olmedo & Santa Cruz, 2010). In this sense, a particular school is measured by the academic results of its pupils and the existence and effectiveness of mechanisms of internalization of the "habitus that will lead them to success, in competition with children who have not had these advantages" (Jordan, Redley, & James, 1994, p. 142). Given their constant insecurity and fear of failure, academic results are a key characteristic that gives the schools a certain social prestige and reputation and contributes to consolidating their process of "distinction" and "active differentiation."

> That's why I wanted a school with a reputation, that was known to have social status and, as well, had results, statistically speaking, with few failures as against passes in June, when *Selectividad* [A-levels] come round. (Elsa)

And not only the academic level.... Although the school was new, it still had the prestige of the schools in this company. And, well, we decided that the kids should go there and it was a pretty good decision. (Tito)

This search for high academic standards could take the parents to the limit in some cases. Elisa, for instance, found herself with a difficult dilemma when she discovered that the environment in which the family was living at that time because of her job could not offer the ideal conditions for her child's intellectual development. A decision was taken and the new situation forced her to drive daily for more than 2 hours a day to get to her job in the village, as she explains:

I was a teacher appointed in Periana [village], and they [her children] came with me. There was only one school there, a public school. Then, my son Pablo did all his primary education in that school. We had no other option, it was what it was. When he finished primary school, at 6th grade, we decided that the school had become [too] small for us. We also saw some hints in the boy. He was very studious, read a lot, and he liked it ... he was studying and got always very good marks with little effort. Then I decided to go back to the city [to live] and travel to Periana every day ... in order to keep Pablo in Granada already where the standards were higher, because in the public schools the standards are always influenced by the type of students that attend them. (Elisa)

A prestigious school should therefore guarantee good results, promoting and urging its pupils not to accept prospects beneath their capabilities but to aim for the highest positions that their personal and family potential allows. It should set mechanisms that help its students to internalize a specific culture: the culture of competition. This point clearly exemplifies the intimate relationship between the *instrumental* and *expressive* orders:

One teacher told me once, and it is true!, when you see kids talking in the street, youngsters of 18 or 19 years old, you can tell instantly which school they attended. My son told me that even he knows. When he goes out with his friends he says: "Dad, I go to talk to my friends (the ones that are not from the school) and they tell me: "Shit! All of you from Agustinos [subsidized-private school] and Maristas [subsidized-private school] are always saying the same thing: I got a nine [out of ten] and could have got a ten! I got a seven and could have got an eight!" In the public schools, instead, they say: "Shit! I passed" or "I failed three subjects." I mean, the way they see their education is different in some schools than others. For some of them a five [pass] is heaven, while for others a seven is not enough. And I want to bring up my children in this way. (Jose)

According to these families, the social prestige of the school is related to the type of population that it enrolls. School choice policies encourage the internal homogeneity of schools in social terms by increasing the possibility of children from the area attending the same local schools.[6] Considering that distribution in cities corresponds to homogeneous socioeconomic profiles, we can observe that such school choice policies serve to draw a particular social class to a specific area, more than other dynamics traditionally considered as segregationist (Van Zanten, 2005). The *instrumental* and *expressive* orders converge here once more, as Marcos explains:

> Well! I think that, if the parents have studied [i.e., have a college degree], the quality and the level of the class, with some few exceptions, are higher than in those ones where the parents don't have any degree.... I am not saying they should all be the children of professors, not at all, but that I would like that my children have friends who are children of people that … I mean, whose parents have studied and have knowledge. And, of course this influenced me! I have been teaching for 25 years and, my god! I know that the children of teachers, or doctors, lawyers, vets, etc., are generally 100% better in school than [the children of] those without education. (Marcos)

This is an important dimension of their social closure strategies resulting in the direct or indirect exclusion of other social groups. These parents filter schools as they search for those where they find "people like us," as Maria puts it. In this respect, private education appears as a "refuge," thanks to the ease of control over their children's school environment and a certain degree of pupil selection according to social class. There is an initial conviction that families from the same class will share the same habitus, which implies a similar set of values as well as a common trajectory and prospects.

> And you do have some statistics: "How many children in public schools have a moped in high school?" Well, surely about 80%. If you go to a religious school it is only 30%. Why? Well, simply because the parents there say: "You being 18 years old don't need to have a moped; neither have I to buy it for you, so I won't buy it; and, if I do buy it, it is because you deserve it." I mean, in the public schools, in almost all of them … a building worker or a plumber makes more money than a doctor, because this is the reality. And, then, they lack what others like ourselves fortunately had … then they say: "Since, as a child, I didn't have this and that, I want my children to have it...." And they are buying stuff for their children who are 16 or 17. So what is happening? It is that the education, the scale of values that we have is different … this is the one that we [people from our class]want to give to our children in the other schools. (Miguel)

Families with sufficient economic capital to make the "investment" can avail themselves of private education, thus guaranteeing an initial filter based on the economic resources of the families of their children's companions:

I'm going to say something terrible here, because it's not like that, but the friends my son can find in that school are different from the friends he'd have in other schools. The social class is different and I ... if my son can have a friend whose father is a doctor, well, listen, it's a harsh thing to say, but I prefer.... Listen, I don't mean that I'm ... a builder's son is great, but socially different than a doctor's son. If they're both nice people I don't care which friend he has, if they're nice people, but, normally, he has more chance of having a future relation with a doctor's son than with a builder's. If I need, for example, to go to hospital to a specialist and it just happens that the father of one of my son's friends is a surgeon, well, in a selfish way, I think it's better for me than if my son's friend's father is a builder, because I won't need to use that contact. That's the way it is. The friendship my son might have is completely different from the relationship he could have in a public school, normally. (Juan)

These words emphatically speak for themselves and, hence, do not need further comments. For this reason, we stop deliberately at this specific point and reconsider some of our initial assumptions in the light of these final pieces of discourse.

Concluding ... or Opening New Starting Points?

Well, I am saying this from an advantageous perspective because I think that in my children's school the standards are higher. Obviously there are others that are left behind. But my children are not behind because they have always been very good students and because I kept an eye on them. And if the level goes higher ... it always happens, doesn't it? If you demand too much, if the level is high, there are always people left behind. There is no other choice. (Pilar)

The final aim is not only to get the "best" for one's own children. The "best" implies "being above" or "gaining advantage over" others, with a constant dialectic process occurring between principles of social justice, a certain concept of "fairness" and ideal equity on the one hand, and the ideas of individualism and competition, on the other. As Kohn (1998) suggests:

It isn't just that these parents are *ignoring* everyone else's children, focusing their efforts solely on giving their own children the most desirable education. Rather, they are in effect *sacrificing* other children to their own. It's not about success but victory, not about responding to a competitive environment but creating one. (p. 572)

Therefore, against the one-sided criticism of the school, which is made principally responsible for the dynamics of social exclusion, we should also place the action of the families, as political actors in decision-making processes, fomented by the implementation of market policies in education. From this position it is important to avoid adopting a substantialist view, as described by Bourdieu (1998), that does not consider the influence of aspects indirectly related to the process, such as the presence of different habitus making up expectations and trajectories that are in turn different, or the role of social class and other variables concerning gender, race, or ethnicity. As suggested by Gewirtz and her colleagues (1995), this substantialism is the one found in studies based on a "list of factors focus," that consider parents only as rational actors. As we have shown, the "'reasons' are ambiguous" and the meanings are "contextually specific" (Gewirtz et al., 1995, p. 7). The parents' actions will change and be defended from different positions depending on the different situations their children find themselves in throughout their education. Various factors, such as a particular methodology, insistence on exams, discipline and values, personalized attention or heterogeneity in the children's class are ambiguous reasons that are used differently according to the specific circumstances faced by these families. Their advantage over the rest resides in the balance of their different types of capital but this does not guarantee them successful outcomes. Throughout our interviews, we also encountered some "discontent" with the operation of the system, specifically among parents whose children are having some problems during their educational trajectory. These situations represent an interesting future line of research. The study of such families' reactions to situations of failure can offer an important insight regarding the social reproduction mechanisms of the middle classes.

In short, we would like to stress at this point that, even though the research on school choice has increased during the last decade in Spain, the lack of qualitative approaches is significant, not allowing us to explain the different rationalities, discourses, and imaginaries that different actors involved in the process are developing in order to make their choices. The valuation of schools by these middle-class families indicates the need to consider the influences and possible effects of school choice more broadly, as part of more profound dynamics in search of "distinction" and the reproduction of the social position of certain groups. Educational policies thus represent an opportunity for the state to mediate and control such dynamics. This requires knowledge of the strategies and instruments the various actors are putting to use with specific ends and results that are not always desirable for the equity of the system. So, through the creation of quasi-markets in education, as is the case in Spain, if we obviate the actions and development of strategies by middle-class families, we shall thereby be empowering new mechanisms for the transmission of privilege and the creation of inequality.

Notes

1   Due to space limitations, we will not analyze the Spanish legislation on school choice, school funding, and management here. For a more detailed discussion of the implementation and

effect of those policies see Bonal (1995), Calero and Bonal (1999), Olmedo (2008a), and Villarroya and Escardíbul (2008).

2 The funds would cover both the cost of the teachers' salaries and other costs derived from school budget needs. And both the number of teachers and the amount of those expenses will be calculated as a function of the number of "units" (complete classrooms) in each course.

3 The most relevant aspects in these first scales were annual family income (favoring families with lower incomes) and the proximity of the family home to the school. Less important were other variables, such as siblings attending the school and other complementary criteria (returning emigrant families, disability of student or family member, large families, and a single point awarded at the school's discretion for "objective criteria").

4 This is part of a broader research project founded by the Spanish Ministry of Education (I+D Program) during the period 2006 to 2010. The codification and analysis methods are based on the analytical procedures proposed by grounded theory (Strauss & Corbin, 1998). In order to facilitate the various processes and analyses, the interviews were transcribed and the NVivo 8 software program was used for the codification and generation of trees of categories and diagrams resulting from the analysis.

5 The selected parents belonged to the managerial and professional categories of the ISCO-88 international classification.

6 Interesting research has been conducted in Spain analyzing variables related to the demographic and geographical distribution of the population of different types of schools. The more relevant variables that arise when trying to explain segregation dynamics are social class and the percentage of immigrants in schools. See, for example, Pérez and González Balletbó (2007), and Alegre, Benito, and González (2010).

References

Allatt, P. (1993). Becoming privileged. The role of family processes. In I. Bates & G. Riseborough (Eds.), *Youth and Inequality* (pp. 139–159). Buckingham, England: Open University Press.

Alegre, M. Á., Benito, R., & González, I. (2010). Measures and determinants of student body socioeconomic diversity: Evidence from Spain. *Journal of School Choice, 4*(1), 23–46.

Ball, S. J. (2003a). *Class strategies and the education market: The middle classes and social advantage.* London: Routledge Falmer.

Ball, S. J. (2003b). *The more things change...: Educational research, social class and "interlocking" inequalities.* London: Institute of Education, University of London.

Ball, S. J., Macrae, S., & Maguire, M. (1999). Young lives, diverse choices and imagined futures in an education and training market. *International Journal of Inclusive Education, 3*(3), 195–224.

Ball, S. J., & Vincent, C. (1998). I heard it on the grapevine: "Hot" knowledge and school choice. *British Journal of Sociology of Education, 19*(3), 377–400.

Beck, U. (1992). *Risk society: Towards a new modernity.* London: Sage.

Beck, U. (2002). *Libertad o Capitalismo* [Liberty and capitalism]. Barcelona, Spain: Paidós.

Bernstein, B. (1977). *Class, codes and control* (rev. ed., Vol 3). London: Routledge & Kegan Paul.

Bonal, X. (1995). Curriculum change as a form of educational policy legitimation: The case of Spain. *International Studies in Sociology of Education, 5*(2), 203–220.

Boudon, R. 2003. Beyond rational choice theory. *Annual Review of Sociology, 29*, 1–21.

Bourdieu, P. (1986a). *Distinction: A social critique of the judgement of taste.* London: Routledge.

Bourdieu, P. (1986b). The forms of capital. In J. Richardson (Ed.), *Handbook of theory and research for the sociology of education* (pp. 241–258). New York: Greenwood.

Bourdieu, P. (1998). *The practical reason.* Cambridge, England: Polity Press.

Bourdieu, P., & Boltanski, L. (1978). Changes in social structure and changes in the demand for education. In S. Giner & S. Archer (Eds.), *Contemporary Europe. Social structures and cultural patterns* (pp. 197–227). London: Routledge & Kegan Paul.

Bourdieu P., & Passeron, J. C. (1977). *Reproduction in education, society and culture.* London: Sage.

Brown. (2000). The globalisation of positional competition? *Sociology, 34*(4), 633–653.

Calero, J. (1998). *Una Evaluación de los Cuasimercados como Instrumento de Mejora para la Reforma del Sector Público* [An evaluation of the quasi-market using instruments of growth in order to reform the public sector]. Bilbao, Spain: Fundación BBV.

Calero, J., & Bonal, X. (1999). *Política Educativa y Gasto Público en Educación* [Educational policy and the public cost of education]. Barcelona, Spain: Ediciones Pomares-Corredor.

Castells, M. (2000). *La Era de la Información: Vol.1. La Sociedad Red* [The information age: The networking society] (2nd ed.). Madrid, Spain: Alianza Editorial.

Clark, T., & Lipset, S. (1991). Are social classes dying? *International Sociology, 6*(4), 397–410.

Devine, F. (2004). *Class practices. How parents help their children get good jobs.* Cambridge, England: Cambridge University Press.

Escardíbul, J. O., & Villaroya, A. (2009). The inequalities in school choice in Spain in accordance with PISA data. *Journal of Education Policy, 24*(6), 673–696.

Feito, R. (2010). Democracia educativa frente a segregación y racismo en una época de crisis económica [Democratic education in the face of segregation and racism in a period of economic crisis]. *Revista de la Asociación de Sociología de la Educación, 3*(1), 20–40.

Fernández Esquinas, M. (2004). Elección de escuela: Efectos sociales y dilemas en el sistema educativo público en Andalucía [School choice: Social effects and dilemmas in the public education system in Andalucia]. *Revista de Educación, 334*, 377–390.

Fernández Soria, J. M. (2007). Igualdad y libertad de elección de centro docente: un cuestión polémica para un acuerdo necesario [Equality and freedom of school choice: A polemical question essential for agreement]. *Revista de Educación, 344*, 41–59.

Gewirtz, S., Ball, S. J., & Bowe, R. (1995). *Markets, choice and equity in education.* Buckingham, England: Open University Press.

Hatcher, R. (1998). Class differentiation in education: Rational choices? *British Journal of Sociology of Education, 19*(1), 5–24.

Jessop (2002). *The future of the capitalist state.* Cambridge, England: Polity Press.

Jordan, B., Redley, M., & James, S. (1994). *Putting the family first. Identities, decisions and citizenship.* London: University College London Press.

Kohn, A. (1998). Only for *my* kid. How privileged parents undermine school reform. *Phi Delta Kappan, 79*(8), 569–577.

Lash, S. & Urry, J. (1994). *Economies of signs and space.* London: Sage.

Lareau, A., & McNamara, E. (1999). Moments of social inclusion and exclusion: Race, class and cultural capital in family-school relationships. *Sociology of Education, 72*(1), 37–53.

Lucey, H., & Reay, D. (2002). Carrying the beacon of excellence: Social class, differentiation and anxiety at a time of transition. *Journal of Education Policy, 17*(3), 321–336.

Morgenstern, S. (2003). La crisis de la sociedad salarial y las políticas de formación de la fuerza de trabajo [The crisis of a salaried society and the politics of forming a powerful labor movement]. *Témpora, 3*, 279–306.

Olmedo, A. (2008a). De la Participación Democrática a la Elección de Centro: las Bases del Cuasimercado en la Legislación Educativa Español [On democratic participation in general elections: The basis for the quasi-market in Spanish educational legislation]. *Archivos Analíticos de Políticas Educativas, 16*(21), 1–32.

Olmedo, A. (2008b). Middle-class families and school choice: Freedom versus equity in the context of a "local education market." *European Educational Research Journal, 7*(2), 176–194.

Olmedo, A., & Santa Cruz, E. (2008). Las Familias de Clase Media y Elección de Centro: el Orden Instrumental como Condición Necesaria pero no Suficiente [Middle class families and freedom of choice]. *Profesorado. Revista de Curriculum y Formación del Profesorado, 12*(2), 1–31.

Olmedo, A., & Santa Cruz, E. (2010). El proceso de valoración de los centros educativos por parte de las familias de clase media: el papel del orden expresivo en la búsqueda de la "distinción." [The process of valorizing school choice for middle class families]. *Papers: Revista de Sociología, 96*(2), 515–537.

Parkin, F. (1979). *Marxism and class theory: A bourgeois critique.* London: Tavistock.

Pérez, R. B., & González Balletbó, I. (2007). *Políticas de acceso escolar y equidad educativa: Un análisis de la incidencia de la zonificación sobre la segregación escolar* [The politics of school access and equality in education: An analysis of the role of zoning in school segregation]. Paper presented at the ninth Congreso Español de Sociología.

Rhodes, R. A. W. (1996). The new governance: Governing without government. *Political Studies, 44*, 652–667.

Rose, N., & Miller, P. (1992). Political power beyond the state: Problematics of government. *The British Journal of Sociology, 43*(2), 173–205.

Strauss, A., & Corbin, J. (1998). *Basics of qualitative research: Techniques and procedures for developing grounded theory* (2nd ed.). Thousand Oaks, CA: Sage.

Van Zanten, A. (2003). Middle-class parents and social mix in French urban schools: Reproduction and transformation of class relations in education. *International Studies in Sociology of Education, 13*(2), 107–123.

Van Zanten, A. (2005). New modes of reproducing social inequality in education: The changing role of parents, teachers, schools and educational policies. *European Educational Research Journal, 4*(3), 155–169.

Villarroya, A., & Escardíbul, J. O. (2008). Políticas públicas y posibilidades efectivas de elección de centro en la enseñanza no universitaria en España [Public policy and the likelihood of actual school choice in higher education in Spain]. *Profesorado, 12*(2), 1–26.

Wacquant, L. J. D. (1991). Making class: The middle class(es) in social theory and social structure. In S. G. McNall, R. F. Levine, & R. Fantasia (Eds.), *Bringing class back in: Contemporary and historical perspectives* (pp. 39–64). Boulder, CO: Westview Press.

Wright, E. O. (2000). *Class count: Comparative studies in class analysis.* Cambridge, England: Cambridge University Press.

10

EDUCATING SUPRANATIONAL CITIZENS

The Incorporation of English Language Education into Curriculum Policies[1]

Yun-Kyung Cha and Seung-Hwan Ham

Introduction

English language education is now a global phenomenon. The transnational diffusion of policy discourses on English language education across non-English-speaking countries deserves close scholarly attention from various theoretical frameworks so as to further understanding of the relationship between globalization and education. While the importance of providing schoolchildren with English language education has been widely acknowledged in the context of an increasingly globalized world (Crystal, 2003; Grabe, 1988), a range of critical perspectives has also evolved that problematizes the global dominance of English and its impact on the individual and society at multiple levels (Pennycook, 1998; Phillipson, 1992; Tsuda, 1999). Considering that the rise of English as the most dominant international language undergirds today's global clamor for teaching and learning English, the institutionalization of English language education around the world constitutes a key and critical topic that must be explored in relation to the larger global context, a context that brings about both new hopes and fears about the possibility of equitable distribution of power and opportunity not only within countries but also internationally.

In this chapter, we investigate the cross-national institutionalization of English as a regular school subject over the past century and discuss how the rise of English as a global language in today's curricular policy models around the world reflects an expansive conception of supranational citizenship that emphasizes the empowerment of the individual in global society. We also extend our discussion to the possible problem that the discursive rationalization of English language education as an indispensable tool to help children become supranational citizens can also lead to the legitimation of some new forms of social inequality both within and across countries, especially if curricular policies on English language education are not accompanied by sustained and shared efforts to constantly identify and minimize their unintended consequences.

In recent decades, English has been widely depicted as a useful medium of international communication in various spheres of society. The often-used categories of the developing and the developed do not appear so meaningful when considering the perceived importance of this language in many different countries. In such a global context, English language education has emerged as an important policy issue that "needs to be taken into account in its language policy by any nation-state" (Spolsky, 2004, p. 91). Although the rise of the United States as the world's superpower after World War II seems to have facilitated the rapid diffusion of English language education across national education systems, the association between English and some particular Western cultures, if it still exists, is becoming much weaker today.[2] Despite challenges from other languages, English is not only the most frequently used language in various international agencies and transnational companies; it is also widely seen as the most useful language for accessing information and scientific findings (Crystal, 2003; Grabe, 1988).[3]

Of course, such usefulness of English seems to be an important factor driving countries to promote the language in their education systems. Enhancing the English proficiency of future citizens has, in many countries, been conceived as a vital means for promoting national development, especially in the context of an increasingly integrated global economy. However, it is also important to understand that the virtues of providing English language education to schoolchildren have been taken for granted in most national education systems, despite varying degrees of actual utility of English depending on country-specific societal needs. Educational researchers and policymakers in non-English-speaking countries decry limited opportunities for schoolchildren to learn this foreign language, but the taken-for-granted nature of its usefulness tends to make scholars devote relatively little effort to reaching a deeper understanding of the macrohistorical context involved. This study is intended to be a systematic examination of the cross-national diffusion of English language education over the past century, with special analytic attention given to its institutionalization after World War II when the nation-state system became consolidated as the world model in international institutional arrangements.

Although systematic research on the rapid diffusion of English language education across national education systems is less extensive than might be expected, conventional perspectives tend to expect the incorporation of English into the school curriculum of a country to result from an educational policy decision contingent upon the country's concrete societal condition. Despite the various ways to define the concept of societal condition depending on theoretical orientations of different perspectives, one might reasonably speculate from such perspectives that English is expected to be taught in schools to the degree of its substantive utility under the economic, political, and cultural conditions of a given country. Obviously, such views convey useful insights on some national variation. However, they often have difficulty accounting for the influences from the wider environment that provides institutional rules and values to which nation-states are likely to conform to promote their structural legitimacy (Meyer, Boli, Thomas, & Ramirez, 1997). In order to provide a more balanced analysis, we attempt to examine some competing, yet complementary explanations through a series of empirical analyses. After examining several hypotheses derived from different theoretical perspectives, we discuss implications for educational policy and practice.

Theorizing the Spread of English Language Education

The diffusion of English as a legitimate component of curricular content in schools around the world provides a concrete context to which different conceptual perspectives on the sociohistorical nature of the school curriculum can be applied. Three different perspectives are briefly presented here that provide useful insights into the spread of English in the school curriculum. They represent a rational-functionalist perspective, a neocolonialist perspective, and an institutionalist perspective. This categorization, as many taxonomic frameworks do, probably overstates the degree of difference among perspectives. We should note that exceptions and complexities abound within each theoretical approach. Despite this limitation, it will be helpful to identify the main defining qualities of different approaches and their underlying assumptions so that we may derive a set of hypotheses that can be empirically tested and further explored.

First, the most popular account of the spread of English comes from a rational-functionalist perspective, in which English is understood as a practical commodity that brings various kinds of concrete benefits to individuals and society. This perspective posits that the incorporation of English into the school curriculum of a country is a result of a deliberate policy decision influenced by concrete societal needs for it. With the increasing consolidation of the global economy and the intensification of complex economic interdependency among different countries (Castells, 2000; Coe, Dicken, & Hess, 2008), promoting English language education is widely regarded as a rational policy choice to address societal demands for international communication. For example, one might expect that countries whose economic conditions are heavily dependent on international trade are more likely to incorporate English into the school curriculum (hypothesis 1). English as an important medium of communication in international business is akin to a common currency whose use increases economic efficiency through reduced transaction costs (Grin, 1996). Considering that the use value of a language may be sensitive to the size of its speaker population as a potential network of communication (de Swaan, 2002), the widespread use of English in international business may well motivate those countries with a strong orientation toward international trade to make efforts to join the network. In a similar vein, one might reasonably assume that a country whose largest export partner speaks English as the national language is more likely to incorporate English into the school curriculum (hypothesis 2). As part of attempts to boost exports, national governments might want their future citizens to be more sensitive to the languages spoken by their major export partners (Stanley, Ingram, & Chittick, 1990). In addition, among linguistically diverse countries, the decision to teach English as a regular school subject has often been made in order to "avoid the problem of having to choose between competing local languages" (Crystal, 2003, p. 85). English in those countries serves as a "neutral" means that not only unifies different linguistic groups into national citizens but also minimizes undue advantage for a particular group. In this respect, one might plausibly postulate that the incorporation of English into the school curriculum is more likely in countries of high linguistic diversity (hypothesis 3). Regardless of different forms of rational-functionalist thought, the core proposition is that the incorporation of English into the school curriculum is a result of its fitness to the economic and social conditions of a given country. A close relationship between what is taught in schools and the constituency is a central assumption of this line of thought.

Second, from a neocolonialist perspective, historical trajectories of national societies in relation to international politics account for a great deal of why a particular country's school curriculum is in its current shape. Indeed, many newly independent countries have tended to inherit, with minimal changes, the educational system set up by the former colonial rulers because of a shortage of educational resources and a paucity of alternatives (Altbach & Kelly, 1984; Carnoy, 1974). The school curriculum in the third world or peripheral areas has been influenced by the legacies of colonial education and neocolonial penetration from the advanced metropolitan centers. The spread of English language education across many third-world countries is often seen as resulting from deliberate policies of the advanced metropolitan centers to maintain neocolonial relations with the third world (Phillipson, 1992; Whitley, 1971). Many neocolonialist accounts of the spread of English provide useful insights for understanding various mechanisms through which colonial discourses on English language education function to disseminate and perpetuate the image of English as a superior language. Such mechanisms have often been associated with the neocolonial development of English, not only in everyday life but also in academic and political discourse, for example (Mühleisen, 2003; Pennycook, 1998). The core proposition of this perspective is that the incorporation of English into the school curriculum in a country is contingent upon the country's colonial legacy. Following the central logic of this perspective, one might reasonably expect that countries are likely to incorporate the language of their former colonizer, if any, into the school curriculum insofar as it is an internationally used language (hypothesis 4). Despite a unique theoretical orientation, the neocolonialist perspective shares a central underlying assumption with the rational-functionalist perspective; both perspectives assume that there exists a close relationship between what is taught in schools and the concrete societal conditions of a given country.

Finally, an institutionalist perspective posits that "education is an institution … that at a deeper level is strongly affixed to global norms and rules about what education is and how schools should operate" (Baker & LeTendre, 2005, p. 8). Understanding education as deeply grounded in global institutional ontology and rationalization, this perspective highlights that the school curriculum is constantly influenced by institutional dynamics of the wider environment in which general models of curricular formations are constituted and elaborated globally. Based on this perspective, the incorporation of English into the school curriculum is understood largely as an institutional embodiment of world-level educational norms and values and not simply as an instrumental means on the part of individual societies to meet idiosyncratic local requirements. With the modern nation-state model consolidated as a taken-for-granted political unit of sovereignty in the world polity, nation-state purposes have been increasingly rationalized around common principles of progress and justice (Meyer et al., 1997). Such a homogeneous cultural construction of nation-states has been an important institutional condition for rapid diffusion within the world system (Strang & Meyer, 1993). Indeed, the institutional environment in contemporary world society provides solid ground for the rapid diffusion of English as a curricular subject. For instance, English language education is widely regarded as important not only to facilitate the spread of modern scientific and technological discoveries but also to contribute to the economic and cultural development of nations. The association of English with such collective meanings and values embedded in modern world culture undergirds the legitimacy of English as an appropriate curricular subject across countries. In this respect, it is reasonable to expect from an institutionalist perspective that countries with more ties to global civil society are more likely to incorporate English into the school curriculum (hypothesis 5). Extensive empirical evidence suggests that world models often diffuse through international linkages of global civil society with assistance from various international nongovernmental organizations (Boli & Thomas, 1999). In the modern world system, where various policy discourses flow through expanding networks of global civil society, national education systems and their school curricula are likely to be quite isomorphic across countries in accordance with worldwide epistemic models of education despite pervasive "loose couplings" between official models and actual implementations.[4]

Data and Method

In order to see the global patterns of institutionalization of modern foreign languages in school curricula, we have collected and updated cross-national and historical data.[5] The accumulation of the data gathered for our prior exploratory studies conducted over the past two decades allows us to systematically examine the cross-national contextual factors that have contributed to the spread of English as the most popular foreign language in primary and secondary school curricula.[6] Our data analysis involved five historical periods between 1900 and 2005.[7] In each period, countries were treated as either an adopter or a nonadopter of English as the first foreign language, both at the primary and at the secondary level.[8] Since curricular standards and guidelines are susceptible to change over time, the adopters in a given period were not automatically assumed to be adopters in succeeding periods but were assessed regarding whether or not they continued to have English as the first foreign language in the school curriculum. Since we were interested in English taught as a foreign language, English-speaking countries were excluded from the sample.[9]

Using a series of descriptive statistics, we first traced the historical patterns of the incorporation of English into school curricula across countries. Next, differences in the historical trend of diffusion of English language education were found among countries, depending on the experience of colonization by an English-speaking country. Regional variations were also examined by analyzing the data according to world regions. Finally, we used ordered logit regressions to assess the effects of different national characteristics on the incorporation of English into school curricula. In our regressions, we were interested in the diffusion of English language education across countries that were never under colonial rule by an English-speaking country in order to examine the diffusion mechanism through which "voluntary" adoption of English language education occurred as opposed to "inherited" adoption. The dependent variable was an ordinal categorical variable indicating the degree of adoption of English language education in a given country. For this ordinal variable, we coded two for a given country in a certain period of time if English was incorporated into the school curriculum as the first foreign language at both the primary and secondary levels (i.e., full adoption); we coded one if English was incorporated into the school curriculum as the first foreign language only at the primary level or only at the secondary level (i.e., partial adoption); we coded zero if English was not incorporated into the school curriculum as the first foreign language either at the primary level or at the secondary level (i.e., nonadoption).

Seven independent variables were entered into our regressions according to the three perspectives reviewed earlier. Table 10.1 presents the descriptive statistics and definitions of the independent variables used in the ordered logit regressions. The variables used from the rational-functionalist perspective were international trade, English-speaking export partner, and linguistic diversity, based on hypotheses 1, 2, and 3, respectively. In connection to the neocolonialist perspective, we used the international language-speaking colonizer variable to test hypothesis 4. In relation to the institutionalist perspective, we included

TABLE 10.1 Independent Variables with Descriptive Statistics, among Countries that Were Never under Colonial Rule by an English-Speaking Country, 1945–2005

Variable	Description	1945–69		1970–89		1990–2005	
		Mean (SD)	N	Mean (SD)	N	Mean (SD)	N
International trade	International import and export divided by gross domestic product; 1960, 1980, and 1995 for the first, second, and third periods, respectively.	4.663 (2.699)	71	6.164 (3.175)	80	7.070 (3.092)	106
English-speaking export partner	Is English the national language used by the largest export partner? Coded one if yes, otherwise coded zero; 1960, 1980, and 1995 for the first, second, and third periods, respectively.	.375	80	.310	87	.336	110
Linguistic diversity	Linguistic diversity index ranging from zero for no diversity to near one for high diversity; 1961, 1985, and 2000 for the first, second, and third periods, respectively.	.329 (.279)	83	.350 (.281)	87	.396 (.281)	111
Int'l language-speaking colonizer	Was the country once under colonial rule by a French, German, Russian, or Spanish-speaking country? Coded one if yes, otherwise coded zero.	.446	83	.414	87	.438	112
Global civil network	Number of international nongovernmental organizations to which individuals or organizations belong in the country (× 100 memberships); 1966, 1980, and 1995 for the first, second, and third periods, respectively.	3.086 (3.094)	83	4.152 (3.897)	86	9.016 (8.061)	109
Economic development	Gross domestic product per capita (× $1,000); 1960, 1980, and 1995 for the first, second, and third periods, respectively.	3.162 (4.813)	78	5.764 (8.812)	82	6.381 (10.741)	106
Recently acquired sovereignty	Independence after 1920, 1945, and 1970 for the first, second, and third periods, respectively. Coded one if yes, otherwise coded zero.	.373	83	.356	87	.196	112

Note. Descriptive statistics in this table are based on countries for which data on English language education are also available at both primary and secondary school levels.

the global civil network variable to examine hypothesis 5. Two additional variables, economic development and recently acquired sovereignty, were entered into the regression equation as control variables. These two control variables were added because, considering the costs involved in providing English language education for schoolchildren, most conventional perspectives would expect countries in better economic conditions to be more able to incorporate English into the school curriculum; in addition, countries of recently acquired sovereignty might temporarily prioritize establishing a solidary national community over educating supranational citizens.

Results

Overall Historical Patterns

Table 10.2 shows the percentage of countries teaching English as the first foreign language in primary and secondary schools over the period from the beginning of the 20th century to the present. Our historical data indicate that English was not a strong candidate for a modern foreign language as a regular curricular subject in schools before the mid-20th century. Less than 1/10th of independent countries taught English as the first foreign language in primary schools before 1945. Even in secondary schools, where the instruction of modern foreign languages was firmly institutionalized by the end of the 19th century (Cha, 1989), the proportion of countries where English was incorporated into the curriculum as the first foreign language was less than one of out of three countries before 1945. However, the proportion sharply increased to 32.2% at the primary level and 59.5% at the secondary level in the 1945 to 1969 period; the proportion finally reached 68.1% at the primary level and 78.5% at the secondary level in the 1990 to 2005 period.

Our data reported in Cha and Ham (2011) provide additional information about historical patterns of the incorporation of English compared to French, German, Russian, or Spanish as the first foreign language. The data show that the ratio of countries that taught English as the first foreign language to those that taught French, German, Russian, or Spanish was only 0.2 at the secondary level in the 1900 to 1919 period, meaning that English was seldom the first choice. However, the situation dramatically changed: the ratio increased to 1.5

TABLE 10.2 Percentages of Countries Having English as the First Foreign Language in the School Curriculum, 1900–2005

School level	1900–19		1920–44		1945–69		1970–89		1990–2005	
	%	N	%	N	%	N	%	N	%	N
Primary	5.4	37	9.6	52	32.2	115	44.2	138	68.1	163
Secondary	18.2	33	32.7	49	59.5	116	65.5	139	78.5	163

in the 1945 to 1969 period and to 4.3 in the 1990 to 2005 period. It is thus possible to say that, in the 1990 to 2005 period, the number of countries teaching English as the first foreign language at the secondary level was more than four times the number of countries teaching other foreign languages. The situation was not very different at the primary level: the ratio was 1.0 or less before 1945 but increased dramatically from 1.1 in the 1945 to 1969 period to 4.0 in the 1990 to 2005 period.

Some may plausibly suspect that the rapid spread of English language education was due in part to the addition of newly independent former British or U.S. colonies to the sample. This appears true in our data presented in Table 10.3. Consistent with hypothesis 4, a substantial difference persisted at the world level in terms of the percentage of countries choosing English as the first foreign language in the school curriculum, depending on the experience of colonial rule by an English-speaking colonizer. Our data show that, among societies that were once under colonial rule by an English-speaking country, the proportion of countries having English as the first foreign language at the primary level was already more than four-fifths in the 1945 to 1969 period. The proportion in the same period, however, was far less than 1/5th among societies that were never under colonial rule by an English-speaking country. The situation was not very different at the secondary level. As a proportion, more than 9 out of 10 former colonies of an English-speaking country chose English as the first foreign language in the 1945 to 1969 period, whereas less than half of other countries did so in the same period.

However, it is important to note that the rapid spread of English language education has another facet. Our data clearly show that countries that were never under colonial rule by an English-speaking country have also been increasingly attentive to the incorporation of English into the school curriculum over the past half century. Notably, as the proportion of countries that incorporated English into the school curriculum increased, the rate of increase became even greater. Among those countries without any historical experience of colonization by an English-speaking country, the percentage that had English as the first foreign language at the primary level increased exponentially

TABLE 10.3 Percentages of Countries Having English as the First Foreign Language in the School Curriculum, Depending on the Experience of Colonial Rule by an English-Speaking Country, 1945–2005

School level	Colonial rule by an English-speaking country?	1945–69		1970–89		1990–2005	
		%	N	%	N	%	N
Primary	Once under colonial rule	80.6	31	85.4	48	98.0	51
	Never	14.3	84	22.2	90	54.5	112
Secondary	Once under colonial rule	93.3	30	87.8	49	98.0	51
	Never	47.7	86	53.3	90	69.6	112

from 14.3% in the 1945 to 1969 period to 54.5% in the 1990 to 2005 period. At the secondary level, following a modest increase from 47.7% in the 1945 to 1969 period to 53.3% in the 1970 to 1989 period, the percentage sharply increased to 69.6% in the 1990 to 2005 period.

A further breakdown of the data by world region in Table 10.4 once again clearly show that the legitimate status of English in the school curriculum is evident across most world regions, even with former colonies of English-speaking countries excluded from the sample. In particular, countries in Asia and Oceania, despite huge cross-national differences within this region in terms of history and economic development, appear to converge on teaching English as the first foreign language at both primary and secondary levels. An illustrative case of such enthusiasm for English language education in this region is South Korea, where a variety of policy strategies have been employed to enhance the quality of English language education for schoolchildren despite controversies regarding their actual impact on educational practices in local contexts (Nunan, 2003; Shin, 2007). Some examples of such policy items include intro-

TABLE 10.4 World-Regional Patterns of the Diffusion of English as the First Foreign Language in the School Curriculum, among Countries that Were Never under Colonial Rule by an English-Speaking Country, 1945–2005

School level	Region	1945–69		1970–89		1990–2005	
		%	*N*	*%*	*N*	*%*	*N*
Primary	Africa South of the Sahara	16.7	18	9.5	21	20.0	25
	Asia and Oceania	9.1	11	23.1	13	80.0	15
	Central Europe and the former USSR	11.1	9	12.5	8	65.0	20
	Latin America and the Caribbean	20.0	20	25.0	20	47.6	21
	Middle East and North Africa	12.5	8	22.2	9	40.0	10
	Western Europe	11.1	18	36.8	19	81.0	21
Secondary	Africa South of the Sahara	15.8	19	20.0	20	28.0	25
	Asia and Oceania	50.0	12	66.7	12	100.0	15
	Central Europe and the former USSR	11.1	9	12.5	8	70.0	20
	Latin America and the Caribbean	80.0	20	76.2	21	90.5	21
	Middle East and North Africa	55.6	9	70.0	10	70.0	10
	Western Europe	58.8	17	63.2	19	76.2	21

ducing an increasing number of English native speakers into public schools as English teachers, encouraging Korean teachers of English to use only English as the language of instruction, and even setting up English-only villages exclusively for educational purposes. English is now taught as the only required foreign language in virtually every school in South Korea from the third year of primary education to the end of the upper secondary level.

Also noticeable is the dramatic increase in the number of countries teaching English as the first foreign language in Western Europe at the primary level. The rapid spread of English in this region seems largely due to the consolidation of the European Union as a supranational political, economic, and cultural entity, where English functions as de facto the most important working language notwithstanding the Council of Europe's "plurilingualism" policy that celebrates linguistic diversity in Europe (Breidbach, 2003; van Parijs, 2001). An interesting example in this respect is Zurich, the most populous canton of Switzerland. In Zurich, where German is the official language, French had long been taught in schools as the most popular second language because it is one of the "national" languages of Switzerland along with German, Italian, and Romansh. However, the canton of Zurich decided in the late 1990s to increase the share of English in the school curriculum while reducing the share of French (Grin, 1998). Despite concerns that it might damage the Swiss model of national unity, English in Zurich's schools is now given more curricular emphasis and is even taught from an earlier age than French. Zurich's decision has recently triggered many other cantons, especially in German-speaking Switzerland, to consider similar educational plans.

It is also notable that a great proportion of countries in central Europe and the former USSR incorporated English into the school curriculum as the first foreign language at both primary and secondary levels during the 1990 to 2005 period. The rise of the United States as the world's unchallengeable superpower with the fall of the Soviet Union during this period seems to have contributed to this sudden increase in the percentage of countries teaching English in this region. It is an illustrative example of educational change that "all countries in central and eastern Europe in which Russian was a mandatory [foreign] language [in the school curriculum at a particular stage of compulsory education] in 1982/83 abandoned this policy from the beginning of the 1990s" (Eurydice, 2005, p. 37).

Sub-Saharan Africa, which shows a relatively moderate increase in the percentage of countries incorporating English as the first foreign language into the school curriculum, is the only exception. This phenomenon is probably due to the fact that most countries in this region inherited, upon independence, the metropolitan languages of their former colonizers as their official languages (i.e., French, Portuguese, and Spanish as well as English). Since these languages are de facto foreign languages for the speakers of local languages, these countries may have difficulties accommodating an additional foreign language in the school curriculum. Nevertheless, it is important to note that many of these countries also teach English as a required foreign language in schools in addition to the metropolitan languages inherited from their former colonizers. Former French colonies in this region, such as Central African Republic, Congo, Madagascar, Mauritania, Niger, and Togo, for example, teach English as well as French as a compulsory subject in secondary schools, although slightly less curricular emphasis is devoted to English compared to French.

Cross-National Diffusion Patterns

Another issue of interest here is how well the incorporation of English as a regular school subject can be explained by national characteristics. The coefficients in Table 10.5 indicate the amount of increase in the predicted ordered log odds of moving to the next higher level in our ordinal dependent variable by a one-unit increase in an independent variable, with all other independent variables held constant. In our regression analyses, we focused on examining the effects of the independent variables among countries without any experience of colonial rule by an English-speaking country. As already shown in Table 10.3, almost all former colonies of an English-speaking country adopted English as the first foreign language at both primary and secondary levels as soon as they became independent; since this is a ubiquitous postwar pattern, the increasing rate of transnational diffusion of English language education in the past several decades is mostly due to its institutionalization across countries that were never under colonial rule by an English-speaking colonizer.[10]

Considering the prevailing assumption of a tight linkage between curricular contents and country-specific conditions, the results in Table 10.5 are quite suggestive. With regard to the effects of the individual variables, with other variables held constant, most of the independent variables describing national characteristics did not stably increase the expected ordered log odds of moving to the next higher level of incorporation of English into the school curriculum. Inconsistent with hypothesis 1, there was no statistically significant effect of international trade in any period from 1945 to 2005. Similarly, although the English-speaking export partner variable had a significant positive effect in the 1945 to 1969 period in line with hypothesis 2, the effect disappeared in the succeeding periods. These insignificant or unstable results suggest the possibility that the diffusion of English language education around the world may have been rather independent of individual countries' actual needs for English, as expected from the institutionalist perspective.

The effect of linguistic diversity was also not significant, except in the 1990 to 2005 period, when its effect was significantly negative, meaning that linguistically more diverse societies were less likely to incorporate English into the school curriculum in this most recent period. Hypothesis 3 was not supported. One possible explanation of this significant negative association may be that

TABLE 10.5 Ordered Logit Regressions for English as the First Foreign Language in the School Curriculum, among Countries that Were Never under Colonial Rule by an English-Speaking Country, 1945–2005

	1945–69	1970–89	1990–2005	
	(A1)	(B1)	(C1)	(C2)
International trade	-.022 (.134)	-.136 (.083)	.029 (.077)	.028 (.077)
English-speaking export partner	1.386 (.721)*	.588 (.487)	.303 (.469)	.353 (.484)
Linguistic diversity	.389 (1.102)	-.469 (.916)	-2.380 (.804)**	-1.533 (.874)
Int'l language-speaking colonizer	-.534 (.606)	-.424 (.496)	-1.885 (.485)***	-2.004 (.513)***
Global civil network	-.057 (.153)	-.009 (.103)	.166 (.053)**	.124 (.052)*
Economic development	-.004 (.094)	.011 (.047)	-.107 (.038)**	-.101 (.037)**
Recently acquired sovereignty	-1.360 (.884)	-1.695 (.620)**	-.733 (.578)	-.597 (.600)
Sub-Saharan Africa				-1.973 (.649)**
Threshold 1	-.364 (1.130)	-1.725 (.844)*	-2.044 (.847)*	-2.492 (.863)**
Threshold 2	1.780 (1.164)	-.114 (.822)	-.812 (.822)	-1.154 (.828)
Parallel lines test χ²	3.500	5.909	10.354	7.610
Nagelkerke R^2	.280	.278	.394	.462
N	68	80	104	104

Note. Standard errors are in parentheses. The dependent variable is an ordinal categorical variable indicating the degree of adoption of English language education in a given country: full adoption, partial adoption, or nonadoption. Full adoption = English was the first foreign language at both primary and secondary school levels; partial adoption = English was the first foreign language only at the primary level or only at the secondary level; and nonadoption = English was not the first foreign language at either the primary level or the secondary level. For χ² tests of the parallel lines assumption, df = 7 in all models except for model C2, where df = 8. All χ² values are statistically insignificant at the level of p ≤ .05, suggesting that the assumption is not violated.

*p ≤ .05; **p ≤ .01; ***p ≤ .001.

many sub-Saharan African countries, where high ethnolinguistic fractionalization is normal, tend to place relatively moderate curricular emphasis on English compared to countries in other world regions, as already shown in Table 10.4. Our further analysis in model C2 of Table 10.5 supported this explanation. We added the sub-Saharan Africa dummy variable to our regression and found linguistic diversity insignificant after controlling for this dummy variable. The inclusion of this dummy variable, however, did not meaningfully alter other results. The effect of another language-related variable, the international language-speaking colonizer, was consistently negative in line with hypothesis 4, but it was statistically significant only in the 1990 to 2005 period. What this significantly negative effect in this latest period also means is that English language education has become highly institutionalized to the degree that only some countries that inherited other international languages from their former colonizers compose the majority of nonadopters of English as the first foreign language.

Overall, the results in Table 10.5 show that the structuration of national education systems often exceed, or are "loosely coupled" with, concrete societal needs of individual countries (Meyer et al., 1997). In addition to such loose couplings, the institutionalist perspective expects countries with more ties to the global civil network to have a greater tendency to incorporate English into the school curriculum (Boli & Thomas, 1999). Since a certain high level of English proficiency has been emphasized increasingly in world discourses as a basic literacy skill for tomorrow's supranational citizens, a country's institutionalization of English language education is likely to be associated with the extent to which a country is connected to the cultural construction of world discourses. The results in Table 10.5 provide some evidence that supports this explanation. There was a significant positive effect of the global civil network on the tendency to incorporate English into the school curriculum as the first foreign language in the 1990 to 2005 period. In line with hypothesis 5, the transnational diffusion of English language education in the recent phase appears to have been facilitated by international linkages of global civil society. However, its effect was not significant in earlier periods. One plausible explanation of this insignificance may be that the prevalence of international discourses emphasizing English proficiency as part of basic literacy skills is rather a recent phenomenon. Indeed, contrasting discourses have been present concerning the prevalence of English and its impact on various spheres of society, with associated fears of linguistic domination by a particular culture.[11] Today's new vision of education as contributing to unlimited progress and justice throughout the world, however, appears to give increasing legitimacy to English as an integral curricular subject, whose significance in empowering the individual as a capable and responsible member of global society has become an institutionalized rule or "myth" in international policy discourses.[12]

In addition, we found the effects of our control variables very interesting, too. With regard to the effect of economic development, it was not significant from 1945 to 1989. In the 1990 to 2005 period, when this variable was statistically significant, the direction of its effect was negative. Such an insignificant or negative effect of this variable would not be expected from most conventional perspectives that expect the feasibility of an educational policy to be contingent upon the country's economic condition under which to afford the costs involved in formulating and implementing the policy. However, even the negative effect of this variable is not surprising from the institutionalist perspective because the universal meanings of teaching English to future citizens may have more intense significance for those countries that are anticipating development than for other countries already seen as economically advanced economies.[13] Similarly, the effect of recently acquired sovereignty was statistically insignificant except for the 1970 to 1989 period. This insignificant result is very suggestive because it implies that newly independent societies were also very attentive to the provision of English language education to their future citizens despite the possibility that establishing a solidary national community might have been their immediate political priority, at least temporarily, upon independence.

Discussion and Conclusion

In the modern world, an important role of schooling is to provide universal education in order to equip children with basic skills that are necessary to learn advanced knowledge and skills in the future. Today, English appears to have joined this category of basic skills in the sense that English is no longer seen narrowly as a language of particular Western countries, although it once used to be. As our data show, English is becoming a regular school subject whose legitimacy is taken for granted in most national education systems, largely regardless of individual countries' immediate societal needs. As Meyer (2006) puts it, "the modern world society is built around an expansive conception of the rights and capacities of the individual human person, seen as a member of human society as a whole rather than principally as the citizen of a nation-state" (p. 264). Children around the world are not only learning English language skills; they are changing their identities into new ones through which they are better positioned within a larger social context beyond national borders. It seems that English language education around the world has been increasingly linked to the expanded notion of citizenship that emphasizes the centrality of the individual as a primordial member of the greater civil society, rather than as a member of a bounded national territory, which we may call "supranational" or "transnational citizenship" (Meyer, 2006; Ramirez, 2006). That is, one of the legitimate and desirable roles that education systems around the world are expected to play involves "the construction of collective identities" (Koenig, 2008, p. 95) that empower future citizens in global society.

Extensive cross-national and historical data analyzed in this study suggest that teaching English in schools has become an institutionalized routine across diverse countries. Only small percentages of countries incorporated English into the school curriculum up until the first half of the 20th century. Within half a century, however, English achieved a legitimate status in the school curriculum in most countries around the world. Most conventional views explain the popularity of English language education in terms of its economic and political functions in a given society. Such explanations proffer useful insights from a realistic stance. However, an educational phenomenon is not only a functional or political response to meet substantive societal needs; it is also an institutional embodiment of transnational cultural rules and values. By gaining legitimacy from universalistic world models and principles, English language education appears to have consolidated its status in curricular policies across countries. Reflecting worldwide rationales regarding the significance of English proficiency in the increasingly globalized world as well as international discourses emphasizing the empowerment of the individual as a capable and responsible member of global society, the importance of English language education is being taken for granted across non-English-speaking countries. A certain high level of English proficiency appears to be increasingly conceived as a basic skill for everyone, rather than as something that privileges particular social strata, although the latter was once the case, especially in many postcolonial societies.

In support of linguistic diversity around the world, the theorization of language as inseparable from human existence extends to growing concerns about the "ecology" of languages, and such concerns are now framed in terms of how to preserve indigenous local languages and promote linguistic human rights (Hornberger & Hult, 2008; Skutnabb-Kangas, 2000). The celebration of linguistic diversity in world discourses, however, is not necessarily in conflict with the worldwide discursive promotion of English language education. Indeed, both ways of discourse formation are grounded in the common notion of the individual whose personhood is seen as being constituted independent of national citizenship. That is, an individual person is theorized as a member of subnational and transnational communities in addition to being a national citizen. Increasing attention has been given to both indigenous and global languages along with national languages because the nation-state as a societal unit is no longer conceptualized as the primary boundary for an "imagined community" (Anderson, 1991). Further, both linguistic diversity and English language education are commonly "invoked with ... the world interest in mind" (Ramirez, 2006, p. 382), rationalized around universalistic principles of progress and justice. While linguistic diversity is seen to contribute to the richness of the cultural heritages of the world, English is assumed to serve as a useful tool for international communication and global cooperation.

Education is a futuristic project in character. Contemporary political conceptualizations of education continue to expand the purposes of public education far beyond providing direct or immediate functional utility to individuals or to society (Gutmann, 1987; Labaree, 1997). Education systems around the world are constantly responsive to new visions of society, not only within but also beyond national boundaries. They have integrated various educational aims into their educational policies, with increasing emphasis placed on education for world citizenship and sustainable development, for example (Banks, 2008; Cha, Dawson, & Ham, 2010; Fiala, 2006). In this respect, the incorporation of English language education into curriculum policies around the world can be seen largely as an embodiment of ideas that have been constituted in various "transnational spaces" (Gough, 2000) for educational discourses, symbolically reflecting institutional dynamics of the modern international system. As economic and cultural globalization processes intensify, an individual child in even a remote peripheral nation-state is now expected to become a capable and responsible member of a new "imagined community" that may be called "world society" (Meyer et al., 1997). Current world-cultural values that celebrate individual personhood as the fundamental basis of one's distinctive and special roles in society undergird various educational policies for empowering all individual children regardless of their circumstances (Frank & Meyer, 2002). In this context, the potential effect of educational policies for English language education extends not only to their contribution to meeting some concrete societal needs within individual countries but also to their institutional impact on our cognition by which every individual is seen as having the ontological status as a primordial member of global civil society.

Given the unprecedented spread of English instruction across national education systems, reflective evaluations of current curricular policies on English language education are necessary in order to better assess their intended and unintended effects on nations, local communities, and, most importantly, individual children. Without such reflective procedures, English language education incorporated into the school curriculum might remain only as an official policy element whose impact on lived experiences in the classroom might be limited in many parts of the world, especially where an adequate teaching force or other necessary educational resources are not present. Further, close attention needs to be given to the possibility that new forms of social inequality and exclusion may arise due to uneven access to English language education, which can lead to what may be called the "English divide" between different groups of people. That is, the access to quality English language education should not be determined based on children's socioeconomic backgrounds or on other socially constructed categories of difference that serve to privilege some groups over others, either within or across nation-states.

In this respect, the world institutionalization of English language education poses both promises and challenges to educational policymakers and practitioners all around the world. Sustained and shared policy efforts should be directed toward pondering how to better design English language education as an empowering tool to help all schoolchildren develop a heightened sense of both cultural diversity and common humanity in the context of today's world society. As the incorporation of English language education into national education systems has become a world model, educators and policymakers should become reflective enactors of this curricular policy model in order to achieve its intended educational goals while constantly identifying and minimizing its unintended consequences. Future research needs to attend to the importance of developing an empirically based research agenda to examine the possible disparity in opportunity structures for different groups of children in the global context of English education policies and practices.

Notes

1   Adapted from Cha & Ham, *American Journal of Education, 117,* 2 "Educating Supranational Citizens: The Incorporation of English Language Education into Curriculum" (2011), pp. 183–209. Used with permission of University of Chicago Press.

2   Although there have been some critical views on the growing impact of English on local cultures and languages around the world, a certain high level of ability to communicate in English seems to be becoming in many countries a new kind of basic literacy that no longer conveys narrowly Western ideological connotations (Crystal, 2003; Graddol, 2006; Honna, 2005). In this respect, English proficiency may be comparable to the new digital literacy for information and communication technologies, which is now part of basic competency for tomorrow's global citizens (Ham & Cha, 2009).

3   See also Tsuda (1999), who notes that the rise of English as the most dominant international language may create communicative inequality and discrimination among people with different linguistic and cultural backgrounds, giving an unearned advantage to the speakers of English as their mother tongue.

4   It is important to note that the transnational isomorphism in educational policy discourses inevitably involves the pervasiveness of various "loose couplings" (Meyer, et al., 1997; Weick, 1976) within individual countries. The reason is that imported models may be "indigenized" or "hybridized," at various levels of policy and practice, into innovations extensively different from the original models that have been officially adopted and institutionalized (Anderson-Levitt, 2003; Paine & Fang, 2006). Such institutional isomorphism accompanied by local or national recontextualization processes is primarily due to the "structural duality of educational policy" (Ham, Paine, & Cha, 2011) through which nation-states successfully incorporate and display elements that conform to global epistemic models of education and yet preserve considerable autonomy of state action.

5   For data sources, see notes 5 and 10 in Cha and Ham (2011).

6   For a bibliography of our prior exploratory studies, see the "References" section in Cha and Ham (2011).

7   Only independent (or self-governing) countries were included for analysis; societies under colonial rule were not included until they became formally independent. Including all societies for analysis wherever data were available regardless of formal sovereignty did not change overall historical patterns, however.

8   In our data, either a compulsory or compulsory elective subject taught in primary or general secondary schools was considered as a regular school subject in this study, but an optional subject was excluded from analysis.

9   If English was an official language in a given country and, at the same time, was the first language of more than half of the population, we regarded the country as having English as

the first/national language and thus excluded the country from the sample. In other words, unless English was used as the first language by more than half of the population in a given country, we regarded it as de facto a foreign language even if it had an official status in the country.

10 The effects of interest did not much differ if countries that were once under colonial rule by an English-speaking country were added to the sample. The results are available on request.

11 The linguistic diversity of the world is often seen to be threatened by the rise of English as a global language. Such a view is based on the analogy between an increasingly reduced number of living languages in the world and an increasing number of endangered species in the natural ecology. Of course, this ecology metaphor is useful to draw attention to diverse linguistic heritages around the world. However, many sociolinguists today observe a variety of modern Englishes that have evolved in different parts of the globe (Davies, 2005; Kachru, 1990), thereby questioning the traditional assumption that English has some unidirectional influence from one particular culture to another. As Honna (2005) notes, "the spread of English as a language for multinational and multicultural communication utilized by an enormous number of non-native speakers shows that English is becoming more and more de-Anglo-Americanized in many regions of the world" (p. 76).

12 We use the word *myth*, derived from Meyer and Rowan (1977), to emphasize that an institutionalized rule often conflicts with practical efficiency but persists as a taken-for-granted routine.

13 In other words, some countries that are highly developed and modern may delay adopting innovations; since they are already deeply integrated into world society, conforming to additional world standards may not be their immediate political priority. For example, Rauner (1998) provides some evidence supporting this hypothesis with respect to the cross-national incorporation of global civics content into social studies curricula.

References

Altbach, P. G., & Kelly, G. P. (Eds.). (1984). *Education and the colonial experience.* New Brunswick, NJ: Transaction.

Anderson, B. (1991). *Imagined communities: Reflections on the origin and spread of nationalism* (2nd ed.). London: Verso Press.

Anderson-Levitt, K. M. (Ed.). (2003). *Local meanings, global schooling: Anthropology and world culture theory.* New York: Palgrave Macmillan.

Baker, D. P., & LeTendre, G. K. (2005). *National differences, global similarities: World culture and the future of schooling.* Stanford, CA: Stanford University Press.

Banks, J. A. (2008). Diversity, group identity, and citizenship education in a global age. *Educational Researcher, 37*(3), 129–139.

Boli, J., & Thomas, G. M. (1999). *Constructing world culture: International nongovernmental organizations since 1875.* Stanford, CA: Stanford University Press.

Breidbach, S. (2003). *Plurilingualism, democratic citizenship in Europe, and the role of English.* Strasbourg, France: Language Policy Division, Council of Europe.

Carnoy, M. (1974). *Education as cultural imperialism.* New York: David McKay.

Castells, M. (2000). *The rise of the network society* (2nd ed.). Oxford, England: Blackwell.

Cha, Y.-K. (1989). *The effect of global integration on the institutionalization of modern foreign languages in the school curriculum, 1812–1986* (Unpublished doctoral dissertation). Stanford University, Stanford, CA.

Cha, Y.-K., Dawson, W. P., & Ham, S.-H. (2010). *Global civil society and the cross-national adoption of multicultural education policies.* Paper presented at the 14th World Congress of the World Council of Comparative Education Societies, Istanbul, Turkey.

Cha, Y.-K., & Ham, S.-H. (2011). Educating supranational citizens: The incorporation of English language education into curriculum policies. *American Journal of Education, 117*(2), 183–209.

Coe, N. M., Dicken, P., & Hess, M. (2008). Global production networks: Realizing the potential. *Journal of Economic Geography, 8*(3), 271–295.

Crystal, D. (2003). *English as a global language* (2nd ed.). Cambridge, England: Cambridge University Press.

Davies, D. (2005). *Varieties of modern English: An introduction.* London: Pearson-Longman.

de Swaan, A. (2002). *The world language system: A political sociology and political economy of language.* Cambridge, England: Polity Press.

Eurydice. (2005). *Key data on teaching languages at school in Europe.* Brussels, Belgium: Eurydice European Unit.

Fiala, R. (2006). Educational ideology and the school curriculum. In A. Benavot & C. Braslavsky (Eds.), *School knowledge in comparative and historical perspective* (pp. 15–34). Hong Kong, China: CERC-Springer.

Frank, D. J., & Meyer, J. W. (2002). The profusion of individual roles and identities in the postwar period. *Sociological Theory, 20*(1), 86–105.

Gough, N. (2000). Locating curriculum studies in the global village. *Journal of Curriculum Studies, 32*(2), 329–342.

Grabe, W. (1988). English, information access, and technology transfer: A rationale for English as an international language. *World Englishes, 7*(1), 63–72.

Graddol, D. (2006). *English next: Why global English may mean the end of "English as a foreign language."* London: British Council.

Grin, F. (1996). The economics of language: Survey, assessment, and prospects. *International Journal of the Sociology of Language, 121*(1), 17–44.

Grin, F. (1998). *Language policy in multilingual Switzerland: Overview and recent developments.* Paper presented at the Cicle de Conferencies sobre Política Lingüística, Barcelona, Spain.

Gutmann, A. (1987). *Democratic education.* Princeton, NJ: Princeton University Press.

Ham, S.-H., & Cha, Y.-K. (2009). Positioning education in the information society: The transnational diffusion of the information and communication technology curriculum. *Comparative Education Review, 53*(4), 535–557.

Ham, S.-H., Paine, L. W., & Cha, Y.-K. (2011). Duality of educational policy as global and local: The case of the gender equity agenda in national principles and state actions. *Asia Pacific Education Review, 12*(1), 105–115.

Honna, N. (2005). English as a multicultural language in Asia and intercultural literacy. *Intercultural Communication Studies, 14*(2), 73–89.

Hornberger, N. H., & Hult, F. M. (2008). Ecological language education policy. In B. Spolsky & F. M. Hult (Eds.), *The handbook of educational linguistics* (pp. 280–296). Oxford, England: Blackwell.

Kachru, B. B. (1990). World Englishes and applied linguistics. *World Englishes, 9*(1), 3–20.

Koenig, M. (2008). Institutional change in the world polity: International human rights and the construction of collective identities. *International Sociology, 23*(1), 95–114.

Labaree, D. F. (1997). Public goods, private goods: The American struggle over educational goals. *American Educational Research Journal, 34*(1), 39–81.

Meyer, J. W. (2006). World models, national curricula, and the centrality of the individual. In A. Benavot & C. Braslavsky (Eds.), *School knowledge in comparative and historical perspective: Changing curricula in primary and secondary education* (pp. 259–271). Hong Kong, China: CERC-Springer.

Meyer, J. W., Boli, J., Thomas, G. M., & Ramirez, F. O. (1997). World society and the nation-state. *American Journal of Sociology, 103*(1), 144–181.

Meyer, J. W., & Rowan, B. (1977). Institutional organizations: Formal structure as myth and ceremony. *American Journal of Sociology, 83*(2), 340–363.

Mühleisen, S. (2003). Towards global diglossia? English in the sciences and the humanities. In C. Mair (Ed.), *The politics of English as a world language: New horizons in postcolonial cultural studies* (pp. 107–118). Amsterdam, Netherlands: Rodopi.

Nunan, D. (2003). The impact of English as a global language on educational policies and practices in the Asia-Pacific region. *TESOL Quarterly, 37*(4), 589–613.

Paine, L. W., & Fang, Y. (2006). Reform as hybrid model of teaching and teacher development in China. *International Journal of Educational Research, 45*(4), 279–289.

Pennycook, A. (1998). *English and the discourses of colonialism.* London: Routledge.

Phillipson, R. (1992). *Linguistic imperialism.* Oxford, England: Oxford University Press.

Ramirez, F. O. (2006). From citizen to person? Rethinking education as incorporation. In D. P. Baker & A. W. Wiseman (Eds.), *The impact of comparative education research on institutional theory* (pp. 367–387). Oxford, England: Elsevier.

Rauner, M. H. (1998). *The worldwide globalization of civics education topics from 1955 to 1995* (Unpublished doctoral dissertation). Stanford University, Stanford, CA.

Shin, H. (2007). English language teaching in Korea: Toward globalization or glocalization? In J. Cummins & C. Davison (Eds.), *International handbook of English language teaching* (pp. 75–86). New York: Springer.

Skutnabb-Kangas, T. (2000). *Linguistic genocide in education—Or worldwide diversity and human rights?* London: Routledge.

Spolsky, B. (2004). *Language policy.* Cambridge, England: Cambridge University Press.

Stanley, J., Ingram, D., & Chittick, G. (1990). *The relationship between international trade and linguistic competence.* Canberra, Australia: Department of Employment, Education, and Training.

Strang, D., & Meyer, J. W. (1993). Institutional conditions for diffusion. *Theory and Society, 22*(4), 487–511.

Tsuda, Y. (1999). The hegemony of English and strategies for linguistic pluralism: Proposing the ecology of language paradigm. In M. Tehranian (Ed.), *Worlds apart: Human security and global governance* (pp. 153–167). London: I. B. Tauris.

van Parijs, P. (2001). Europe's linguistic challenge. *European Journal of Sociology, 45*(1), 113–154.

Weick, K. E. (1976). Education organizations as loosely coupled systems. *Administrative Science Quarterly, 21*(1), 11–19.

Whitley, S. (1971). English language as a tool of British neocolonialism. *East Africa Journal, 8*(12), 4–6.

11

CULTURAL POLITICS IN THE "NEW" INDIA

Social Class, Neoliberal Globalization, and the Education Paradox

Ruchira Ganguly-Scrase and Timothy J. Scrase

Introduction

It is 6:00 p.m. on a Wednesday evening and in South Kolkata many students are waiting to enter a rather dingy looking ground-floor office in a nondescript apartment building. The children are around 8 to 9 years old and they are all tired from a long school day. Heavy looking backpacks, full of books, are strewn on the ground. The air is hot and muggy, and the noise from passing motorists and pedestrians, as well as local shoppers, is almost deafening. The children are, of course, attending an after-school private coaching college, specializing in English tuition.[1] The sign hanging precariously over the entrance "A-1 Coaching College: Your Passport to a Better Future" sums it up completely. Competition for places in the best schools, and thereafter colleges, in Kolkata is furious and only the top 10% of graduates will ever gain such places. English proficiency is essential for future college and professional success. This scene is repeated daily in Kolkata and in literally thousands of large and small towns across India. The commodification and privatization of education in the country is inexhaustible and demand easily exceeds supply, despite the relatively high costs of coaching for ordinary households, let alone for the poor and marginalized for whom such opportunities remain but a distant dream.

The increasing expense of education in India, and its resultant politicization in uncertain and increasingly costly times, is analyzed in this chapter from the perspective of the lower middle classes. Framed by the early 1990s policy shifts in India, and in the state of West Bengal in particular, which have led to the integration of India into the global capitalist economy and the subsequent opening-up of its economy and institutions, we outline and analyze the ways in which cultural politics is expressed in the context of education. The modernist project of providing an educated, skilled, and trained elite stands in contrast to the rhetoric and policy of mass literacy and schooling in a country with inadequate resources and training and fundamental inequities between cities and towns, and the various states and regions. The cultural politics of education is then highlighted in our discussion and analysis of the teaching of English controversy in West Bengal. Discussion focuses on the cultural formation of lower middle-class identity and the way English proficiency emerges as a form of cultural capital that serves to secure middle-class status. The pragmatism and instrumentalism accorded to English language proficiency within the context of a globalizing economy is significant, and for many, an expense which often reaps no great reward due to lack of access to the necessary networks and severe competition for the few opportunities. Interestingly, despite their objective class and economic superiority to the poor, segments within the middle classes see themselves as victims of the opening-up of the Indian economy. Interwoven throughout this chapter are narrative accounts by informants that were gathered during long-term ethnographic fieldwork conducted by the authors in the state of West Bengal during the 2000s.

Neoliberal Globalization in India

One cannot understand the tensions and debates around class and education in India without first considering the impact of 20 years of radical economic reforms. Neoliberalism, essentially involving deregulation of state institutions, privatization of state assets, and widespread market reforms, has become normative in both the developed world and the Global South, imposing new norms for development and policymaking based around "rational" free-market principles and thus regulating and imposing conditions for community progress (e.g., Green, 2000; Miraftab, 2004). Neoliberal development has now been established as hegemonic, an ideology utilized to underpin development policies, programs, and growth strategies at the level of international institutions, national governments, businesses, nongovernment organizations, and to a lesser extent, local communities. Throughout the 1990s a series of International Monetary Fund (IMF)-derived, neoliberal structural adjustment programs were implemented. In July 1991 the New Economic Policy (NEP) was formulated in India and in 1994 in West Bengal. In a dramatic reversal of protecting domestic industrial capital, economic reforms were aimed at freeing the economy from various bureaucratic regulations and controls that were said to have stifled growth in the past. Making the economy more efficient through increased market orientation was the major goal of the reforms. In addition, other changes proposed included reduced public sector employment, limitations on agricultural subsidies, denationalization of banks and insurance companies, and reductions in public expenditure.

West Bengal, which had been ruled by a Left–Front coalition government from 1977 to 2011, dominated by the Communist Party of India-Marxist (CPM), has both a fraught center-state relationship, as well as tense capital–labor relations, especially because there is strong industrial unionization and peasant organizations at the village level (Kohli, 1987). Over the past few years, the Left Front faced enormous difficulties in reconciling its electoral loyalties, "Marxist" ideology, and the perceived "political rationalism" in an era of liberalization. The growing schism between its ideological predilections and the reality of its economic problems has resulted in growing unrest in the state, and within the CPM party hierarchy. The state assembly elections of May 2011 saw the Left-Front coalition finally losing political office after 34 years in power. Nevertheless, within West Bengal parents still demand and expect greater opportunities for their children, particularly because the expansion of Indian commerce and trade is integral to India's place in the global economy. Education, as we shall see in the next section, thus continues to be an important site of cultural politics as various classes vie for access to it and its control, and ultimately success for their children.

Social Class and the Cultural Politics of Education in India

In March 1835, a member of the Supreme Council in India, Lord Macaulay, brazenly declared that the task of the British in India was to "do our best to form a class who may be interpreters between us and the millions we govern; a class of persons, Indian in blood and colour, but English in taste, in opinions, in morals, and in intellect" (1919, p. 16). In essence, the colonial superiority of Western civilization was to be filtered-down to a newly created "middle mass" by way of the education system and mediated by the English language. In other words, the economic subjugation of the Indian subcontinent was to be reinforced by the concomitant hegemonic project of British colonization—to create a willing and culturally servile class of administrators, clerks, and other civil servants (essentially, the middle classes) who could skillfully and professionally administer the country. There were two consequences of this linguistic shift to privilege English. First, it resulted in a further social and cultural division in India which led to "the linguistic stratification of Indian society, further separated the elite classes from the lower castes and classes, and divided the urban populations from the rural" (Parameswaran, 1997, p. 24). Second, it led to the inculcation and absorption of Western liberal values of liberty, individuality of mind and spirit, and freedom of thought—ironically, the essential ideological bases for the later independence struggles in India. Significantly, however, it failed to completely colonize the "native" mind.

Schools were to play an important role in the creating of this new class of English educated bureaucrats. For the elite, the founding of a number of English-style public (i.e., independent, nonstate) schools such as the Doon

School in Northern India were the pinnacle of transposing English ideals of modernity and the cultural superiority of European ideas and British "liberalism" (Srivastava, 1998, p. 5). In postindependent India, modern education was central to Jawaharlal Nehru's[2] vision of a secular, democratic, and prosperous nation-state. A defining feature of the modernist project in India was that all levels of government would assume the responsibility for providing the resources and modes of education that would prepare them for their future while expanding the possibilities of inclusive democracy. Moreover the centrality of the state necessitated a large public sector, and created secure employment opportunities therein. The "old" educated middle classes had interests closely aligned with those of the state. However, in the 1980s and 1990s when the economy stagnated, the middle class sought alternatives to the state and its policy of nation building. At the same time the power and status of the public sector declined and the costs of social reproduction were increasingly placed upon the individual and households (Fernandes, 2006).

The future direction for the education of young people is critical at this juncture. Youth under the age of 21 now comprise 25% of the nation's population, some 300 million children and teenagers. Yet, the status of educational opportunities is severely limited. Bardhan (2006, pp. 3–4), comparing growth and development in India and China, highlights the fact that in India within the 18 to 23 age group only 7% are enrolled in higher education institutions, compared to more than 15% in China. Within the general population high levels of inequality are also found in the adult schooling years. This, coupled with the withdrawal of state support for public institutions (compared to China's growing investment in higher education), makes it increasingly difficult for young people to realize their aspirations. Recent studies from both North and South India have pointed to the growing frustration and difficulties for younger Indian lower middle class and lower caste youth to gain an education and subsequent professional jobs (Jeffrey, Jeffery, & Jeffery, 2004, 2005; Rogers, 2008).

The Politics of an English Education

> English is not only important in getting a better job, it is everywhere in social interactions. If you can't speak it then you are a nobody.
>
> *(Rekha, 31-year-old female clerk)*[3]

Historically, and in more contemporaneous times, the role of English in Indian education is an exemplar of the cultural politics of education in India. The rise and place of English in India has been discussed in several key writings (Kachru, 1983; Mishra, 2000; Trivedi, 1995) emphasizing its hegemonic role in creating a "colonial subjectivity" (Viswanathan, 1989). For most postcolonial states, the colonial language policies and approaches to education have continued relatively unchecked and fundamentally serve the interests of both the West and the indigenous elite (Phillipson, 1992; Pennycook, 1994). From the 1950s onwards in India the desire to learn English remained and it was also taught in most state schools but mainly due to a lack of resources, well-trained teachers, or motivation by parents, the majority of students failed to gain proficiency. The language divide between those proficient in English and those who were not became a mirror image of broader class and spatial divisions in India; between the elite and urban professional classes and the rest. Recognizing this, in 1981 the Left-Front government in West Bengal officially abolished the teaching of English as a compulsory language at the primary level of schooling. Basically, learning English in primary school was seen as inappropriate for the majority of children and therefore teaching it was a waste of government resources.

Over the next 15 years or so, the Left-Front government came under increasing political and cultural pressures to overturn this decision, mainly from the urbanized middle classes. In 1998, after a special committee was formed to investigate the teaching of English at primary level in West Bengal, headed by Professor Pabitra Sarkar (a CPM ally) it was decided that from the year 2000 English language learning would be formally reintroduced into state (government) primary schools to be taught from Class 3 onwards. Importantly, economic liberalization and globalization were two of the main reasons cited for justifying this reversal of policy. In the words of the committee: "the opening-up of the country's economy to foreign multi-national and trans-national corporations as a precondition for economic liberalization, has also contributed to the high profile of English which it enjoys" (Sarkar, 1998, p. 35). Furthermore, the Sarkar Report (1998, p. 21) notes that "due to economic globalization and the expanding operations of the transnational corporations, as with the faster speed of technology transfer, the role of 'business English' has received a boost." In acknowledging the influence of cultural globalization, the committee also describes how it has bowed to the increasingly demanding aspirations of a growing, largely urbanized middle class, with powerful middle–class aspirations, "fed, fostered and often swayed by the dream-peddling fares and advertisements of the print and electronic media" (Sarkar, 1998, p. 33).

The politics of education, especially concerning English in India, also raises several theoretical issues in regard to middle–class cultural politics. The lower middle classes in Bengal (among whom our fieldwork was carried out), despite their objectively higher economic position, nevertheless perceived themselves to be victims of globalization, particularly in terms of economic pressures, diminished job security and employment options, and increasing moral-political concerns over the cultural fabric of Bengal (and India) being eroded by Westernization, consumerism, and sexualization, especially due to the impact of the media and advertising (see Ganguly-Scrase & Scrase, 2009). Retaining English, and education privileges, is one sure way in which the lower middle classes can hope their children can prosper and so reproduce their cultural power. Similar to the arguments outlined in Bourdieu's (1984) book *Distinction*, the processes of class and cultural reconfiguration in India reflect the situation in which a subtle, but nevertheless distinct, differentiation emerges between the various class factions and their cultural practices together with their mobilization of cultural resources, or "cultural capital."

As in West Bengal, all across India the demand for English is increasing. Findings from Southern India reveal the increasing importance of the English language as the dominant marker of status in higher education and the white collar employment sector has entrenched feelings of marginalization and alienation among scheduled caste (SC) students (Rogers, 2008). In the North East region of India, a politically volatile area that is just now becoming embedded into the globalized, Indian national economy, Sen Gupta (2008) argues that: "Privatization and commercialization of education can be seen to be happening in the form of private tuitions, coaching classes and vocational training.... The competitive ethos that globalization created has made [the] entire private business in tuition and coaching classes a concurrent reality along with formal education" (p. 168). In terms of the place of English in West Bengal, what is significant is that not only do all respondents we interviewed basically agree that English is an important language to learn, but also they raise many additional sociocultural and politicocultural issues which need to be considered. It must be acknowledged that English is one of the official national languages of India and is basically the language of government business, science, technology, and private enterprise, especially in large corporations. As such, it unites educated Indians who come from various regional, ethnic, and language groups.

The Middle Classes: The Socioeconomic Background of Informants

Many recent studies of the middle classes in India under globalization have focused on the new rich (e.g., Fuller & Narasimhan, 2007). In response, Nijam (2006) provides empirical evidence disputing the exaggerated claims about urban India's rise of a "great middle class." For the purposes of our study, we largely researched people who can be classified as lower middle class, and this category in Bengal can be defined in terms of both belonging to a particular economic bracket and a cultural milieu. For those that we studied, their average household income at the beginning of our fieldwork in 1999 was just under Rs 10,000[4] per month and during the course of our research over the next 10 years that figure nearly doubled. Within cultural hierarchies of Bengal, these people form part of the Bengali *bhadralok* (or, "respectable people"), a group which traditionally values culture and education above income and materialism. Significantly, across India, in each region or state, one can find clear class hierarchies permeated by cultural nuances defined by ethnicity, culture, and education. Thus, we would argue that many of our findings concerning the formation and expression of class-based cultures in West Bengal can be similarly examined in other regions, but with notable "cultural twists" and local nuances (e.g., van Wessel, 1998). The *bhadralok* in Bengal still seek the best quality education for their children, and attempt to maintain a veneer of their once high social status by engaging in writing, music, and the arts. However, the economic realities of the present mean that educational achievements and cultural pursuits, traditional status symbols, are now insufficient to maintain their relatively high social standing.

Over the past decade or so, the entrepreneurial and moneyed upper middle class has expanded in West Bengal and so, as in other major urban centers of India, conspicuous consumption has become an increasingly important determinant of status. Our informants constantly pointed out that they are not well-off, that they feel increasingly under financial pressure, and that their lives are far removed from the lives of the entrepreneurial and upper middle class, the "new rich," the entrepreneurs and businesspeople of India. Moreover, the key elements of middle-class cultural capital are being redefined along with the changing economy. Increasingly, financial capital is used to purchase an English-medium private education and to send a child abroad for university education, and so to build one's stock of cultural capital. In contrast, many of our respondents' life trajectories have been associated with the downward mobility of the *bhadralok*, which began several decades ago following the partition of Bengal and has been exacerbated by neoliberal reforms. Many had struggled through education to obtain secure employment in the public sector, but now they are increasingly feeling squeezed out of their "rightful" place in educational institutions and government jobs. Our respondents were clerks, lower-ranking professionals and administrators, sales and service personnel. However, sociological attempts to derive class from occupational categories and income are only partially successful at explaining the position of our informants; these groups are best understood as class fractions. Neo-Marxist accounts (Wright, 1985; Wright et al, 1989) shed some light on the social location of a marginal middle class consisting of nonmanual wage earners and low-grade technicians: they may be seen to be in a contradictory class location—semiautonomous, professional employees situated somewhere between the proletariat and the petite bourgeoisie. Others have referred to these groups as "lower white collar classes."[5] We use these categories to specify the respondents' market capacity, given the significance of that capacity in defining the emerging middle classes. Throughout our research, we were particularly concerned to document their consumption and household survival strategies, which subsequently revealed their limited household budgets. However, we also recognize that complex linkages between economic position, status and caste relations, and the dynamics of political power continue to shape the formation of social classes in India, and so we do not claim that any fixed definitions are going to be entirely adequate in analyzing class relations.

When we first started thinking-through the complexity of "middle class," we relied on the self-ascription of our informants. Historically, they self-identified as belonging to the middle class, yet some specifically referred to themselves as "lower middle class." Indeed, when describing themselves in that way, they mostly expressed themselves in English, although some used the Bengali term *nimno moddhobitto* (lower middle class) to depict their neighborhoods. This occurred especially when they intended to describe their surroundings in a self-deprecating way or to signify a fall from grace. We believe this to be a significant departure from other studies of emerging middle-class groups carried out in recent years and it forms the central distinguishing feature of our study. Presenting a striking contrast to the real poor, other terms our informants used were "ordinary folk," or "common folk," or "people of limited means." People invariably described their situation, or their lifestyles, as "normal" although in the context of Indian social hierarchies, they are in fact relatively privileged. What is distinctive is their subtle awareness of internal class divisions and their distancing of themselves from the wealthy or rich. Some simply described themselves as "those dependent on a salary." The image of a regular salary earner is a powerful one in the Bengali cultural context, suggesting a distinction from both menial waged work and earnings gained from trade. However, it also disguises the real incomes of those civil servants who supplement household income by taking bribes. During our fieldwork, no respondents claimed that they were poor, despite their lack of material wealth.

Schooling and Class in India: English as Commodity

In the preceding discussion we have underscored the importance of education and schooling, and the historical importance of English proficiency, as significant in the delineation of class reproduction in contemporary India. Additionally, we argue that fluency in English in a globalizing India benefits the middle and upper classes through their historical control over, and access for their children, to the elite schools, universities, and colleges. The abundance of after-school English language coaching colleges and tutoring centers in the various neighborhoods, together with numerous daily newspaper advertisements for private coaching in English, bears testimony to the commodification of English in India. Our informants also spoke of the stiff competition to get their children enrolled in high quality, English-medium schools and the disappointment for their children when they could not pass the rigorous psychological tests, examinations, and interviews, all at the tender age of 4! Kanika Datta (2006) notes, for instance, that:

> Economic liberalization has certainly changed attitudes, but that is yet to trickle down to the important business of providing quality education. Like so many business schools of doubtful provenance that proliferate in abundance in response to the explosion in demand, English-medium

schools have become all the rage. Most of them charge extortionate fees to provide the rudiments of English literacy rather than a meaningful grasp of the language.

English nowadays becomes an essential commodity for two fundamental reasons; first, because there is practical necessity for having a good command of English in India; and second, because it is an important national language that can eventually open job opportunities nationally and abroad. For Subhas, a lower level administrator aged 34, English is significant because it enables one to work in other states in the country, to work in professional jobs, and to earn a good income:

> We need English because we're a huge country. You can't expect that you're going to stay in West Bengal forever. If you speak Bengali who will understand you in Madras? Our common language has to be English. We may speak Hindi, but the Tamils won't. So, we have to have English. Without it you will miss out every time. So what if you have got a degree? You may have an MA or an MSc, all in Bengali, but when you get an interview in Delhi, what are you going to do? Who is going to give you a job? You're worth nothing in the job market without good command of English!

Ali, aged 40, is also concerned for his children's future careers. He highlights the fact that those without political connections, or who lack the income and wealth to afford private tuition and a private school education—in other words, those just like him—would struggle unless English was offered freely at government schools. His support of English in the curriculum from Class 1 onwards is convincing:

> In the world of work English is absolutely important. To succeed in your career English is a must. Our politicians say that: "English is not essential. Your opportunities aren't going to be closed off because you can't speak English. That all transactions can be in Bengali." The reality is different! *They* don't have to struggle to get a job. *We* do! Among my friends, a number of them were disqualified (from a job) on the grounds that their spoken English was poor. They met all other criteria. English is an international language.... If someone asks you a question in English and you can't answer, you feel bad about yourself and your sense of worth is diminished.

For some of our informants, who came from better-off middle-class families, the support for English was just as strongly felt. The following response is from Amit, a project officer in his mid-30s, in a semigovernment organization. His daughter, only 6 years old, attends Loreto'School, one of Calcutta's more exclusive girls' schools. "My child is going to an English-medium school. I went to an English-medium school. The main reason is that, if we go outside of West Bengal, is there an alternative other than to communicate in English? English is universal." The situation of many middle-class parents spending an excessive proportion of their incomes on the private school education of their children, in preference to public schooling which is generally free, is mirrored in many countries around the world. In particular the 2009 debt crisis has led to government cutbacks on public schooling and a subsequent overcrowding of classrooms, fewer teachers, and a general strain on school resources in many countries.

Those parents who never attended an English-medium school are nevertheless keen to help their children to excel in English. Ajoy, an accounts officer in a semigovernment organization, remarks that:

> English should be taught at primary level. The government's initiative was a complete flop. Most students were unable to learn English properly if they started at Class 6. My child is learning English since kindergarten. The primary section taught English from the start. I help her out with tenses, writing paragraphs. Now if she were to start learning the alphabet at Class 6, she would have been in trouble. It is also more "natural" to start learning from the start.

Ajoy obviously has the resources to afford to send his daughter to an English-medium school. He does not want the situation that faced Anju, aged 28, who sees herself as a victim of the policy that abolished the teaching of English at the primary level. She is an underemployed graduate who has been working as an assistant in an ISD (telephone/telex) booth for many years. She feels that she has been disadvantaged as she cannot converse in English.

> We are so weak in English. People all around us don't have a grasp of the English language. In my view if English was introduced from the start, it would be very beneficial. To get a firm grounding in English you have to start right at the beginning. You don't teach the alphabet at Class 6! Our generation didn't get this, but the next generation when they learn English from the beginning, they will be better off. English is very important in the world of work.

In this instance, a working-class girl recognizes the personal disadvantages accorded to her by the government's "proworking-class" policy of abolishing the teaching of English! Whether, in reality, she would have advanced in her education and career with fluency in English, particularly as she lacked social and cultural capital, remains debatable, but undeniably in her mind the opportunity for social advancement was forgone and she remains an embittered victim of this earlier policy on compulsory English.

Among our informants, few were willing to show outright support for the government and its teaching of English policy. Debdas is a 45-year-old male, employed as a clerk at a regional university, and holds generally critical views on most things political. In stark contrast to the younger Anju, he feels that he has benefited greatly from the policies of the CPM. Importantly, too, he points to the role of cultural capital (educated parents, home support, etc.) in fostering educational success.

> We had English in our curriculum. Then it was removed. Did we learn good English when it was compulsory? 90% of my colleagues cannot speak English, even though it was compulsory in their schooling. People learnt good English because of their family environment, because of the additional support they received, not because it was taught at school.

Debdas's colleague, Ganesh, aged in his early 50s and who works as a registrar's secretary in the university, was also generally supportive of the CPM's education policy decision. His view reflects more of a sense of national pride, that it should not be so important to learn English simply because English is a dominant international language.

> There are so many countries in the world where they do not speak English. Are they backward, tell me? We in the Commonwealth countries were ruled by the British. In non-Commonwealth countries they go about their business in their own language. They do not feel compelled to learn English. In this country, however, there are double standards. There is the rhetoric of using the mother tongue at all official levels. The reality is that English still dominates. So parents feel that they have to teach their children English. If they do, there are lots of avenues for them. They can learn English via private education. I do not believe that English has to be compulsory in primary schools.

Both these supportive views of the policy are illustrative of the way class cultures and worldviews vary according to generation. Many of the older generation of middle-class Bengalis, those aged over 40, were direct beneficiaries of progovernment, prosocialist policies for state employment and mass state education in the 1970s. For them, the policies and programs the government planned and enacted were generally seen to be in the best interests of the state and its vast and diverse population. For the subsequent generation, their children, who grew up in the 1980s and 1990s, there were fewer job opportunities, the state was economically stagnating, and unemployment and underemployment were rife, especially among the middle classes who remain averse to manual forms of labor. The generational contestation and tension within classes remains to this day, not just with respect to politics but in the many and varied ways of cultural consumption, recreation, fashion, media use, and the like.

Apart from the diverse, sometimes generationally divided opinions about the teaching of English policy, observations in the daily press and by various commentators exposed the folly of short-term populist policies by various state governments, not just the regime in West Bengal. For instance, Datta (2006), in a critical newspaper piece comments that:

> True, the burden of responsibility for the decline in standards of English education lies with the state governments. Local populist chauvinism in the seventies and eighties drove English out of the compulsory curriculum of state schools, subordinating it to an optional second language at the high school level. This sometimes created comic situations. In West Bengal, for instance, Shakespeare was interpreted for school-leaving children in Bengali. The impact of the Left Front government's policy, now reversed, was brought into sharp relief in the eighties and nineties as a growing number of young job seekers found themselves trapped in a state in which economic opportunity was steadily shrinking.

This view is clearly echoed by the young Anju in her criticisms noted above, and by Rinku, aged 27, who commented that:

> Some of my friends went to English-medium schools and they fared much better than me. Those who try to pick up English later find it very difficult to catch up. If you know English you get access to a lot more information. You need English because it is everywhere! I have to know English because some of my clients don't know Bengali.

The quest for learning English in India, and improving on one's efficiency in the language is one that is highly competitive, contested, and contextual. The quest demands one's cultural and economic resources, one's cultural and social capital as it were, and also involves perseverance, disappointment, and sacrifice on behalf of both individuals and their families.

The selection of narratives from some of our informants which we have presented above demonstrates their degree of critical insight, reflection, and evaluation of the government's previous education policies toward the language. Moreover, they reveal their knowledge of the strategies they need to employ for for English language proficiency—to read, write, understand, and speak with preferably an "English," or even more preferably nowadays, American accent. The struggle to attain English language proficiency is as much a struggle about one's ability to learn well a difficult language as it is about broader class-based, cultural struggles taking place in a nation that is rapidly globalizing and where, for the most part, entrepreneurialism and an emerging moneyed class is rapidly surpassing the older, established middle class order that once controlled India's major cultural institutions.

CONCLUSION: NEOLIBERAL GLOBALIZATION AND THE PARADOX OF EDUCATION

English is an international language. You feel humiliated if you can't speak English. People think you are dumb.

(Ali, a 39-year-old male accounts officer)

The Indian middle classes see a distinct social advantage in maintaining English proficiency in the increasingly deregulated Indian economy. The struggles over the teaching of English in West Bengal, the language wars, were clearly established during the long period of colonialism, with the establishment of the British system of education and the subsequent employment of the educated, Indian middle classes in the civil service and in private enterprise. Nevertheless, the language divide, as a reflection and extension of broader social class and cultural division, is not unique to India. The cultural politics of education in India is indeed part and parcel of the broader political struggles over scarce and valued resources. English language proficiency in a globalizing India is an essential component of one's cultural baggage, a resource that can eventually open doors into the world of professional employment in both India and abroad. For the middle classes, English is a resource that must be defended and maintained at all costs.

Our research reported in the preceding paragraphs, together with a range of studies of schooling and inequality in the subcontinent, points to the paradox of providing mass education and literacy in the context of neoliberal globalization. In terms of social class, for example, while one class seeks to harness the social advantages of an internationalized education, proficiency in English, and attending university, other marginalized classes measure the educational success of their children purely in terms of attaining literacy, or completing primary level schooling. In terms of cultural capital, marginalized groups still lack the essential cultural capital necessary for future education success. Middle-class informants clearly indicated to us the ways they act as brokers and intermediaries of their children's schooling—dealing with the school bureaucracy, helping with their children's homework, and the like. In other words, devoid of the sort of income and wealth necessary to send their children to the most exclusive schools, they are able to subsidize their lack of financial capital with their relatively high degree of cultural capital.

In terms of English in particular, our informants emphasized the way English is recognized now as a lingua franca, the dominant national and global language of culture, entertainment, technology, and business in the "new" India. English has become the language of opportunity, for university entrance, well-paying professional careers, and migration abroad. Conversely, there is the slow devaluation of regional languages and dialects whose speakers are predominantly confined now to the rural Indian towns and villages—the places where one sees much fewer realistic and quality educational opportunities. For the majority of our informants, they are very much engaged in the practice of negotiating globalization. As "modern" Indian citizens they recognize they must move forward and not look back to the past, even though for many they are culturally more attuned with the ideals of a broadly socialist, secular nation. Yet, they are also savvy enough to engage, and strategically negotiate, with those social institutions in which they appreciate and wield some degree of symbolic power, namely education and government bureaucracy, and so are able to mitigate the extent to which the paradoxes of modern Indian education and the neoliberal economy impact on their daily lives.

Notes

1 The term *tuition*, meaning to teach, to coach, to instruct, is commonly used in the Britain, Australia, and India to refer to the work that a teacher does when he or she teaches a particular subject, particularly to one person or to a small group. Here we use "English tuition" to refer to private coaching colleges that specialize in teaching English.
2 India's first Prime Minister.
3 Note that fieldwork was conducted during the early 2000s so the ages noted for informants were their ages at the time of interview.
4 The approximate exchange rate during fieldwork was Indian Rupees (Rs) 40.00 = U.S.$1.00. Thus, their monthly household income ranged from U.S.$250 to U.S.$500. This exchange rate is similar at the time of writing (March 2011), although the purchasing power of the rupee in India is fast diminishing due to high inflation of up to 8 to 12% per annum in recent years.
5 In the neo-Weberian stratification model developed by Goldthorpe and Hope (1974) following the sevenfold (seven scales), this group forms part of Class II (lower professionals; technicians; lower administrators; small business managers; supervisors of nonmanual workers) and Class III (clerks; sales personnel).

References

Bardhan, P. (2006). Awakening giants, feet of clay: A brief assessment of the rise of China and India. *Journal of South Asian Development, 1*(1), 1–17.
Bourdieu, P. (1984). *Distinction: A social critique of the judgment of taste* (Trans. R. Nice). Cambridge, MA: Harvard University Press.
Datta, D. (1998, September 12). Lesson in primary folly. *The Telegraph* (India), p. 12.
Datta, K. (2006, October 22). The language barrier. *Business Standard*. Retrieved April 10, 2010, from http://www.businessstandard.co.in/india/news/kanika-dattalanguage-barrier/245642/
Fernandes, L. (2006). *India's new middle class: Democratic politics in an era of economic reform*. Minneapolis: University of Minnesota Press.
Fuller, C., & Narasimhan, H. (2007). Information technology professionals and the new-rich middle class in Chennai. *Modern Asian Studies, 41*(1), 121–150.
Ganguly-Scrase, R. & Scrase, T. J. (2009). *Globalisation and the middle classes in India: The social and cultural impact of neoliberal reforms*. London: Routledge.
Goldthorpe, J., & Hope, K. (1974). *The social grading of occupations*. Oxford, England: Clarendon.
Green, M. (2000). Participatory development and the appropriation of agency in southern Tanzania. *Critique of Anthropology, 20*(1), 67–89.
Jeffrey, C., Jeffery, R., & Jeffery, P (2004). Degrees without freedom: The impact of formal education on Dalit young men in North India. *Development and Change, 35*(5), 963–986.
Jeffrey, C., Jeffery, R., & Jeffery, P (2005). "A useless thing!" or "nectar of the gods?" The cultural

production of education and young men's struggles for respect in liberalizing North India. *Annals of the Association of American Geographers, 94*(4), 961–981.

Kachru, Braj B. (1983). *The Indianization of English: The English language in India.* New York: Oxford University Press.

Kohli, A. (1987). *The state and poverty in India.* Cambridge, England: Cambridge University Press.

Macaulay, T. B. (1919). Macaulay's minute on education, 1835. In *Calcutta University Commission Report* (Appendix II, pp. 8–17). Calcutta, India: Government of West Bengal.

Miraftab, F. (2004). Making neoliberal governance: The disempowering work of empowerment. *International Planning Studies, 9*(4), 239–259.

Mishra, P. K. (2000). English language, postcolonial subjectivity, and globalization in India. *ARIEL: A Review of International English Literature, 31*(1&2), 383–410.

Nijam, J. (2006). Mumbai's mysterious middle class. *International Journal of Urban and Regional Research, 30*(4), 758–775.

Parameswaran, R. (1997). Colonial interventions and the postcolonial situation in India: The English language, mass media and the articulation of class. *Gazette, 59*(1), 21–41.

Pennycook, A. (1994). *The cultural politics of English as an international language.* Harlow, England: Longman.

Phillipson, R. (1992). *Linguistic imperialism.* Oxford, England: Oxford University Press.

Rogers, M. (2008). Modernity, "authenticity", and ambivalence: Subaltern masculinities on a South Indian college campus. *Journal of the Royal Anthropological Institute, 14*(1), 79–95.

Sarkar, P. (1998). *Report of the one-man committee on English in primary education in West Bengal.* Calcutta, India: Government of West Bengal.

Sen Gupta, S. (2008). Globalization and its impact on society: Some reflections. in B. J. Deb, K. Sengupta, & B. Datta-Ray (Eds.), *Globalization and north east India* (pp. 156–170). New Delhi, India: Concept Publishing/North-East India Council for Social Science Research.

Srivastava, S. (1998). *Constructing post-colonial India: National character and the Doon School.* London: Routledge.

Trivedi, H. (1995). *Colonial transactions: English literature and India.* Manchester, England: Manchester University Press.

Van Wessel, M. (1998). Wealth and its social worth: Consumers in the land of Gandhi. *Amsterdam Sociologisch Tijdschrift, 25*(4), 562–567.

Viswanthan, G. (1989). *Masks of conquest: Literary study and British rule in India.* New York: Columbia University Press.

Wright, E. O. (1985). *Classes.* London: Verso.

Wright, E., Brenner, J., Buroway, M., Burris, V., Carchedi, G., Marshall, G., … Van Parijus, P. (1989). *The debate on classes.* London: Verso.

CONTRIBUTORS

Richard Arum is Professor of Sociology and Education at New York University, and director of the Education Research Program at the Social Science Research Council. He is coauthor of *Academically Adrift: Limited Learning on College Campuses* (University of Chicago Press, 2011), the author of *Judging School Discipline: The Crisis of Moral Authority in American Schools* (Harvard University Press, 2003), and coeditor of *Improving Learning Environments: School Discipline and Student Achievement in Comparative Perspective* (Stanford University Press, 2012).

Azeem Badroodien is a Senior Lecturer in the Department of Education Policy Studies within the Faculty of Education, University of Stellenbosch where he teaches and does research in sociological and historical perspectives in education. His publications include articles in the *International Journal of Education and Work*, and the *International Journal of Educational Development*.

Yun-Kyung Cha is Professor of Education at Hanyang University, Seoul, and he is currently serving as president of the Korean Association for Multicultural Education and as editor of its international journal, *Multicultural Education Review*. Having received his PhD in the sociology of education from Stanford University, he has published extensively on the institutionalization of policy models for school curricula, teacher preparation, and multicultural education.

Yan Zhao Ciupak received her PhD in social foundations of education at the State University of New York—Buffalo. She established and taught a three-course series in the Chinese Language and Culture Program at Kettering University. She currently works with the Educational Testing Service. Her research focuses on international education and education of immigrant youth. Her new book, *On the Nexus of Local and Global: Chinese Higher Education and College Students in the Era of Globalization*, will be published by AMC Press in 2012.

Catalina Crespo-Sancho is a lecturer in the Department of International and Transcultural Studies at Teachers College, Columbia University. Her research interests include immigration, social stratification, human rights education, and international educational development. Her current work focuses on elite/upper class immigration and its effects on both the community in the host and home land. In addition, she has been working with the Costa Rican government on education reform.

Luis Eduardo Santa Cruz is a Chilean sociologist and researcher at the University of Granada, Spain. He is currently finishing his PhD. He is also a researcher at the Interdisciplinary Research Program in Education (PIIE) and the Research Centre in Education in the University UCIFN, both in Chile. He has published several articles and contributions to books in the field of sociology of education, education policy, education reform, media and citizenship.

Nadine Dolby is Associate Professor of Curriculum Studies and Affiliated Faculty, Cultural Foundations of Education at Purdue University, Indiana. Her most recent book is *Youth Moves: Identities and Education in Global Perspective* (edited with Fazal Rizvi, Routledge, 2008). Her other publications include *Constructing Race: Youth, Identity, and Popular Culture in South Africa* (State University of New York Press, 2001), and *Learning to Labor in New Times* (edited with Greg Dimitriadis, Routledge, 2004). She has also published in numerous journals including *Review of Educational Research*, and *Harvard Educational Review*. Her areas of research interest include international education, higher education, and global youth culture and she has conducted research in South Africa, Australia, and the United States.

Daniel Faas is an Assistant Professor in Sociology at Trinity College, Dublin. He was a Fulbright-Schuman Fellow at the University of California at Berkeley (2009) and Marie Curie Research Fellow at the Hellenic Foundation for European and Foreign Policy in Athens (2006–2008). His research interests focus on migration and education, citizenship and identity politics, multiculturalism and social cohesion, ethnicity and racism, curriculum and policy developments, and comparative research within and between Europe and North America. Faas is author of *Negotiating Political Identities: Multiethnic Schools and Youth in Europe* (Ashgate, 2010).

Caroline Foubister is a remedial/community teacher. She runs a learning support and advocacy project for 200 refugee students at a school in Cape Town. Caroline completed her master's degree in 2010 at Stellenbosch University. Her thesis, *Navigating Their Way: African Migrant Youth and Their Experiences of Schooling in Cape Town,* explores how African migrant youth navigate their lives both in and out of school.

Adam Gamoran is the John D. MacArthur Professor of Sociology and Educational Policy Studies and Director of the Wisconsin Center for Education Research at the University of Wisconsin-Madison. His research focuses on inequality in education and school reform. With Yossi Shavit and Richard Arum, he coedited *Stratification in Higher Education: A Comparative Study* (Stanford University Press, 2007), and with Andrew Porter, he coedited *Methodological Advances in Cross-National Surveys of Educational Achievement* (National Academies Press, 2002). He is an elected member of the U.S. National Academy of Education and was appointed by President Barack Obama to serve on the National Board for Education Sciences.

Ruchira Ganguly-Scrase obtained her doctorate in anthropology from the University of Melbourne. She is Professor of Anthropology and the National Course Director for International Development, Australian Catholic University, Melbourne. She is the author of numerous articles on the impact of neoliberal reforms, the ethnographic method, forced and labor migrations, childhood and schooling, and gender relations in Asia. Her book-length publications include *Globalisation and the Middle Classes in India* (Routledge, 2009; with Timothy Scrase) and *Global Issues/Local Contexts: The Rabi Das of West Bengal* (Orient Longman/Sangam Books, 2001).

Seung-Hwan Ham received his PhD in educational policy from Michigan State University, where he also taught social foundations courses in education. He now teaches at Hanyang University, Seoul. His research interests include schools as organizations as well as educational policy formulation and implementation as social and institutional processes.

Anna Hickey-Moody is a Lecturer in Gender and Cultural Studies at Sydney University. She previously taught at Monash University and the University of South Australia. Her research interests lie at the intersection of cultural studies and the sociology of youth. She is currently completing a book called *Youth, Arts and Education* (forthcoming from Routledge), which is an investigation into the arts practices of young people at risk of leaving school early. Her books include *Unimaginable Bodies* (Sense, 2009), and coauthored with Kenway and Kraack, *Masculinity Beyond the Metropolis* (Palgrave Macmillan, 2006).

Jane Kenway is an Australian Professorial Fellow of the Australian Research Council, a Fellow of the Australian Academy of Social Sciences, and a Professor in the Education Faculty, Monash University, Australia and is recognized internationally for her research on the politics of educational change in the context of wider social, cultural, and political change. Her more recent coauthored books include *Haunting the Knowledge Economy* (Routledge, 2006), *Masculinity Beyond the Metropolis* (Palgrave, 2006), and *Consuming Children: Education-Advertising-Entertainment* (Open University Press, 2001). Her more recent coedited books are *Globalising the Research Imagination* (Routledge, 2008), *Globalising Public Education: Policies, Pedagogies and Politics* (Peter Lang, 2005), and *Innovation and Tradition: The Arts, Humanities, and the Knowledge Economy* (Peter Lang, 2004).

Shumin Lin is a Postdoctoral Fellow in Anthropology at the University of South Florida. She received her Ph.D. in Educational Psychology in 2009 from the University of Illinois at Urbana-Champaign. Her research focuses on the role of language in socialization and in the construction of social inequity. She has published her work in *Language in Society* and co-authored a monograph *How Socialization Happens on the Ground: Narrative Practices as Alternate Socializing Pathways in Taiwanese and European-American Families* (Monographs of the Society for Research in Child Development, 2012).

Antonio Olmedo is Senior Lecturer of Education Policy at the University of Granada, Spain and Visiting Fellow at the Institute of Education, University of London. His research focuses on different areas related to the fields of education policy and sociology of education, with a special interest in different dimensions of the interrelations between social class and education dynamics. He has authored a book on school choice strategies and middle-class families in local education markets. He has also published articles and contributed to books in areas relating to the implementation of the quasi-markets and privatization dynamics in and of education. He has recently finished a study based on the analysis of social geographies of local schooling processes and school choice strategies of families from different social backgrounds. Currently, he is working on two new research projects: the first one explores "new regimes of regulation," the implementation of different "policy technologies," and the introduction of different forms of "privatization(s)" in the Spanish education system; the second is based on the analysis of global policy and philanthropy networks within the field of education.

Josipa Roksa is Assistant Professor in the Department of Sociology at the University of Virginia (UVA), with a courtesy appointment in the Curry School of Education. Her research examines social stratification in educational and labor market outcomes, with a specific focus on higher education. Roksa has published in a wide range of sociology and education journals, and is a coauthor of *Academically Adrift: Limited Learning on College Campuses* (University of Chicago Press, 2011).

Timothy J. Scrase is Professor of Sociology and Associate Dean for Research at the Australian Catholic University in Sydney, Australia. He has been a visiting research fellow at the International Institute for Asian Studies (IIAS), University of Amsterdam. He has published widely on development and social change in Asia in a range of leading academic journals and edited book collections, and has previously published five books including: *Social Justice and Third World Education* (Garland, 1997) and *Globalisation and the Middle Classes in India* (Routledge, 2009; coauthored with R. Ganguly-Scrase).

Yossi Shavit is the Weinberg Professor of Sociology of Inequality and Stratification at Tel Aviv University. He was previously on the faculty of the University of Haifa and the European University Institute (EUI), and joined Tel Aviv University in 1996. His main interests are in the areas of social inequality and the sociology of education. He is coauthor of *Persistent Inequality* (with H-P. Blossfeld, Westview Press, 1993), *From School to Work* (with W. Müller, Clarendon Press, 1998) and *Stratification in Higher Education* (with Richard Arum and Adam Gamoran, Stanford University Press, 2007).

Amy E. Stich is a Postdoctoral Research Associate at the State University of New York—Buffalo. Her research focuses on knowledge differentiation, the social process of democratization, and resultant inequality of opportunity in higher education. She has published numerous articles, including a recent paper in *Review of Educational Research*. Her forthcoming book, *The Social Debt of Democratization: Class, Knowledge, and Capital in Higher Education*, will be published by Lexington Books in 2012.

Lois Weis is State University of New York Distinguished Professor of Sociology of Education at State University of New York—Buffalo. She is the author or editor of numerous books and articles relating to race, class, gender, education, and the economy. Her most recent volumes include *The Way Class Works: Readings on School, Family and the Economy* (Routledge, 2008); *Class Reunion: The Remaking of the American White Working Class* (Routledge, 2004); and *Beyond Silenced Voices: Class, Race and Gender in United States Schools* (coedited with Michelle Fine, SUNY Press, 2005). She is a Fellow of AERA, winner of the outstanding book award from the Gustavus Meyers Center for the Study of Bigotry and Human Rights in North America, as well as a seven-time winner of the American Educational Studies Association's Critic's Choice Award, given for an outstanding book.

INDEX